FEATURE AND MAGAZINE WRITING

FEATURE & MAGAZINE WRITING

David E. Sumner and Holly G. Miller

ACTION, ANGLE AND ANECDOTES

SECOND EDITION

WILEY-BLACKWELL

A John Wiley & Sons, Ltd., Publication

This second edition first published 2009
© 2009 David E. Sumner and Holly G. Miller

Edition history: Blackwell Publishing Ltd (1e, 2005)

Blackwell Publishing was acquired by John Wiley & Sons in February 2007. Blackwell's publishing program has been merged with Wiley's global Scientific, Technical, and Medical business to form Wiley-Blackwell.

Registered Office
John Wiley & Sons Ltd, The Atrium, Southern Gate, Chichester, West Sussex, PO19 8SQ, United Kingdom

Editorial Offices
350 Main Street, Malden, MA 02148-5020, USA
9600 Garsington Road, Oxford, OX4 2DQ, UK
The Atrium, Southern Gate, Chichester, West Sussex, PO19 8SQ, UK

For details of our global editorial offices, for customer services, and for information about how to apply for permission to reuse the copyright material in this book please see our website at www.wiley.com/wiley-blackwell.

The right of David E. Sumner and Holly G. Miller to be identified as the authors of this work has been asserted in accordance with the Copyright, Designs and Patents Act 1988.

Wiley also publishes its books in a variety of electronic formats. Some content that appears in print may not be available in electronic books.

Designations used by companies to distinguish their products are often claimed as trademarks. All brand names and product names used in this book are trade names, service marks, trademarks or registered trademarks of their respective owners. The publisher is not associated with any product or vendor mentioned in this book. This publication is designed to provide accurate and authoritative information in regard to the subject matter covered. It is sold on the understanding that the publisher is not engaged in rendering professional services. If professional advice or other expert assistance is required, the services of a competent professional should be sought.

Library of Congress Cataloging-in-Publication Data

Sumner, David E., 1946–
    Feature and magazine writing : action, angle, and anecdotes / David E. Sumner, Holly G. Miller. — 2nd ed.
        p. cm.
    Rev. ed. of: 1st ed., Feature and magazine writing: action, angle, and anecdotes, 2005.
    Includes bibliographical references and index.
    ISBN 978-1-4051-9204-0 (pbk. : alk. paper) 1. Feature writing. 2. Journalism—Authorship. I. Miller, Holly G. II. Title.
    PN4784.F37S86 2009
    808'.06607—dc22
                                                            2008055191

A catalog record for this book is available from the British Library.

Set in 10.5 on 13 pt Minion by SNP Best-set Typesetter Ltd., Hong Kong
Printed in Singapore by Ho Printing Singapore Pte Ltd

03 2010

CONTENTS

PREFACE: THE FUTURE OF MAGAZINES IS BRIGHT

Five times in the past 100 years, skeptics have predicted the decline or demise of magazines. First, after World War I when automobiles became popular and affordable, some people feared the newly mobile population would spend more time driving and less time reading. Second, when commercial radio stations flourished in the 1920s, some thought radio would lure advertising dollars away from magazines. Third, the Golden Age of film during the 1930s again convinced skeptics that magazines had a dim future as the public became fascinated with this dramatic new medium. Fourth, television's introduction and its spectacular growth in the 1950s and 1960s again made people wonder whether magazines could survive. Finally, the introduction of the Internet during the 1990s and the phenomenal growth of the Web since 2000 again brought out the "death of print" chorus to sing its eulogy to magazines. Frequent media reports about circulation declines and staff cutbacks at daily newspapers have fueled skepticism about the future of print journalism in general. Yet the magazine industry has remained remarkably buoyant.

Newspapers produce a broad range of news stories aimed at an audience of all ages, professions and interests within a specific geographic area. This form of journalism—often called "history's first draft"—has been seriously hurt by the Web because news has become a free commodity instantly accessible to anyone with a laptop or portable device.

Magazines, on the other hand, have taken advantage of the Web in ways that touch more readers and attract more advertisers. That's because most magazines are built on a simple formula and business model: They provide specialized information to a narrowly defined audience that advertisers want to reach with their products. Magazines have been able to transfer that formula to their Web sites with measurable success. Now we see print versions directing readers to their electronic versions and vice versa. Rather than compete, they complement each other.

In recent years we've seen the number of magazines in the U.S. expand from 18,000 to more than 19,500. Simultaneously the amount of advertising revenue at magazines has doubled from $12.7 billion to $25.5 billion, according to the Magazine Publishers of America. Consumer magazines' share of the media advertising market has increased from 17 percent to 19 percent within five years, and the number of magazine readers has grown by 5 percent, while the average number of issues read by each reader escalated by 6 percent. The percentage of Americans who read magazines has remained stable at about 85 percent as the population continues to swell.[1]

The economic crisis that began in the United States and spread to the world economy during the latter months of 2008 threatened many magazines as some were forced to make staff layoffs while others cut back on the number of pages or frequency of publication. This damage, however, resulted from cancellations and cutbacks from advertisers, not from online competition. The long-term impact of this economic crisis remains unseen at the time we write these words.

The power of magazines stems from the personal identity that they convey as well as their color, design and editorial tone. Magazines are the most intimate form of media because they can establish a relationship with their readers unequalled by newspapers, television or radio. A magazine becomes a friend, a reflection of and integral part of the reader's personal and professional life.

The Web has, indeed, hurt the circulation and revenue of some high-circulation magazines that focus on breaking news and facts easily available on the Web. However, magazines focusing on travel, food, lifestyle and specialized hobbies and interests continue to gain popularity. In short, magazines succeed when they provide stories and information that readers can't get anywhere else.

There will always be a demand for original stories that inform, inspire or entertain, whether they are published in print, on Web sites or both. This book is based on that long-time formula for successful magazines: provide stories and information that readers can't get anywhere else. Between the covers of this textbook we explore the entire process—from identifying a good idea to creating an original angle, and from finding primary sources to constructing a final draft.

The success of the first edition of *Feature and Magazine Writing* has been gratifying. We've received positive feedback from students and professors using it at major universities from Florida to California and from as far away as Australia. Because we're convinced that every good product can be better, we've updated this second edition with fresh facts and examples, and we've integrated ideas and suggestions that we've gleaned from teachers, students, professional writers and editors. No chapter has remained the same, and we've added two new chapters: One offers a checklist for preparing a final draft of an article; the second reviews strategies to help students find jobs in the magazine industry.

As working professionals, we continue to learn about the fascinating business of feature writing. Our joint experiences outside the classroom include overseeing the lifestyle section of a daily newspaper, serving on the staffs of several magazines, creating and editing Web site copy, supervising an award-winning campus magazine, producing a corporate tabloid, fulfilling hundreds of freelance feature assignments and judging regional and national journalism competitions. Yet writing is not a skill you ever master. Each article and every issue present new challenges. The goal of this book is to help equip the next generation of feature writers with the tools to successfully meet those challenges.

David E. Sumner
Holly G. Miller

December 2008

ENDNOTE

[1] Magazine Publishers of America, *The Magazine Handbook 2008–2009.* Accessed at www.magazine.org/advertising/handbook/Magazine_Handbook.aspx, Nov. 2, 2008.

PART I

PREPARING TO WRITE FEATURE AND MAGAZINE ARTICLES

The process begins with an interesting and fresh idea so tightly focused that the writer can summarize it in a single sentence. The research phase follows and takes two forms: a thorough exploration of existing materials, and thoughtful interviews conducted with knowledgeable and quotable sources.

1

CAPTURING READER ATTENTION

Your takeaway . . .

Characteristics of compelling stories include strong action, specific angles and plenty of anecdotes. This chapter will tell you why these are important ingredients in your writing recipes. You will learn the five most common mistakes of beginning writers and how to avoid those mistakes. You also will learn the differences between newspaper and magazine writing and why you should learn as much as you can about your readers.

> *"Do you know, Madam, that I would rather write for a magazine for $2 a page than for a newspaper at $10? I would. One takes more pains, . . . looks nicer in print and . . . has a pleasanter audience."*
> [Mark Twain in a letter to Mary Fairbanks, May 29, 1870]

"China's Instant Cities" in *National Geographic* chronicles the booming growth of cities and factories along China's northern coast where newly constructed factories churn out everything from playing cards and neckties to table-tennis paddles and socks. To illustrate the country's growth, reporter Peter Hessler told the story of the creation and growth of a family-owned company named "Lishui Yashun Underdress Fittings Industry Co., Ltd.," which makes wire fittings required in the manufacture of women's bras.[1]

"Pat Dollard's War on Hollywood" in *Vanity Fair* told the story of Dollard, a wealthy Hollywood agent and filmmaker, who abandoned Hollywood's "inner circle" to travel to Iraqi war zones, where he was injured and almost killed while producing a documentary that supported

America's war effort. His story was later made into a movie with the same title.[2]

An article in *Atlanta Magazine*, "You Have Thousands of Angels Around You," told a heart-tugging story about Cynthia Siyomvo, a 17-year-old refugee from Burundi who, after arriving in Atlanta without any family, faced the threat of deportation. But soon she discovered a circle of new friends who helped her find a home and began pursuing a biology degree and a career in medicine.[3]

These three stories won National Magazine Awards, the magazine industry's most prestigious awards—equal to the Pulitzer Prizes among newspapers. "China's Instant Cities" won the NMA for Reporting, "Pat Dollard's War on Hollywood" won the top award for Profile Writing, and "You Have Thousands of Angels Around You" won the NMA's top honor for Feature Writing.

These stories also provide rich examples of *action, angle* and *anecdotes*, which comprise the three primary ingredients of *interesting* writing. "There is a principle of writing so important, so fundamental that it can be appropriately called the First Law of Journalism and it is simply this: be interesting," wrote Benton Patterson, a former *Guideposts* editor and author of *Write To Be Read*.[4] This book's title includes *Action, Angle and Anecdotes* because we believe that lively action, a fresh, creative angle and lots of anecdotes characterize interesting writing that keeps readers interested and involved.

Action. These stories tell about Chinese cities and factories that grew out of nowhere, a street-side bomb that injured a Hollywood filmmaker in Iraq, and a Burundi teenage girl who discovered a new circle of friends and support from a southern American city.

Action is one characteristic of interesting stories. "Readers love action, any kind of action, and the story that does not move, that just sits there stalled while people declaim, explain, elaborate and suck their thumbs is justly labeled by some editors as MEGO—My Eyes Glaze Over," said William Blundell, in *The Art and Craft of Feature Writing*.[5]

Angle. These stories don't vaguely describe "Chinese industrial growth" or the "status of refugees in the United States." They have a focus—an angle on specific people who have a story to tell that illuminates larger issues, such as the war in Iraq.

An angle makes a story interesting because it provides enough detail about a subject to give the reader some fresh, original information. Broad subjects are vague, fuzzy and boring. Fresh angles give insight into old topics. You have to find a tiny slice that no one has cut before from a broad topic (such as "time management" or "weight loss") to make a publishable article out of it.

Anecdotes. These three stories contain dozens of anecdotes, which is another way of describing real-life examples and illustrations. They tell *specific* stories about *specific* people doing *specific* things at *specific* times and in *specific* places.

Anecdotes make articles interesting by telling true stories about people doing things. Many articles begin with an anecdote for a good reason: anecdotes tell a story—a tiny tale that draws us into the larger one. They illustrate the meaning of the information that follows. Nothing is more involving or revealing than human drama, and anecdotes capture drama with impact.

Best American Magazines

Over the past 25 years, these 10 magazines have won more National Magazine Awards than any others. The National Magazine Awards—given by the American Society of Magazine Editors—are the magazine industry's top honors.

The New Yorker
National Geographic
Newsweek
Vanity Fair
Esquire
Sports Illustrated
Rolling Stone
Wired
Time
BusinessWeek

SIDEBAR 1

Feature stories are sometimes called "human-interest stories." Good writers understand people as well as they know the language. They are sensitive, socially connected individuals who have an innate sense for finding and writing stories that interest humans. The more you talk to people, the more you understand what people are interested in hearing and discussing.

When most people pick up a magazine or the feature section of a newspaper, they're looking for entertainment or information. If a guy snoozes with an unfinished feature article on his lap, then the publication hasn't done its job. You can't argue that he's too lazy to understand the challenging content. Our sympathies are with the reader. If he got bored, it's because the writers didn't do their job. Great writing is all about reaching the reader through the use of compelling action, specific angles and colorful anecdotes.

FIVE MISTAKES OF BEGINNING WRITERS

After reading thousands of student-written articles for more than 30 years, we've created a list of the most common mistakes we've seen. We will start by explaining these five common mistakes and tell you how this book will teach you to avoid them.

Staying safe in your own backyard

Too many new writers rely on home-grown situations for article ideas and personal connections for interviews. They want to write about themselves, their parents, brothers and sisters, aunts and uncles or grandparents. Probably every person has a couple of good stories that originate among relatives. But once you write those stories, your tank is empty. You can't become a successful writer by staying in your own backyard. You can't rely on personal experience for more than a few article ideas or limit interviews to those people you know.

The main problem with writing about friends or family members is the writer's lack of objectivity and detachment. For example, what seems fascinating to you about your father may, in fact, be commonplace and boring to most readers. The Model Code of Ethics published by the Associated Collegiate Press says collegiate journalists "Should not cover ... or make news judgments about family members or persons with whom they have a financial, adversarial or close sexual or platonic relationship." Another reason for avoiding these convenient sources is that they fail to challenge you to venture outside your backyard and find the article ideas and sources you will need to discover week after week and year after year if you want to become a successful journalist. You also won't be challenged to work in your professional mode as you prepare and execute a probing interview.

Meg Grant, former West Coast editor for the *Reader's Digest*, says: "You really have to be fearless about approaching people and getting them to give you what you need. I think they will often give it to you if you ask them." She says that years ago when she worked for *People* magazine, an editor assigned her to interview the families of three children killed by a drunk driver, who was also a celebrity athlete:

> The editor told me, "You have to knock on their door and talk to some of these victims' families. I know you think they don't want to talk to you, but the truth is they do. They want to talk to someone and they want to tell you about their kids." So I had to go bang on those people's doors and say, "Would you talk to me?" And he was right. They did want to talk.[6]

Some students don't read enough outside of class assignments to know the difference between an original and an unoriginal idea. We know a journalism professor who begins each semester with a student survey that asks class members to list the magazines and newspapers that they read on a regular basis. The vast majority report that they don't read *any* print publication but depend on the Internet to give them the headlines of the day. Not only should future magazine writers read publications, they should read high-quality publications that contain in-depth articles. (See our list of "Best American Magazines.") If you don't read much outside of classes, what you consider a groundbreaking idea may have already been written about dozens of times.

Broad topic that lacks an angle

Second, some beginning writers want to write about a vague topic with an unfocused angle. When we ask for proposals for story ideas, many come up with a vague topic that interests them—but not a story idea. For example, some suggest writing about "the benefits of vegetarianism," on which many books have been written. "What can you tell us about this subject that hasn't been written before?" and "What is your specific angle?" are always the first questions we ask when someone comes up with an unfocused idea. Instead of writing about "the benefits of vegetarianism," we'd rather see a narrower angle on "the best vegetarian choices in fast-food restaurants."

Many magazine articles have been written about the advantages or disadvantages of alternative medicine. *Cat Fancy* took this same topic and gave it an angle aimed directly at its niche readership: In "Traditional vs. Alternative Medicine: Which Is Best for Your Cat?" the writer said, "You might be able to improve your cat's quality of life and hasten recovery from illness by including complementary and alternative medicine."[7]

The prevalence of this second mistake is why we're spending two chapters on developing and focusing ideas. Chapter 2 contains a dozen specific ways to come up with an idea while Chapter 3 gives some suggestions for whittling it down into a publishable angle.

Failing to dig deep

Strong, creative writers do a lot of digging. They've learned to be aggressive in seeking interviews and asking probing questions. Jack Kelley, a former senior editor for *People*, says, "Many of the best magazine writers liken their work to mining. They chip and chip until they extract a nugget. Then they chip some more. They are not embarrassed to keep asking questions until they hear what they need. Gold is in the details, and compelling color, quote and detail do not simply materialize."[8] One academic study found that the typical Pulitzer Prize-winning feature story was based on interviews with 53 people.

Scott McCartney, a *Wall Street Journal* reporter, wrote a story about the impact of high gasoline prices on the cost of air travel. He wanted to know what percentage of a ticket price paid for fuel. Airline officials he contacted refused to disclose that information because they considered it confidential. However, he found reports the airlines had filed with the U.S. Department of Transportation that gave him the answer. Six airlines reported an average of 53 to 73 percent of typical ticket prices went for fuel—a dramatic increase over earlier years when fuel prices were considerably lower.[9]

We know student writers who constantly check the word counts on their computers because their goal is to reach the word count that a professor requires. Professional writers typically do the opposite. They do enough research to assemble more than enough good material. Their main problem is "editing down" rather than "pumping up" a manuscript.

Some beginners write articles full of generalizations but lacking detailed evidence that backs them up. Writing skill, while essential, can never carry the article without strong content. Editors want facts, and they love to break stories with news their competitors have missed. Few writers have opinions or personal experiences that are in great demand.

Writing without anecdotes

The fourth mistake is failing to provide colorful, human-interest stories by using anecdotes. Anecdotes are true stories that illustrate the writer's main theme. Some editors have called them the "chocolate chips" of writing because they whet readers' appetite and keep them reading. Anecdotes also add credibility because they give real-life examples to the claims and generalizations made by the writer. For example, *Atlanta Magazine*'s "You Have Thousands of Angels Around You" began with this anecdote:

> She [Cynthia Siyomvo] got off the plane from Paris with nothing more than a couple of small bags. The bags had been packed for days as she waited for Eddie, a stranger who had approached her out of nowhere to say he knew all about her problems and could help. For $155 Eddie had given her a passport in the name of Marie-Therese Ekwa, age 24, from Verviers, Belgium. This young woman, however, was 17, and her journey had not started in Paris, and she had never been to Belgium.
>
> It was just before five in the afternoon. Detroit. September 4, 2001.
>
> The airport agent looked at the passport and asked her to state her business. She spoke very little English and did not understand.
>
> Français?
>
> Oui.
>
> She wore her long hair in braids and had on a T-shirt and pants. She stood five-foot-ten and carried her slender height gracefully, almost gliding. Despite the long flight, she had not slept but rather spent the transatlantic journey in conversation with herself: Where am I going? What am I doing? Have I done the right thing?[10]

Anecdotes are so essential and so difficult to find that they deserve their own chapter in this book. Anecdotes come from the people you interview. Chapters 5 and 10 explain how to find sources and phrase questions that will bring out the most humorous and compelling anecdotes.

Boring articles that lack action

Boring, windy articles lacking any action constitute the fifth mistake. We have read dozens of student articles that sound like condensed research papers or encyclopedia articles. Many beginning writers use stiff, long-winded content that doesn't fit the tone of today's magazines. Other symptoms of this disease occur with too many passive voice verbs, long and convoluted sentences, runaway adjectives and adverbs and an academic tone.

Editors eagerly look for stories that move, outrage, alarm, delight or inspire readers. They want to make their readers laugh, cry or get angry. They would rather receive angry letters to the editor than none at all because that means people are reading their publication. A plodding, formal style is a turnoff to every editor.

Chapter 9 tells you how to avoid boring stories by building action into characters and content. It shows you how to create action by increasing the use of tension, using people to illustrate abstract ideas and increasing the use of narrative, dialogue, action verbs and active voice.

DIFFERENCES BETWEEN NEWSPAPERS AND MAGAZINES

Good magazine and news feature stories connect with the reader in a way that differs from a news story. They tug at the heart at the same time they inform and inspire the mind. Is there any difference between newspaper and magazine features? Here's our consensus:

First, newspaper feature writing is shorter and more closely related to current events than magazine feature writing. There is, of course, much overlap and many fine newspaper features could easily appear in magazines. Generally speaking, magazine features may find a common theme in a series of events over time while a newspaper feature investigates one or two recent events. The features in magazines are also closely related to the niche topics of interest to their specialized audiences, while newspaper features more closely relate to current events or topics of interest to a broad audience. Consequently, magazine articles have a longer shelf life than newspaper articles. For example, magazines in public libraries remain on display shelves for at least a month, while most newspapers are changed daily.

Second, newspaper writing aims to please a geographically restricted audience with a broad range of ages, interests and socioeconomic backgrounds. It's like "shotgun writing." Magazine writing is directed toward a geographically diverse, but narrow target audience who has specific interests and demographic characteristics. It's like "rifle writing." With such a broad range of readers, newspapers must appeal to the lowest common denominator of interests, while magazines can cater to the special interests of their narrowly defined audience.

Third, newspaper feature writing is generally detached and objective. The personality of the writer remains hidden. Magazine writers have more freedom to display viewpoint, voice, tone and style in their writing. While newspapers aim for objectivity and neutrality in their reporting, the reputation of many magazines is built upon a particular political or religious point of view.

Fourth, newspapers employ large staffs of reporters and a few editors. Magazines employ large staffs of editors and few full-time writers. Most magazines rely on freelance writers for most of their stories. They don't just do this to save money. Because most magazines have a national readership, they want content from a wide range of contributors who resemble their readers. Although large consumer magazines are typically published in New York City, their editors really want their content to reflect the interests of all types of people in all types of places. That's why freelance writers are important to them.

Finally, newspaper writing requires daily deadlines; magazine writing has monthly deadlines except for a few weeklies and quarterlies. Readers expect more from their magazines: more complexity, analysis, originality, depth, sources and accuracy. Magazine writing is more intellectually challenging for the reader and the writer.

CHARACTERISTICS OF MAGAZINE READERS

Successful salespersons spend a lot of time nurturing relationships with their customers. Likewise, successful writers nurture relationships with their readers. When you write, you always need to ask yourself: "How will the reader react to this? Will this sentence cause the reader to laugh or roll his eyes? Will this paragraph fascinate the reader or send her quickly to another article?"

Good writers need to develop two personalities as they write. The first is the sensitive creator of words and eloquent ideas. But the second is the critical editor, acting on behalf of the reader, who savagely scours the page looking for mistakes and unnecessary content. The editor part of you must be precise and demand perfection.

Readers roam the aisles of supermarkets and department stores and browse through their magazines. Wal-Mart, for example, now accounts for 15 percent of all single-copy magazine sales. Readers sit at computer terminals surfing through Web sites. They browse through an airport newsstand while waiting for their connection. If a title or headline attracts their attention, they pick it up and read. If it holds their attention, they read to the end. Think about this happening millions of times every week, and you get the picture. Editors are paid, writers are paid, magazines are published, Web sites stay in business, and everyone is happy.

Large magazines hire research companies to determine the characteristics of their readers since this information is crucial to advertisers. These characteristics, known as demographics, may include (but are not limited to) their readers' ages, incomes, gender breakdown, educational levels, race and ethnic backgrounds, and percentage of homeowners. You can often find this information on a magazine's Web site under links for potential advertisers. Sidebar 2 includes an illustration of reader demographics of *The New Yorker*, *Rolling Stone*, and *TV Guide*.

We chose these three magazines to illustrate different types of reader characteristics. They have such differing readers that an article written for one magazine would never be publishable in the other two.

Demographics of Magazine Readers

	The New Yorker	Rolling Stone	TV Guide
Median age	55	28	44
Median household income	$154,933	$64,032	$49,466
Male	52%	59%	41%
Female	48%	41%	59%
Graduated/ Attended College	80%	60%	45%

Source: Magazine Web sites and Mediamark Research, Inc.

SIDEBAR 2

You will succeed as a writer if you assume that people who might read your work are:

✓ **Busy**. Unless assigned to read for school or job, they are not forced to read magazines, newspapers or the Internet. People use their discretionary time to read feature articles. It's your job to attract their attention and keep it.

✓ **Knowledgeable**. They probably know more than you do. People who read a lot of magazines generally have achieved higher educational levels than the general public. Therefore, you must work hard to give them information they haven't seen or heard before.

✓ **Easily distracted.** In today's multimedia world, readers have many sources of information from which to choose. Therefore, you can't assume they will finish reading what they begin. You have to find color and human-interest material to include in your stories.

These characteristics may not describe each reader. If you assume that they do, however, you will work harder and get published more quickly than your peers. An interesting article that will attract and hold the reader begins with an interesting idea. So to find an interesting idea, just turn to Chapter 2, and we'll get started.

ENDNOTES

[1] Peter Hessler, "China's Instant Cities," *National Geographic*, June 2007, 87.

[2] Evan Wright, "Pat Dollard's War on Hollywood," *Vanity Fair*, March 2007.

[3] Paige Williams, "You Have Thousands of Angels Around You," *Atlanta Magazine*, Oct. 2007.

[4] Benton Rain Patterson, *Write to Be Read* (Ames: Iowa State University Press, 1986), 6.

[5] William Blundell, *The Art and Craft of Feature Writing* (New York: Penguin Books, 1986), 54.

[6] Telephone interview with David E. Sumner, Nov. 29, 2003.

[7] Narda G. Robinson, DVM, "Traditional Vs. Alternative Medicine: Which Is Best for Your Cat?" *Cat Fancy*, July 2008, 30–33.

[8] Telephone interview with David E. Sumner, Jan. 19, 2004.

[9] Scott McCartney, "Flying Stinks, Especially for the Airlines," *The Wall Street Journal*, June 10, 2008, D1.

[10] Paige Williams, "You Have Thousands of Angels Around You."

2

THE HUNT FOR FRESH IDEAS

Your takeaway . . .

In searching for an idea, you have to keep in mind its angle, form and audience. In this chapter, you will learn why it's important to begin with an audience in mind and the possible "form" of an article as you search for an idea. Finally you will learn about a dozen specific places to look for article ideas.

Every magazine article idea has three specific components: *angle, form* and *audience*. The angle is the particular "slice" of the broad topic that you pursue, as we discussed in the last chapter. The "form" is the type of article, such as profile, how-to, inspirational, travel and so forth. The "audience" consists of the particular demographic group who reads the magazine where you intend to publish the article. When challenged to find an idea, most beginning writers think about the topic and the angle. These three components, however, form a triangle and none can be considered apart from the others. Before we discuss the angle, let's begin with audience and form.

FIGURE OUT YOUR AUDIENCE

The first step in developing an idea is figuring out who you are writing for. At least that's the first step professional writers take. Beginners often don't think of an audience for the article until after they've written it. If you've taken news or creative writing courses, you should remember the different characteristics of magazine articles. Newspaper and many Internet articles are written for the same, general audience. In news writing courses, you learn to write one way for a standard, vaguely defined audience. Among the first tasks when you create a magazine article idea is deciding who your readers are and which magazines you are aiming for. Here are some possible audiences and some sample magazine titles that serve them:

- college-aged males (*Maxim*)
- single women (*Cosmopolitan*)
- middle-aged women (*More*)
- business entrepreneurs (*Entrepreneur Magazine*)
- pro football fans (*Pro Football Weekly*)
- turkey hunters (*Turkey and Turkey Hunting*)
- adherents of specific religions and faiths (*U.S. Catholic*)
- managers of printing businesses (*Printing Impressions*)
- restaurant owners and managers (*Nation's Restaurant News*)
- residents of the South or New England (*Southern Living* or *Yankee*)

Most writers naturally start out by wanting to write articles for people like themselves. They stay in their own backyards. College students want to write articles for college students; those interested in fashion want to write about fashion; and those interested in sports want to write for sports fans. As you progress in writing experience, however, you learn to detach yourself from your personal interests and write articles that will interest people of vastly differing ages, professions and outlooks.

FIGURE OUT YOUR FORM

The second step in writing an article is deciding on form, which determines the format, structure and organization of the article. Magazine articles have these forms: profile, question-and-answer interview, trends and issues, dramatic stories, inspirational, reviews, how-to, etc. We will explain most of these types of articles in detail in subsequent chapters, but understanding the differences now will help you establish a framework for figuring out an original magazine article idea. Keep in mind that the boundaries between these categories are not rigid. You can easily find examples of features that blend two or more types.

Blurbs, briefs and brighteners (Chapter 13)

The best way to break into a publication today is with short, self-contained items that range from 50 words (for a joke) to 750 words (for a mini-profile). Readers like "shorts" because they are quick to absorb, less intimidating than a multi-page article, offer variety, can be clipped and saved and play to the current preference for skip-and-scan media.

Profile articles (Chapter 14)

Interviews produce three types of profile articles: the portrait, the photograph and the snapshot. Chapter 14 will offer tips on creating the well-balanced profile, often called a "warts-and-all" study of an interesting person.

Dramatic stories (Chapter 15)

The dramatic story tells about one person and one specific event in his or her life. In some cases, the focus may be on two or three people who encountered a dramatic experience together. A true-life narrative differs from a profile that describes an individual's personal interests, hobbies or insight into his or her personality.

Service and "how-to" articles (Chapter 16)

Service journalism offers readers useful, practical information that they can take and apply in their everyday lives. This type of article provides a service to readers by giving them practical information to help them live their lives, raise their families, prepare for a career, etc. They often focus on consumer information such as personal finance, shopping, health, career preparation or education. Readers are always looking for new ways to save, spend, make and invest money.

Seasonal and calendar-related stories (Chapter 17)

Most publications look for particular types of articles at special times of the year—Christmas, back-to-school, tax season and so forth. This chapter explains how to tune in on a publication's seasonal needs. It also gives practical tips on writing anniversary stories to commemorate special events, dates and historical markers.

Trends and issues (Chapter 18)

This type of news feature describes some recent trend, issue or controversy and quotes experts and participants who give their opinions about it. The distinguishing characteristic of this genre of writing is, first, that it focuses on an issue or trend and not upon a particular person and, second, that you bring together a variety of sources to shed light on an important topic. Issues and trend stories require a complex blend of analysis, facts, anecdotes and human interest.

Writing to inspire and motivate (Chapter 19)

People need all kinds of encouragement simply to get through life. You don't have to write for a religious publication to write an inspirational article. Hundreds of magazines and feature sections of newspapers look for articles that provide motivation and inspiration toward career success, religious faith or meaning in life.

Trades, organizations and associations (Chapter 20)

The common characteristic of these articles is the nature of the audience: they are written for people in particular jobs and careers or for people who belong to specific organizations and associations. This audience has specialized and narrow interests within a specific field. In general, both sectors publish the same types of articles as consumer magazines: profiles, dramatic stories, trends and issues, how-to, calendar-related, etc. Their articles employ the same principles and techniques of writing that we teach throughout this book. Freelance writers use the same techniques of publishing articles by studying the market and writing query letters.

FIGURE OUT YOUR ANGLE

The most difficult task beginning writers face is finding an original idea with a clearly focused angle. Many beginning writers can organize words, sentences and paragraphs using good punctuation and grammar. What most struggle with, however, is coming up with a strong angle that has a chance of being published.

Editors today insist on new material because they know their readers don't want a rehash of what's already out there. *Woman's Day* advises prospective writers in its guidelines: "We want fresh articles based on new material—new studies, new statistics, new theories, new insights—especially when the subject itself has received wide coverage. Any article that could have been published three years ago is not for *Woman's Day*."

Ellen Levine, former editor of *Good Housekeeping*, advises writers, "Give readers information unavailable elsewhere" and "strive for exclusive stories."[1] Everything a writer produces needs an original angle supported by information not already in print. Being original means that each article should "smell fresh" when it arrives in front of the reader. It shouldn't sound like it's been pulled from an "article warehouse" shelf somewhere. That's why you can't write an original article simply by regurgitating material from existing magazines, newspapers or Internet articles.

Let's put it this way: if you don't do any background reading before you develop an idea, you're likely to come up with an unoriginal idea. The best way to find an original idea is by reading. If you don't know what's been published in magazines, newspapers and books, then you have no way of recognizing an original idea when you find one. Successful feature writers have an insatiable appetite for reading. If you don't, you should question whether journalism is the right field for you.

For example, suppose you're interested in writing an article about the benefits of cat ownership. So you read through some back issues of *Cat Fancy* to get some ideas. In one issue, you find "Clergy Cats: An Exclusive

Look Into the Lives of Religious Leaders and Their Feline Companions." The writer interviewed a Catholic bishop, a rabbi and two Protestant ministers about their cats.[2] About a year later, the same magazine ran an article titled, "The Writer's Muse: Cats Help Inspire Their Owners' Creativity." This writer interviewed two professional writers about their cats and how cats inspire their creativity.[3] These two articles suggest that *Cat Fancy* likes to run articles about how and why people in particular kinds of work like cats. So why not propose a story about "Firefighters and Their Cats" or "Police Officers and Their Cats"?

"The real importance of reading is that it creates an ease and intimacy with the process of writing," writes Stephen King. "It also offers you a constantly growing knowledge of what has been done and what hasn't, what is trite and what is fresh, what works and what just lies there dying (or dead) on the page."[4]

A few years ago, this author interviewed more than a dozen syndicated magazine and newspaper columnists about their craft. One of the first questions was: "Where do you get ideas for your columns?" Their unanimous answer was "reading."

For example, humor writer and Pulitzer Prize winner Dave Barry says, "I read *The New York Times* and *The Miami Herald* every day. When I can, I read *The Wall Street Journal*, which I love. It's different from every other paper. I read *Newsweek, Esquire, Sports Illustrated, Harpers* and *The Atlantic*. I sometimes read the *New Republic* and balance it by reading the *National Review*. I just like to read."[5]

Kathleen Parker's feature column appears in more than 350 newspapers. When asked how she comes up with ideas, she said, "I read and read and keep reading until I feel a metabolic shift. I have to feel my blood pressure rise a little bit. The subject, whatever it is, has to evoke some emotion. . . . I have to feel something before I can write. I have to care. No passion in the writer, no passion in the reader."[6]

Anyone who hopes to maintain a steady flow of ideas has to read continuously, including publications that few others read. Ideas may come from unexpected sources: professional quarterlies, association newsletters, academic journals, annual reports and almanacs. While they seem boring, such sources often contain the most original thinking and latest developments long before they reach the general public. Here are more specific items to read or places to look as you dig for ideas for your feature articles.

Yellow Pages® of telephone books

The Yellow Pages® of small and large communities offers a plethora of businesses and individuals who can lead you to dozens of ideas. The best place to start is the "A" listings and browse until an inspiration hits you. However, here are some tips:

- Profiles of successful businesses or professionals. Every business, industry and profession has at least one magazine for people who work in that field. These magazines look for profiles of people in their field with unusual accomplishments or innovations.
- Profiles of people engaged in out-of-the-ordinary endeavors. General interest magazines may have an interest in profiles of practitioners of unusual jobs, such as magicians, chimney sweeps or insurance fraud investigators.
- Look for practitioners to interview for expert advice for a "how-to" article. For example, you can interview apartment building managers for advice on questions to ask before you sign a lease. You can interview auto dealers for advice on the most reliable used-car models or how to negotiate the best deal. You can interview dermatologists about the dangers and risks of tanning salons.
- Think about "what's up?" and "what's down?" All business cycles produce winners and losers, and even a dismal economy has some who profit from the downturn. RV and luxury car sales suffer with high gasoline prices, while train and bus travel increases. In recessionary times, thrift, discount and second-hand stores do well. Think about trends or cycles in your local economy and write about businesses affected by them in positive or negative ways.
- Look under "social service organizations" for details on groups that serve the underprivileged or engage in humanitarian causes that interest you. Call and ask about notable volunteers or recipients of their services who have inspiring or newsworthy stories. For example, our community has a place called "Stepping Stones for Veterans," which provides a residence for veterans who are unemployed or face substance-abuse problems.

You can also browse through the Yellow Pages® for any city in the United States through online services such as www.switchboard.com. These are excellent resources for finding ideas and sources for articles outside your immediate geographic area.

Weekly newspapers

Check local and area newspapers for small news items that you can develop into long feature stories for a magazine. Focus on locally written stories, not Associated Press or national stories. Look for brief articles about people who have received awards. The award itself may simply culminate an interesting series of events or achievements leading up to it. Many of our students have found their story ideas in small-town weekly newspapers. "Newspapers are filled with undeveloped stories, announcements of meetings and events, or tiny clues that could lead to interesting narratives," says Roy Peter Clark, senior scholar at the Poynter Institute for Media Studies.[7]

Old magazines

Magazines have certain perennial or evergreen topics that they revisit at least once a year. Look for seasonal articles related to holidays and anniversaries of major events. If you browse through enough issues, you can discover their perennial topics and come up with a fresh angle. Even if you don't think you have a chance of selling that idea to a prestigious magazine, you can send a query on a similar topic to a competing but lesser-known publication.

Remember that you can't copyright the *idea* for an article—only the particular way in which you write it. If you take an article as inspiration and develop it into something else, then you haven't committed plagiarism. Plagiarism only occurs when you use words from another article without giving credit.

Why You Should Read Old Magazines

Editors frequently complain that freelance writers don't study their publications before they submit unsolicited ideas and manuscripts. Experienced freelance writers pick the magazine or group of magazines they want to write for before they decide on an idea for a story. Then they study dozens of back issues at a library. That's because the best ideas will come from seeing the types of articles that those particular periodicals publish. Beginning writers often write their articles first and then try to find a place to publish them.

SIDEBAR 1

Here are some advantages to choosing your target publications first and reading through some of their previous issues:

- You know what topics have been covered and therefore can recognize an original idea when you see it.
- You know about current trends within the field of interest you want to write about and can pick a topic related to one of those trends.
- You can recognize the most frequent types of articles published in these magazines. For example, some magazines never publish profiles, poetry or personal experience articles.
- You become familiar with the writing style, tone and "personality" of the magazine (see Chapter 6 for more details).

Another advantage to reading old issues of some of your favorite magazines is that you can discover their evergreen topics. Susan Ungaro, former editor of *Family Circle*, once said:

Certain "evergreen" articles are published in every magazine over and over again. For instance, we constantly tell readers different ways to make the most of their money or to take charge of their health. I do a story every spring and fall on spring-cleaning your house, how to get organized, how to deal with clutter in your life. Romance and marriage secrets—how to make your marriage closer, more intimate, more loving—are probably addressed in every issue of every women's magazine.[8]

Public bulletin boards

Bulletin boards contain notices of future events, concerts, speakers or meetings of organizations. Musical performers or nationally known speakers may be visiting your area. You may find them very accessible to an interview. To obtain an interview, contact the sponsoring group for contact information on people you wish to interview.

Schedules of meetings, conventions and conferences

Most newspapers, city magazines, TV and radio stations publish an online calendar of upcoming speakers, conventions, hobby and trade shows and meetings. Web sites sponsored by city governments and visitors' bureaus contain the same information. A hobby or trade show, for example, will give you access to dozens of experts. These listings may also publicize meetings of self-help groups, hobby and service clubs and include meeting times and contact numbers. For example, support groups exist for families of murder victims, the mentally ill and drug abusers. These groups may allow you to visit if you promise to protect individual identities.

Faculty biographies on university Web sites

Go to any university's Web site and look for biographical sketches of faculty members. Colleges are the homes of some the nation's best minds, and the writer who doesn't tap this source of free information will miss a great opportunity. For example, a Florida zoology professor is an expert on alligators and often treks through the state's swamps with a camera and notebook. After getting an idea through reading faculty biographies, you can follow up with a telephone call to the professor. Many professors are nationally known experts in their subject areas and are flattered by requests for interviews.

To find them, click on the "academic programs" link on any university's Web site, and then find a department that interests you. Most departmental Web sites will list the publications and accomplishments of their faculty members along with telephone and e-mail addresses.

Association directories

Association directories are an excellent source for ideas and expert sources. "For every problem you can think of, there is an organization who can guide you to people who have it or have a story to tell. There are support groups for everything you can possibly imagine. There is not a disease or a political cause that is not represented somewhere in some group," says New York-based magazine writer Judith Newman.[9]

You will find thousands of associations. Here are some categories that represent members with broad types of concerns and interests:

- diseases, disabilities and other consumer medical issues
- political causes, environmental issues or rights for various minority groups

- hobbies, leisure pursuits and participatory sports
- faith-related causes and parachurch organizations
- professional organizations representing various jobs and occupations
- fraternal organizations and service clubs

Browse through the thousands of professional, hobby and nonprofit organizations in the association directory at the Internet Public Library: www.ipl.org/div/aon. In the medical category alone, you will find hundreds of organizations such as the Association of Suicidology, National Attention Deficit Disorder Association, Sexual Compulsives Anonymous and the Chronic Fatigue and Immune Dysfunction Syndrome Association. In the entertainment and leisure category, you will find groups such as the American Kitefliers Association, the Unicycling Society of America, the Association of Canadian Mountain Guides, the United Skateboarders Association and the National Woodcarvers Association.

CQ Researcher

CQ Researcher is often the first source that librarians recommend when researchers are seeking original, comprehensive reporting and analysis on issues in the news. Founded in 1923 as *Editorial Research Reports, CQ Researcher* is noted for its in-depth, unbiased coverage of health, social trends, criminal justice, international affairs, education, the environment, technology and the economy. Reports are published weekly by CQ Press, a division of Congressional Quarterly Inc. Although not available as a free Web site, you can find print and electronic editions available through most academic libraries. Each issue of this biweekly resource contains a balanced review with articles and bibliography. Recent topics included the transition to digital television, dealing with the "new" Russia, cyberbullying, gasoline prices and campaign finance reform.

Ask for referrals

Experienced reporters and magazine writers "mine" their sources by continually asking people they know for tips and leads for stories and whom to interview. Start with the people you know—teachers, librarians, religious leaders and the people you do business with. You don't get ideas by staring at a keyboard. Visit unfamiliar places and talk to strangers. Get away from the university and talk to factory workers, taxi drivers and store clerks. Listen to their gripes, problems and stories. Go to a political rally or a professional baseball game. The more you seek new experiences, the more likely you will find something to write about.

An editor once told a writer, "Your manuscript is both good and original, but the part that is good is not original and the part that is original is not good." To make it into print, an article must ooze quality, style and freshness. In short, the most successful magazine and newspaper features inform, provoke thought and introduce the reader to something new.

How to Know if You Have a Great Article Idea

Your idea should answer "Yes" to at least the majority of the following 10 questions:

1 Is this topic so new and original that you can't find any books written on the subject?
2 Is your topic of broad interest to the narrow group who read the particular magazine you are interested in writing for? Or will it just appeal to a narrow group within this narrow group?
3 Does this topic deal with basic life issues? "Basic" issues mean death, love, sickness, money, careers, health—issues that affect millions of people.
4 Do you have a strong, central unifying theme?
5 Can you state your angle in one sentence using an action verb?
6 Does your angle allow you to offer intelligent insight—as opposed to saying something that's obvious, commonsense or that readers have already read about many times?
7 Are there elements of drama or conflict that will attract and sustain the reader?
8 Can your topic generate several colorful and compelling anecdotes from your sources? Can you find human-interest stories about it?
9 Does your theme question or contradict what most people seem to think or assume? The best articles call into question the conventional wisdom about a subject.

SIDEBAR 2

10 Do you have access to the sources you need to write this article? These sources should be participants, keen observers or experts on the topic you are writing about.

ENDNOTES

[1] Quoted in Sammye Johnson and Patricia Prijatel, *Magazine Publishing* (Lincolnwood, Ill.: NTC Contemporary Publishing, 2000), 193.

[2] Sandy Robins, "Clergy Cats: An Exclusive Look Into the Lives of Religious Leaders and Their Feline Companions," *Cat Fancy*, Dec. 2006, 36–39.

[3] Christie Craig, "The Writer's Muse: Cats Help Inspire Their Owners' Creativity," *Cat Fancy*, July 2008, 80–81.

[4] Stephen King, *On Writing: A Memoir of the Craft* (New York: Simon & Schuster Pocket Books, 2000), 150.

[5] Interview with David E. Sumner, Miami, Fla., Nov. 17, 1997.

[6] Interview with David E. Sumner, Camden, S.C., Oct. 27, 1997.

[7] Telephone interview with David E. Sumner, July 21, 2008.

[8] Quoted in Judy Mandell (ed.), *Magazine Editors Talk to Writers* (New York: John Wiley and Sons, 1996), 57.

[9] Telephone interview with David E. Sumner, Dec. 11, 2003.

3

STRONG ANGLES AND FOCUSED IDEAS

Your takeaway . . .

A successful feature has a focused angle on a broad topic. A focused angle can be stated in one sentence and displays unity, action and specifics. In this chapter, you will learn how to recognize if your idea is too broad. You will also learn some techniques to help narrow it into a workable angle. Two exercises to help you do this are the "funnel of focus" and the "angle tree."

Jane Harrigan, former editor of the *Concord (NH) Monitor*, tells a story about a writer friend of hers.

> One day as I was climbing the stairs to her apartment, she yelled down a warning: "Watch out! I'm in the middle of a piece, and the place is a mess." Inside, her writing room looked just like mine, piles of paper covering every horizontal surface. Then something on the windowsill caught my eye. It was an index card with a single sentence written on it.
> "What's that?" I asked.
> "That's the point," Sue replied. "I put it there so I always know where to find it."[1]

Summarizing a story's central idea in a single sentence is a time-tested principle of writing. It's also a time-tested principle for creating a strong angle. Without that sentence, an article has no unifying theme, focus or compelling message. That focus prevents all of the bits and pieces of information you have collected from sprawling into an incoherent mess.

The most frequent problem among story ideas from new writers is broad and unfocused ideas. A *Wall Street Journal* editor put it this way:

Most of us think too big. We try to embrace the circus fat lady, and only well into the effort do we find there is too much of her and not enough of us. The result is a piece impossibly long, or superficial, the reporter frantically skipping from point to point without dwelling on any of them long enough to illuminate and convince.[2]

Some writers come up with vague topics they want to write about (such as physical fitness or a local band), but they don't create story ideas that have any chance of publication. For example, one student wanted to write an article about eating disorders. Her teacher challenged her to come up with a tighter angle on this broad topic. After some conversations with the professor, she decided to focus on treatment and build her story around the experiences of a young woman who acknowledged her problem and sought help. Still another writer chose a gender angle and explored anorexia among men.

ANGLES AND SUBJECT MATTER

Meg Grant, former West Coast editor for the *Reader's Digest*, explained how the magazine's editors narrowed a proposed feature article on foster care for children:

> We didn't want to do the same piece everybody is reading in the local papers about how broken the foster care system is. We picked a section of the foster care issue that was a smaller piece to chew on, which was about those kids who spend their whole lives in foster care and never get out of the system. We decided to look at one of the programs, and then we found one kid and told his story.[3]

A limited tale told clearly has more impact than a sweeping story that lacks depth and insight. The more frequently magazines and newspapers cover a given topic, the sharper and fresher the angle must be. Sidebar 1 provides examples of how to narrow the angle of some broad and unfocused topics.

A focused angle has three characteristics: unity, action and specificity. Let's look at each characteristic.

How to Give a Tighter Angle to a Broad Topic

Too Broad	Tighter Angle
Losing Weight	Teacher Tells How She Lost 100 Pounds
Quitting Smoking	Can Hypnotism Help You Quit the Habit?
Improving Your Home's Security	An Ex-Burglar Tells How to Burglar-Proof Your Home
Traveling on a Budget	Five Ways to Save Money on Hotels and Motels
Choosing a GPS Device	Avoid Buying Extra Features You Don't Need in a GPS Device

SIDEBAR 1

Unity

If you can't explain your article idea in one sentence, you don't have a workable idea. Dozens of editors and authors we have interviewed echo this "one sentence" rule. Why? Unity means that everything "hangs together" around a central idea. This central idea creates an organizing principle to help you determine whom you interview, what to look for in your research, what facts to include and what facts to omit. If you have a sharply focused angle before you begin, then you will save dozens of hours in fruitless research that leads you down the wrong path. Sometimes you find a fascinating anecdote, and you feel as if you just have to include it. But those paragraphs that interrupt the unity of the article will also jar the reader. So go back and remove them.

A good, clear focus means that the title and introduction let the readers know exactly what they are getting into and give them a chance to get off if they don't want to go there. Here's an example of a tightly focused article from *BusinessWeek*:

"Toyota's All-Out Drive to Stay Toyota"

How's this for strange? Toyota Motor, the company that has the rest of the auto industry running scared, is worried. As new hires pour in and top executives approach retirement, the company fears it might lose the culture of frugality, discipline, and constant improvement that has been vital to its success. So management has launched a slew of education initiatives, and even uses a business school in Tokyo to teach Toyota to be, well, more like Toyota.[4]

You can summarize this article in this sentence: "Toyota has launched a slew of education initiatives to teach its employees how to maintain its culture of frugality, discipline and improvement." And everything in the story pertains to that central idea. If it takes two sentences to explain your idea, then you should write two stories.

Unity means unity in content, style, voice and approach. Gary Provost says in *Beyond Style: Mastering the Finer Points of Writing*: "Unity, that quality of oneness in your writing, means that everything you write should look as if it were written at one time, by one person, with one purpose, using one language."[5]

Action

Strong, creative articles contain action. They describe people having fun, helping others, getting a job or making a business succeed. A strong action verb in the title or magazine's cover line attracts the attention of the editor and the reader. Go to a store's magazine display and look at the teasers that are placed above the newspaper's nameplate. Both cover lines and teasers are meant to attract readers, which is why they often contain action verbs.

J.C. Suares, a New York magazine designer, believes that cover lines must contain an action verb. Verb-less cover lines are motionless and boring, he argues: "There's no such thing as a cover line without a verb. If it doesn't have a verb then it's not a cover line. It's a title. You've got to come up with a sentence with a verb in it. I talk myself blue in the face [to editors] about having a verb in the cover line or headline."[6]

Here are some cover lines from recent magazines. Notice that each one contains an action verb.

"*Hazing* Nightmares: You *Won't Believe* These Shocking Stories" (*Teen People*)

"What to *Do* When His Crazy 'Ex' Won't *Let Go*" (*Teen People*)

"Get Lean All Over: A New Diet and Workout Plan to Max Your Metabolism" (Shape)

"Chill Out—How to *Calm* Your Hot Horse" (*Horse and Rider*)

"Cool Wedding Trends: What Other Couples Are *Doing* Coast to Coast" (*Bride*)

"How to *Avoid* the Fat Trap in Fast Food Salads" (*Ladies Home Journal*)

Specificity

Don't write about a person or group simply because they exist. A story shouldn't just be "about" a place or an institution. "What about it?" is the question to ask. Something should happen.

For example, suppose you traveled to Cleveland and wanted to write an article about the Rock and Roll Hall of Fame and Museum. What about it? Since hundreds of articles have been written about it, what has happened recently that is newsworthy? Who has been inducted into the Hall of Fame since last year? Remember that a story should be a verb. Give it a specific angle. *The Boston Globe* wrote about the museum's annual induction ceremony with this title: "Rock and Roll Hall of Fame Show Lacks Luster of Past."[7]

Facts and quotes must include specific dates and places in which they occur. "Unanchored" articles are vague and make it difficult for the reader to visualize their ideas. If you can't cite specific dates and places in an article, then it isn't sufficiently anchored. Tell where your quoted experts are from and who they work for. Avoid the abused words "recent" and "recently" and tell how long ago the interview or event occurred. Even if your story is on some broad "evergreen" topic like tax-saving tips, you have to anchor it with expert sources and examples that occurred in specific places at specific times.

HOW TO NARROW YOUR TOPIC

Before we look at specific steps to narrow the angle of a topic, these guidelines will help you determine if your story idea is too broad. Let's say you're thinking about writing an article on e-mail scams, and so we will use that as an example.

If you can find a book

Never write a feature article from rehashed book content. Editors demand fresh, original stories. They don't want hash that's been ground out of books, Internet or other articles. A search of books using the term "e-mail scams" at Amazon.com turns up more than a dozen books on the topic. Here are some examples:

The Complete Idiot's Guide to Frauds, Scams, and Cons

A Con Man Reveals the Secrets of the Esoteric Trade of Cheating, Scams, and Hustles

E-mails from Hell

Phishing Exposed

Crimes of Persuasion: Schemes, Scams, Frauds

Judging by the number of books, "e-mail scams" by itself is definitely too broad a topic for a feature article.

If someone could write a book

If someone could write a book on a subject, they probably have. About 150,000 books are published every year in the United States according to one estimate. Feature articles can't cover everything because their length usually ranges from 1,000 to 2,000 words. Each story must focus on a small slice of a huge pie.

If your proposed title has no verbs

We've already discussed the importance of action in an angle. Look at the titles of articles from popular magazines. As mentioned, most will include a verb in the title describing something happening. The term "e-mail scams," of course, has no verbs, and we've already ruled it out as a topic. So let's look at how five magazines or TV networks covered the topic from five angles:

1   ***The New Yorker:*** "How a Massachusetts Psychotherapist Fell for a Nigerian E-Mail Scam"
2   ***PC World:*** "In Pictures: How to Spot an E-Mail Scam"
3   ***ABC News:*** "Former Congressman Duped by Nigerian Scams"
4   ***Network World:*** "Whaling: Latest E-Mail Scam Targets Executives"
5   ***The Motley Fool:*** "Do Online Banks Facilitate Fraud?"

If you want to write an article on e-mail scams, we challenge you to read a dozen articles on the topic before you begin writing or interviewing. Then—and only then—will you know what's been covered, what the issues are, where disagreements exist, which questions remain unanswered and what questions to ask. Then—and only then—will you know how to come up with a fresh and original angle on well-worn topics.

While reading about your general topic in other publications is the first step, it only helps you eliminate non-original angles. After that there are no quick and easy steps. However, you can ask at least three questions that will point you in the right direction.

Find a news peg

First, ask yourself, "How can I hang this topic on a news peg?" A news peg is a current event or anniversary of a historic event that illustrates the topic you want to write about. For example, the January birthday of Martin Luther King Jr. offers a news peg to write stories related to civil rights or race relations. An election campaign offers a news peg for stories about controversial issues that the candidates are debating. A recent death caused by a drunken driver offers a peg into several possible angles on the subject of alcohol abuse.

"Any time you're fortunate enough to have a news item related to your topic, the battle for your reader's attention if half over," said author Mary S. Schaeffer in an article in *The Writer.*[8] News pegs offer a way to "get into" or develop a lead for a feature story. To get some ideas, simply browse the headlines of newspapers and news Web sites and see where you can go from there.

"Nationalize" a local topic

Newspaper reporters and editors always try to localize a national story by finding a local source who can give it an angle that's closer to their readers. Magazines sometimes follow the other direction. They write about a story in a small town that illustrates or amplifies an important national issue. *The New Yorker* story mentioned earlier—"How a Massachusetts Psychotherapist Fell for a Nigerian E-Mail Scam"—illustrates this point. The writer found a 57-year-old psychotherapist from Groton, Mass., who lost $600,000 by falling for one of the infamous Nigerian e-mail scams. While telling his story, the writer offered factual background and context about e-mail scams and showed readers how they could avoid making the same mistake.[9] We show you how to nationalize a local story in Chapter 6.

Decide what you want to know

Ask yourself, "What would I like to know about this topic?" Trust your hunch about what angle seems most interesting. One of the biggest myths about writing is the often-repeated aphorism, "Write about what you know." If we only wrote about what we knew, none of us would last more than a week in the publishing business.

If a magazine editor asks you, "What do you know about _____ topic?" then try this answer: "Well, I'm not an expert, but I want to find some experts and ask them the right questions." In other words, you don't have to be an expert to write a good story. You simply need to know where to go to find the experts.

Find a unique source

Another way of deciding how to focus a topic is by asking, "What unique or primary sources do I have access to?" A person with expertise or unique experiences in a particular area is a primary source. Other primary sources are copies of correspondence or official documents. Maybe you know someone who is newsworthy because of a unique accomplishment. Maybe a friend can help you get an interview with a celebrity.

One student wrote about the lifelong romance of a couple who had been married 65 years. Their romance began with writing love letters to each other while he was fighting overseas in World War II. The student obtained copies and quoted the letters they wrote to each other during the 1940s, which brought freshness, originality and poignancy to their story.

David E. Sumner wrote a magazine story about a small Florida town's "Kumquat Festival" that attracts 30,000 people every January (a kumquat is a small citrus fruit). His angle was on a Boston TV celebrity who has visited the festival every year since it began. The story idea originated, however, with a conversation with his nephew, who helps organize the festival and who helped him obtain interviews with the TV celebrity and other festival organizers.

Writer and movie producer Nora Ephron advises, "You must come up with some little thing that you know about that others don't. A good journalist figures that out. It means reading everything possible to keep up with what's going on. You can't merely find a subject that may interest a magazine editor. Find a subject on which you have something interesting, surprising or perverse to say."[10]

THE ANGLE TREE

One of the best ways to focus an idea is to use the "Angle Tree" exercise, which allows you to brainstorm on paper. Start with a broad topic you are interested in covering and write it in the center circle. Then write four directions or angles you could pursue with that topic. If you try to cover all angles your article will lack depth; however, you can choose one angle as your main focus and a second angle to explore as a sidebar. After you've decided on your focus, the next step is to determine whom you should interview and what kind of background research you should gather.

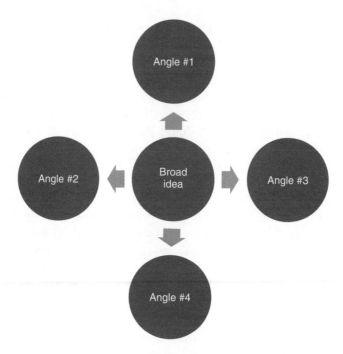

Here is an example using the broad topic of time management. We chose some titles that were actually published in popular magazines.

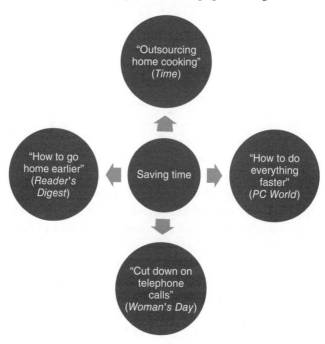

USING THE FUNNEL OF FOCUS

Another way of narrowing an angle is the "funnel of focus" exercise developed by Dr. Gerald Grow, a professor of journalism at Florida A&M University.[11] The purpose of this exercise is the same—begin with a broad topic and narrow it down into a focused angle. Here is an example beginning at the "top" of the funnel and proceeding to the narrow end.

1 *Topic big enough to fill a library*
Example: "College Education"
2 *Topic big enough to fill a book*
Example: "Paying for a College Education"
3 *Theme topic for one issue of a parenting magazine*
Example: "Where to Find Scholarships for Your Children"
4 *A single article in the same magazine*
Example: "Best Scholarships for Children of Military Veterans"
5 *Another article in the same magazine*
Example: "Where to Find Scholarships for Journalism Majors"

To summarize, an angle takes a specific approach to its subject matter. A strong angle can be summarized in one sentence and displays unity, action and specificity. The cover lines on magazines provide examples of focused angles. You can use the "angle tree" or "funnel of focus" as an exercise to narrow your topic. You can narrow your topic by asking yourself what you want to know, what sources you have access to and by finding a news peg that ties your topic to a current event.

The narrower your angle, the more likely you will write a creative, original article. The narrower your angle, the more likely you will find a "scoop" that no one else has written about. Finally, the narrower your angle, the more likely you will get published. Finding a good angle isn't easy, but the more you read what's already been published, the easier it will become.

ENDNOTES

[1]   Jane Harrigan, "Organizing Your Material," in *The Complete Book of Feature Writing*, ed. Leonard Witt (Cincinnati, Ohio: Writer's Digest Books, 1991), 100.

[2]   William Blundell, *The Art and Craft of Feature Writing* (New York: Penguin Books, 1988), 24.

[3]   Telephone interview with David E. Sumner, Nov. 29, 2003.

[4]   David Welch and Ian Rowley, "Toyota's All-Out Drive to Stay Toyota," *BusinessWeek*, Nov. 22, 2007. Accessed at Businessweek.com, June 18, 2008.

[5]   Gary Provost, *Beyond Style: Mastering the Finer Points of Writing* (Cincinnati, Ohio: Writer's Digest Books, 1988), 42.

[6]   Interview with David E. Sumner, New York City, Aug. 5, 2005.

[7]   Sarah Rodman, "Rock and Roll Hall of Fame Show Lacks Luster of Past," *The Boston Globe*, March 8, 2008. Accessed at www.boston.com, June 19, 2008.

[8]   Mary S. Schaeffer, "Take a Potentially Dry Topic and Spice It Up," *The Writer*, July 2007, 27.

[9]   Michael Zuckoff, "How a Massachusetts Psychotherapist Fell for a Nigerian E-Mail Scam," *The New Yorker*, May 15, 2006. Accessed at www.newyorker.com, June 19, 2008.

[10] Quoted in Candy Schulman, "The Idea Ideal," in *Handbook of Magazine Article Writing*, ed. Jean M. Fredette (Cincinnati, Ohio: Writer's Digest Books, 1988), 25.

[11] Gerald Grow, "The Funnel of Focus." Accessed at www.longleaf.net/ggrow, Nov. 2, 2008. Reprinted with permission.

ORIGINAL RESEARCH = ORIGINAL ARTICLES

Your takeaway . . .

Successful nonfiction writers know that digging deep with strong reporting and creative research precedes great writing. This chapter will give you tips on finding expert sources for productive interviews and mining the sources of traditional libraries, electronic databases and the "invisible" sources of the Internet. It explains the difference between primary and secondary sources and how to use different types of primary sources to produce fresh, original articles.

Isabel Wilkerson won the 1994 Pulitzer Prize for feature writing while a reporter for *The New York Times*.[1] In a speech to journalism students, she encouraged them to practice her "40-40-20" rule for writing great stories. She says she spends the first 40 percent of her time doing background research to find her topic, angle and sources to interview, the next 40 percent doing interviews and background research, and the final 20 percent writing the story. She calls this the "up-front" rule of reporting. Writers should spend 80 percent of their time on the "up front" work, so that the writing will follow easily and require no more than 20 percent of their time.[2]

When faced with the challenge of coming up with an idea for a story assignment, many beginning writers follow the "thumb-sucking" rule. That means they sit in their corner, suck their thumb and think, "What shall I write about?"

The problem with this "thumb-sucking" approach is, first, you're not likely to come up with an original idea. You're likely to find only a "backyard topic"—a topic drawn from the narrow perimeters of your personal interests—not one that has any chance of getting published in a national magazine with millions of subscribers.

The most common "backyard topics" for students are male-female relationships, stress, diet, health and fitness, sororities and fraternities, local bands and music, and travel ideas. For example, we've read dozens of student articles on "How to Plan a Spring Break Trip." The first problem with these tired topics is they've been written about hundreds of times. Finding an original angle is difficult. The second problem with tired topics is that they rarely contain original insight or rise above common sense information anyone can figure out or find on the Internet.

Beginning with some background research offers the best way to narrow your focus. If you have a general idea of what to write about, but are puzzled about the focus, then start reading. Read a dozen articles on your chosen topic before doing any interviews. This background research helps you determine the context, focus and angle for an article. It tells you what's been written, what questions have been asked, and—most important—what questions haven't been asked or answered. By discovering these gaps and questions, you can come up with a fresh angle on an old topic.

A few years ago, David E. Sumner surveyed 134 journalism professors who taught feature and magazine writing courses. He asked them to choose, from a list of 20 common writing mistakes, the ones that occurred most often in their students' work. The biggest mistake? An overwhelming number of these professors ranked number one: "Not reading widely enough to distinguish between original and unoriginal ideas," which confirms a point we made in Chapter 1.

How to Test the Originality of Your Idea

SIDEBAR 1

The single biggest improvement students could make to improve their grades in feature writing classes is to spend at least three hours of reading about their chosen topics before coming up with the exact angle or deciding whom to interview. Your reading should look for three kinds of information:

1 Discover what's been written and what angles have been covered before. This reading will help you to create an original angle with new insight. Ask yourself: "How can I give this subject a fresh angle that hasn't been covered before?"

2 Look for a news peg—a recent news event to "hang" your story on to make it more pertinent, timely and publishable. Anyone whose goal is to become a professional writer should read at least one newspaper daily—besides your campus newspaper. We also recommend reading a national daily, such as *The New York Times, The Wall Street Journal* or *USA Today.*

3 When reading, watch for quoted experts whom you may be able to call to do your own interviews. You can often find telephone numbers with the help of an online directory such as Switchboard.com. Remember, you cannot "lift" comments from quoted experts whom you didn't interview.

Many comments from these professors in Sumner's survey reflected students' failure to do substantive research or interviewing. "The main problem I've found is lack of depth in reporting," wrote one professor. Students tend to choose topics that affect them personally and then rely on the Internet or "Googling" for most of their research. One professor said, "If the subject has not affected them personally, they have a hard time relating to it." Another added, "Students want to write first-person columns about their personal feelings or interview friends or people they know."

Comments from a professor at the University of Western Sydney in Australia revealed that these problems are not limited to American students. She said, "The problem that troubles me most is the lack of motivation in students to investigate issues. They seem happy to use information that is readily available rather than ask questions or dig deep."

WHY YOU NEED LIBRARIES

More than 150,000 books are published every year in the United States. These books range in price from $10 to more than $100 and few, if any, are published free on the Internet. Authors who spend their days and weeks doing research, conducting interviews and writing deserve to earn a living like everyone else. So if you want to read about the most recent, break-through discoveries, you may have to go to a library.

Joe Treen, a former managing editor for *People*, says library resources possess three advantages over the Internet: "First of all, they've got books. Second of all, they've got employees who can help you. Third, they have reliability. I don't always trust stuff I see on the Internet. I think bricks and mortar libraries are not going to go away."[3]

Library books and articles are also more likely to be closely scrutinized and fact-checked by professional editors than material you find elsewhere. Academic journal articles are peer-reviewed, which means that two or three experts in their field review and approve each article before it appears in print.

You can save valuable time by taking a few minutes to introduce yourself to a reference librarian. Because librarians enjoy books and reading, they enjoy helping writers and researchers. Their job is to make your library research more efficient and productive.

Libraries have two other advantages not found elsewhere. You can browse the magazine stacks and read articles from back issues. Browsing through their article topics will help you create ideas as well as locate target markets for your stories. The number-one complaint editors make about freelance writers is that they don't study their publications before submitting a query letter or article. The library is the only place to study old print issues of target magazines and really get a "feel" for the kinds of articles they publish.

Second, university libraries subscribe to commercial electronic databases not accessible on the Internet. For example, *Lexis-Nexis News*, *Access World News* and *Newspaper Source* are all commercial databases available only through libraries. *Newspaper Source* contains major newspapers, such as *The New York Times* and *The Wall Street Journal*, while *Access World News* has daily newspapers in smaller cities. You can find the full text of court decisions through *Lexis-Nexis Legal*. *Science Direct* offers full-text access to 900 full-text scientific journals covering such areas as biotechnology, chemistry, computer technology and more. Large libraries pay more than $100,000 a year to subscribe to these databases, but make them free to their patrons. While they're always available through in-house terminals, many libraries also make them available through their Web sites to registered patrons.

WHY INTERVIEWS ARE ESSENTIAL

The most common excuse we hear from students about not getting interviews is, "He never replied to my e-mail." Hello? Just pick up the telephone and call.

While background research adds depth and detail to article writing, personal interviews bring freshness, color and originality. We cannot stress enough the superiority of face-to-face and telephone interviews to online research or e-mail interviews. Face-to-face and telephone interviews cover numerous topics in a relatively short period of time. The time required by e-mail to type on a keyboard slows down communication and discourages your source from giving you as much information as they would in a face-to-face or telephone interview.

"Scary" is how John Brady, a professional-in-residence at Ohio University, describes the prevalence of e-mail interviews and reliance on Internet research among his students. Brady wrote, "Interviewing is the key to effective feature writing. Without enough interviews, reporters are writing on empty. I feel so strongly about this problem, I wrote a book about it."[4] Some students have been known to conduct e-mail interviews with persons who work at the same school that they attend.

Myron Struck, editor-in-chief of Targeted News Service, says, "Eight of 10 interns who have come to us over the past four years from journalism programs do not know how to conduct face-to-face interviews and believe that e-mail and perhaps the telephone are far superior." He encourages teachers to discourage e-mail interviews and "encourage more practice doing face-to-face interviews."[5]

Some people feel self-conscious about poor grammar or spelling ability and don't reply to non-essential e-mail. Or they only offer terse replies. Influential people get hundreds of e-mail messages daily and may brush you off if they reply at all. E-mail also gets lost because of technical problems and disappears when a server is down, a power outage occurs, or the sender makes a typographical error in the address.

Sources cannot avoid a telephone call or personal visit like an e-mail message. While they can hit the "delete" key for unwanted e-mail, they have to say something when you appear at their door or reach them on the telephone. It's just harder to say "no." The more distance you put between yourself and a source, the more information you lose. We cover interviewing techniques in Chapter 5.

Get "Up Close and Personal" with Your Interviews

Face-to-face interviews

When you sit in front of someone, you hear and see: (a) words; (b) tone and voice inflection; (c) pauses; (d) facial expressions; (e) dress, appearance and mannerisms; (f) physical surroundings of the interviewee; and (g) you may also get to talk to people who live or work nearby. In other words, you get the benefit of the whole context of the interview.

Telephone interviews

When you talk on the phone, you hear only: (a) words; (b) tone and voice inflection; (c) pauses. You don't see facial expressions. Face-to-face interviews offer facial expressions indicating skepticism, surprise, approval or disapproval that often prompt you to ask follow-up questions. You miss these on the telephone and in e-mail.

E-mail interviews

You see: (a) words. Your interviewee can use carefully chosen words to evade your questions. You can't ask spontaneous, follow-up questions. You can't detect the mood or tone of voice of your interviewee. Use e-mail for quotes only when you are looking for brief facts. E-mail can also be useful for verifying facts and quotes from people you have already interviewed.

The "Model Code of Ethics" published by the Associated Collegiate Press says writers should verify an e-mail source's identity with a follow-up telephone call. Telephone or in-person interviews always surpass e-mail interviews in the quality of the information that they produce.

SIDEBAR 2

Gay Talese, Pulitzer Prize-winning reporter, wrote in his memoir, *A Writer's Life*,

At least half the time I have devoted to this current book, as well as to my earlier ones, has been spent collecting and assembling information that I obtained from libraries, archives, government buildings where public records are kept, and from various individuals whom I have sought out and interviewed. I believe face-to-face contact is necessary because I want not only a dialogue but a visual sense of the interviewee's personal features and mannerisms, as well as the opportunity to describe atmospherically the setting in which the meeting took place.[6]

PRIMARY SOURCES: ESSENTIAL FOR ORIGINALITY

A *Reader's Digest* editor once advised his writers: "Bullet-proof your manuscript. When a story is scheduled, our fact-checking department begins its work. Our fact-checkers are second to none. We don't use secondary sources. You can't quote from newspapers or magazines. You've got to go back to the primary sources to confirm that they weren't misquoted."[7]

Primary sources and secondary sources are terms that distinguish between information that comes from its original creator and that which an intermediary has edited and filtered. A primary source for an interview comes from a person who directly observed an event. A primary source for a document is one that hasn't been published in its original form—such as a letter or report. Articles from existing magazines and newspapers are "secondary" by definition because another writer has already gathered and edited the facts for readers.

Secondary sources aren't necessarily inferior to primary sources. You need to read them to find ideas, figure out the angle and add context and depth to your material. To get an article published, however, you have to interview and use primary sources to get the "scoop."

The Internet creates both a disturbing threat and an unparalleled opportunity to writers. It threatens good reporting because Web sites offer limitless opportunities for shallow research and plagiarism. You can find hundreds of articles on any topic, rearrange a few facts here, lift a few quotes there and create a 1,500-word article. This patchwork approach to Internet research is easy to recognize because it smells stale; it's also dishonest and illegal.

"I can now see how word processors and the Internet make it easy for writers to cut and paste the work of other authors into their own text. At the same time, the Internet also makes it easy for fact-checkers to catch writers in the act," said Lori K. Baker, a former fact-checker at *Arizona Highways*, in an article in *The Writer*.[8]

The Internet offers a tremendous opportunity to writers because it helps locate expert sources on any topic and makes a great starting point. When properly used, the Internet can offer writers in out-of-the-way places access to nationally known experts. It offers access to millions of government records that used to require a trip to the state capital, U.S. Archives or Library of Congress. The Internet offers a "gateway" to the world that can create a national content for articles written to a national audience. But don't do all of your research on the Internet, or you're likely to end up with outdated information.

Recommended Print Research Resources

SIDEBAR 3

CQ Researcher	Compilations of articles on current events and controversial issues
Contemporary Authors and Writers	Biographies of living and deceased American authors
Current Biography	Biographies of current newsmakers and celebrities
Editorials on File	Editorials from newspapers around the country on current news topics
Encyclopedia of Associations	A three-volume directory of more than 24,000 national and international organizations
Gale Directory of Publications and Broadcast Media (annual)	State-by-state directory of all newspapers, magazines, radio and television stations
International Directory of Company Histories	Histories of major U.S. companies and corporations
The New York Times Index	Indexes of NYT articles published back to 1851
The Wall Street Journal Index	Indexes of WSJ articles published back to 1958
Statistical Abstract of the United States (annual)	Recent government data on all topics related to the U.S. (print and online versions)

Who's Who in America	Biographies and contact information of successful Americans in all fields of endeavor
Hoover's Handbooks	Information on public and private companies, including financial data and trends

Recommended Web Sites for Journalism Researchers

Magportal.com and Findarticles.com	Accessible full-text articles from thousands of online magazines
Journalismnet.com	Gateway site to thousands of useful research sites for journalism researchers
Poynter.org	A private institute offering resources, links and training for professional journalists
Powerreporting.com	Gateway site to thousands of useful research sites for journalism researchers
Reporter.org	Resources and links for investigative journalists and reporters
Ipl.org/div/aon	Internet Public Library's "Associations on the Net" directory

SIDEBAR 4

THE INTERNET—PRIMARY OR SECONDARY SOURCE?

Articles and documents found on the Internet can be primary sources or secondary sources. If the information comes from an article in an online newspaper or magazine, then it's a secondary source. But other types of online information can be used as valuable primary source material. Here are some types of primary source information that you can find online.

Speeches, reports, judicial decisions

Published stories about important speeches summarize and paraphrase that speech. But if you can find the full texts of the original, you have a primary source. The full text of speeches, agency reports, research reports and judicial decisions give you original information not filtered or interpreted by other writers. Public figures, such as political leaders and company presidents, often place the full text of their speeches on their company or office's Web site. Professional associations, nonprofit organizations or government agencies may publish the full texts of research reports on the Internet. The full texts of most judicial decisions at the state and higher levels are available online. If you're writing about a controversial court decision, for example, go to the Internet and find the full text of the decision so you won't have to rely on other writers' interpretations.

Reports from companies, government agencies and nonprofits

A "report" usually results from an in-depth investigation of an issue or problem. Academic scholars, nonprofit foundations and associations and government agencies issue thousands of reports every year on public policy issues. They sometimes contain gems and nuggets of information. Since corporate Web sites focus on putting a "PR" spin on their company, you will most likely find hard-hitting reports at "edu," "org," and "gov" Web sites. Some internal documents may not be public knowledge until a writer finds them, combs through them and pulls out the "bombshell" that officials hoped no one would notice.

Original statistical data

Original statistical data also reveal facts and trends that haven't been interpreted or distorted by other writers. When you find the original data, you can report the story using first-hand interpretations.

Statistics add indisputable credibility. They describe a quantitative relationship between phenomena and help you prove the growth, decline or magnitude of any issue you write about. The U.S. government spends millions of taxpayer dollars every year to compile statistics on every aspect of American life: economics, transportation, health, crime, public safety, labor, manufacturing, birth and death rates and more. All of these results are available at a Web site (www.fedstats.gov) described as "the gateway to statistics from over 100 U.S. federal agencies." You can search for statistics by keyword, agency, topic or state. This Web site also contains an online version of the annual series, *Statistical Abstract of the United States*. Most libraries also have the most recent print edition of the *Statistical Abstract* in their reference section. Over the years, we have used the *Statistical Abstract* as a research reference more often than any other print publication besides *Writer's Market*, which we tell you about in Chapter 6.

If you want to gain a competitive edge over your peers, learn how to summarize and interpret data using Excel or any popular spreadsheet. Spreadsheets allow you to take a large list of data—such as state-by-state averages on various issues—and alphabetize or sort from highest to lowest. You can also calculate year-by-year averages, percentage changes and fluctuations. For example, one writer we know used www.fedstats.gov and a spreadsheet to compare inflation, unemployment and job growth in Republican and Democratic presidential administrations every year between 1900 and 2000. (Neither side had a discernible advantage.)

Most journalists dislike numbers, and you may be among them. Any writer, however, who can examine a table of numbers and detect a trend or find an unreported scoop has a talent that employers value. Today's most successful writers know how to download information into Excel spreadsheets, examine it and find stories. For example, original statistical data from the Census Bureau may yield a story around the rapid increase in birth rates in a particular state, increased worker productivity in another state or a population exodus from other states.

A trend story (see Chapter 18) results when a phenomenon is getting bigger or more popular—or the opposite—getting smaller or losing popularity. For example, these stories may report on birth, marriage or divorce rates, consumer spending habits, lifestyle and career choices. They will originate in statistics you can find at the Census Bureau (www.census.gov) or studies conducted by professional associations that represent these issues.

Academic studies and scholarly journal articles

Scholarly journals containing studies conducted by academic researchers are an exception to the rule that previously published articles are secondary sources. Reports on groundbreaking studies from medical journals are frequently published or broadcast in the media. Don't rely on what a magazine story says about a study from the *New England Journal of Medicine*. Go back and find the original article, which is a primary source. You may find a different angle on the same information. Since scholarly journals usually have low circulations, they offer writers the opportunity to publicize the results of groundbreaking studies to the wider public. Browsing through scholarly journals in psychology, sociology, political science or business may also give you plenty of article ideas. Since most authors are also professors, you can interview them after finding their telephone numbers through university Web sites.

Congressional reports and testimonies

Because of the volume and complexity of its work, the U.S. Congress divides its tasks among approximately 250 committees and subcommittees. They conduct thousands of hearings every year on social, economic and political issues that affect everyone. Testimonies at these hearings come from victims of crimes or injury to nationally known experts on health and safety matters. For example, we used transcripts from committee hearings on identity theft for a magazine article on that topic. Consult the government documents department of your library or look for the transcripts of most congressional hearings on the U.S. Senate (www.senate.gov) or House of Representatives (www.house.gov) Web sites.

Correspondence and papers

Original correspondence from well-known people is a wonderful primary source. When famous people die, they often donate their papers to libraries. These "papers" sometimes consist of hundreds of boxes of correspondence and other personal documents. The papers of more recent U.S. presidents are contained at their respective presidential libraries where anyone may use them. The enormous size of these collections makes it possible for authors to write dozens of books on them, each with a different angle and sources of information. Many celebrities and public figures donate their papers to the libraries of their alma maters. These papers are contained within a library's special collections department. A good place to find ideas for stories may start at your nearest library. Ask about its special collections.

FINAL NOTE: COPYRIGHT AND FAIR USE

Three prominent historians who have written dozens of books and often appeared on television talk shows were all charged with plagiarism between 2001 and 2004. All of them admitted to quoting other authors' material in their books and failing to give proper credit and attribution. While none was taken to court, one was forced to pay an out-of-court settlement with the author she had inadvertently quoted.

While plagiarism can occur unintentionally, it still violates copyright law and its consequences can be just as serious as intentional plagiarism. All three of these historians had damaged reputations and received fewer invitations to television talk shows.

"Lifting quotes" is one of the most common forms of unintentional plagiarism. We know of one writer who interviewed a well-known celebrity and published a profile about him in a national magazine. Another writer lifted one of those quotes and used it in his article without giving proper attribution to the first writer. The original writer protested and forced the second magazine to publish a clarification and proper credit in the next issue.

Proper Attribution for Secondary Quotes

Since journalistic writers don't use footnotes, you have to give proper credit within the context of the article. If you choose to re-quote a source from another publication, you should attribute it this way:

"If we have bad crops, it's going to be a wild ride. There's just no cushion," Joseph Glauber, the Agriculture Department's chief economist, told *The New York Times.*

"He played that record about 10 times, and I said, 'That's it, Wayne; that's the record right there. We hit the lottery,'" said Ronald "Slim" Williams in a *Rolling Stone* article.

"I traveled to Cambodia for the first *Tomb Raider.* I got to this country and expected broken, angry people, and found smiling, kind, warm people," Angelina Jolie told Rich Cohen in a *Vanity Fair* interview.

SIDEBAR 5

The latest edition of the *MLA Handbook for Writers of Research Papers*, published by the Modern Language Association, has an entire section devoted to unintentional plagiarism: "Plagiarism," it says, "sometimes happens because researchers do not keep precise records of their reading, and by the time they return to their notes, they have forgotten whether their summaries and paraphrases contain quoted material that is poorly marked or unmarked."[9]

The *MLA Handbook* goes on to distinguish between three types of plagiarism:

* repeating or paraphrasing a few words without giving credit
* reproducing a particularly apt phrase
* paraphrasing an argument or line of thinking

In each case, the plagiarist misrepresents to readers the intellectual property of others as if it were his or her own.

The purpose of the U.S. Copyright Act is to protect "original works of authorship." Congress purposely chose the broad term "works of authorship" to avoid having to rewrite the Copyright Act every time a new "medium" was developed. That means the Copyright Act (Title 17, U.S. Code) protects Internet pages and articles, computer software and multimedia CDs even though these items didn't exist at the time the law was passed in 1978.

The Internet hasn't changed the copyright laws. It has simply made plagiarism easier and more tempting. If you publish an article on the Internet, whether for a personal or commercial Web site, copyright law protects it as soon as it's published regardless or whether the copyright symbol appears or whether the copyright is registered. If someone else copies and publishes your Internet article elsewhere, you can sue for copyright infringement using the same 1978 Copyright Law.

What copyright doesn't protect

One writer sent a query to a newspaper's feature editor that proposed a story about how people celebrate Christmas when they have jobs that require them to work on the holiday—medical and law enforcement personnel, pilots and flight attendants and so forth. The writer never received a reply, but on Christmas day the newspaper published a feature on that identical topic. Of course, the writer was angered, but there was nothing he could do. He later learned this isn't an original idea since many newspapers and magazines publish articles on this topic every Christmas. Even if it was original, he had no grounds for copyright infringement. That's because ideas can't be copyrighted. At least six types of material are generally not protected by copyright. These include:

1   Unpublished works that have not been fixed in a "tangible form of expression." That could include speeches, conversations or performances never written down or recorded.
2   Titles, names, short phrases and slogans; variations of typographic ornamentation, lists of ingredients or contents. That means you can't copyright song titles or titles of articles.
3   Works from the public domain with no original authorship, such as government documents, calendars, telephone directories. After a copyright expires (currently 70 years after the death of the author), it also falls into the public domain.
4   Press releases. Companies and organizations that send out press releases want their information to be published. They put it in the public domain and allow writers to use anything they want—facts, quotes or anecdotes.
5   Published works of the U.S. government or government employees.
6   Ideas, procedures, methods, processes, concepts.

Number 6 is particularly important for writers. As we previously noted, you cannot copyright the idea for an article; you can only copyright the particular way in which the idea is expressed and written. That's good news and bad news for writers.

The good news

The good news is you're free to browse through newspapers, magazines and Web sites and look for ideas you can use. Take any idea you find, interview your own sources and write your own article. That's legal.

Another "good news" consequence of the dichotomy between ideas and their expression is that copyright offers no protection for basic facts or common knowledge. For example, *Newsweek, The Washington Post* and CNN can all write stories about the latest episode in the Middle East without intruding upon each other's copyright. Copyright does not protect the ideas and facts of any particular news event, but only the arrangement of words and phrases in a particular story.

The bad news

The bad news is that it's conceivable you could send your query letter to an editor who steals your idea and assigns it to a staff writer. It's legal, but rarely occurs, at least among reputable magazines. Some editors will pay for the idea, but assign the article to another writer. That also occurs rarely because few ideas are completely original.

UNDERSTANDING FAIR USE

Section 107 of the U.S. Copyright Law covers "Fair Use." In general, the legal term "fair use" means you can use brief quotes from other sources as long as you give proper credit. The law gives permission to build upon the work of others for: "purposes such as criticism, comment, news reporting, teaching (including multiple copies for classroom use), scholarship or research."

"The primary objective of copyright is not to reward the labor of authors," wrote Justice Sandra Day O'Connor in a 1991 Supreme Court decision, "but to 'promote the progress of science and useful arts.' To this end, copyright assures authors the right to their original expression, but encourages others to build freely upon the ideas and information conveyed by a work,"[10] Justice O'Connor said.

The fair use provision doesn't say how many words or how much information you can borrow without permission from the author. Writers generally agree you should not exceed 400 words in any circumstance and sometimes even less. The law gives four general guidelines that determine whether fair use applies to the use of someone else's intellectual property:

1   the purpose and character of the use, including whether such use is of a commercial nature or is for nonprofit educational purposes
2   the nature of the copyrighted work

3   the amount and substantiality of the portion used in relation to the copyrighted work as a whole
4   the effect of the use upon the potential market for or value of the copyrighted work

Plaintiffs file many lawsuits each year over the meaning of "fair use." In general the courts have ruled that the first criterion (a profit motive for the use) and the fourth (damage to market sales) are the most important. But the courts have also ruled that educational use of copyrighted material doesn't automatically make it "fair use." For example, a state court ruled against a New York school system that made copies and distributed video-tapes to avoid purchasing them from the publisher.

If you copy someone else's intellectual property (electronically or manu-ally) without giving credit or paying for it, then you are violating fair use. Copying a CD and giving it to a friend so that he doesn't have to buy it is a copyright infringement. Prosecutions can and do occur. Think of how you would feel if someone made a copy of your intellectual work to avoid paying for it.

Plagiarism is not only wrong, but bad for your career. To avoid ruining your career, be sure you understand your copyrights and wrongs.

ENDNOTES

[1]   Isabel Wilkerson, "The Mississippi Transformed—A Special Report," *The New York Times*, Nov. 21, 1993 and other dates, and "Children and Their Challenges; Nicholas Whitiker, 10," *The New York Times*, April 25, 1993. Accessed at www. nytimes.com, Sept. 5, 2008.
[2]   Speech at Ball State University, March 1995.
[3]   Telephone interview with David E. Sumner, Nov. 21, 2003.
[4]   John Brady, *The Interviewer's Handbook: A Guerilla Guide: Techniques & Tactics for Reporters & Writers* (Waukesha, Wis.: The Writer Books, 2004).
[5]   Telephone interview with David E. Sumner, Aug. 30, 2004. Mr. Struck was for-merly editor-in-chief for States News Service.
[6]   Gay Talese, *Gay Talese: A Writer's Life* (New York: Alfred A. Knopf, 2006), 47.
[7]   Quoted in Judy Mandell (ed.), *Magazine Editors Talk to Writers* (New York: John Wiley and Sons, 1996), 184.

[8] Lori K. Baker, "What Your Magazine Fact-Checker Wishes You Knew," *The Writer*, July 2008, 28.

[9] Joseph Gibaldi, *MLA Handbook for Writers of Research Papers*, 6th ed. (New York: Modern Language Association, 2003), 68.

[10] Justice Sandra Day O'Connor, Feist Publications, Inc. v. Rural Telephone Service Co., 499 U.S. Code 340, 349 (1991).

INTERVIEWS: GOAL-DRIVEN CONVERSATIONS

Your takeaway . . .

What sets a feature article apart from a class research paper is the new information, never before published, that you gathered during your interviews with key sources. This chapter offers a checklist of interview tips; prepares you to deal with problem scenarios you're likely to encounter; helps you determine when you should use a direct quote and when you should paraphrase; and introduces you to words that are loaded with attitude.

Interviews are as important for the writer as a keyboard is for the pianist, the paintbrush for the artist, or the spreadsheet for the accountant. In other words, you won't succeed unless you master them . . . or at least come close to mastering them. Learning to interview is like learning to drive because it seems easy; overly easy. Once you've done a few interviews, you may think there's nothing more to learn. Then you suffer a major failure and realize how much you don't know. Seasoned journalists, like experienced drivers, approach with some trepidation each new "journey" into unfamiliar territory. They know that steering a conversation in the wrong direction at the wrong time can cause an interview to veer off course or, worse yet, come to a screeching halt.

Creating a list of questions to ask is important, but not the most important aspect of an interview. That's the mechanical part. If you do enough research, you can figure out original questions. But great interviews originate with trust. The more that you can convey your trustworthiness and honorable intent, the more likely it is that your sources will tell you things they have never told anyone else.

Celebrities and public figures often complain about the way reporters and writers treat them. They fear that journalists come to interviews with personal agendas, that reporters will take words out of context or inaccurately quote them. They know that a writer has the ability to make a person look foolish or ignorant by quoting only one sentence and ignoring everything else from the interview. Just as you, the writer, size up the interviewee and make assumptions based on first impressions, so does the interviewee come to quick conclusions about you. If he decides that you are a beginner, are unprepared or are likely to misconstrue his thoughts, he may give terse and predictable answers to your questions.

Here are some of the ways you can "turn off" the person you are trying to interview:

1 arriving late or not dressing professionally. If in doubt, dress "up" and not "down"
2 boring the subject with questions he or she has been asked dozens of times
3 asking for biographical details (i.e., "Where were you born?" or "Do you have a family?") that you could have obtained earlier with more preparation
4 assuming you are "buddies" with this person whom you've never met before and doing too much talking. The interview is never about you; your job is to listen
5 failing to bring a tape or digital recorder and, therefore, frequently having to repeat questions and slow the interview while you try to write down the comments

FIRST, YOU PREPARE

Ask professional writers to share their secrets to successful interviews and among their responses you're likely to hear the word "preparation." Obvious advice? Yes, and equally obvious are the follow-up tips. Among them: Writers should do extensive research on the people they interview (the previous chapter gave you ways to find these people and immerse yourself in their areas of expertise); writers should compile a list of thought-provoking questions based on library and Internet research; writers should phrase questions in a way that interviewees can't possibly respond with simple yes/no answers; writers should . . . And the

Interview with an Interviewer[1]

Veteran National Public Radio journalist Diane Rehm has been conducting insightful two-hour interviews five days a week for 30 years. Her list of interviewees includes U.S. presidents, famous athletes, best-selling authors, as well as lesser-known guests. *The Diane Rehm Show* is distributed internationally and is available online. Based on her wide range of experience, she responds to the following questions.

Q: How do you keep up to date on everything from sports to politics to entertainment? What media do you consume to stay current so you can ask timely questions?
A: As I'm getting ready for work in the morning I listen to NPR's *Morning Edition*; then I come to the office where *The Wall Street Journal*, *The New York Times* and *The Washington Post* are waiting for me. I read everything that my producers give me. When I get home at 6 p.m., I turn on the first half hour of the *News Hour* [PBS]; then I switch to ABC news with Charlie Gibson at 6:30; at 7 p.m., I watch NBC news with Brian Williams, and then I go back for the last half hour of news on PBS.

Q: How do you feel about conducting an interview on the telephone?
A: I really *hate* doing interviews on the phone. I want to see the body language; I want to look into a person's eyes; I want to watch what someone is doing with his hands.

Q: What is your strategy when an interviewee rambles and doesn't answer your question?
A: Sometimes I'll interrupt, or I'll take a breath, or I'll use my hand as a gesture to indicate to the person across the table that I want to say something. People who watch me do an interview tell me I look like an orchestra conductor because I'm waving my hands all over the place.

Q: Do you have any stock questions that you rely on if an interview starts to lag?
A: Sure; I ask "how?" or "why?" Also, if I don't understand something I admit, "I don't get it." I think people appreciate that because if I don't understand something, chances are an awful lot of other people don't understand it either.

Q: Many of your interviews deal with very hot issues. How do you stay objective when you might have a very strong point of view?
A: I *always* have a strong and passionate point of view, but I am not here to give people my opinions. I'm here to elicit various points of view so listeners can make up their own minds. That has been my charge right from the start. I do not wish to become the person who tells others what to do.

Q: What do you do when interviewees lay down ground rules on what they will or will not talk about?
A: We're not interested in interviewing them. The only person who got away with that was [former Secretary of Defense] Robert McNamara who called the night before an interview and said he would not take on-air calls from listeners. The next day, when he came to the studio and the microphones were on, I asked my first question: "Mr. McNamara, you refuse to take questions from our listeners. Why is that?" It was *the* question to ask.

SIDEBAR 1

suggestions go on and on. We include a checklist of familiar interview tips below.

SIDEBAR 2

Checklist for Successful Interviews

1   When setting up an interview, alert your interviewee to the topic that you are researching but don't reveal the exact questions you plan to ask.
2   Request a specific amount of time for the interview—an hour is usually sufficient—and limit the interview to that timeframe.
3   Do extensive background research about your topic and your interviewee before you meet.
4   Prepare a long list of questions based on your research—more than you think you will need.
5   Phrase your questions in a way that encourages the interviewee to offer opinions and feelings.
6   Don't step on the interviewee's answers. If you ask a good question and he needs time to frame an answer, don't jump in and provide one.
7   Include several questions that will elicit anecdotes from your interviewee, such as, "Could you give me an example of when that happened?"
8   Cluster your questions into categories: questions about early years; family; career moves; future projects.
9   Use a tape or digital recorder unless you are pressed for time and won't be able to transcribe the interview session.
10   Listen to each answer that your interviewee gives; prepare to ask follow-up questions that might not be on your list.
11   Take notes on your interviewee's body language.
12   If you plan to ask questions that might anger or alienate your interviewee, save those questions until you have established a rapport.

Barbara Walters once told an interviewer: "I really do a lot of preparation. I write all of my questions out on three-by-five cards. I write each question individually. I have lots of them; I can do 200 of them."[2]

Preparation means defining a clear purpose for the interview. What kind of information do you hope to obtain? Is your purpose learning about your subject's personal life or obtaining information based on his or her professional expertise? Just as every article needs a clearly defined angle, so does each interview. All of the questions you ask should be focused around that purpose.

For all the preparation that you will do as an interviewer and writer, you will never master the art of interviewing. The reason is simple: The writer controls only half of an interview. The interviewee controls the other half, and the writer can never be certain what the interviewee will do or say. Although the advice on our checklist is valid, be aware of another, less predictable secret to a successful interview. You should be willing to move past your preparations and beyond your script if, in the course of the interview, an unexpected but equally interesting story angle surfaces. In short, writers should enter an interview situation with a meticulously detailed roadmap that, when followed, will lead them to the information they need. But they also should be flexible enough to investigate surprise twists and turns that pop up in the course of the interview and take writers into uncharted territory that other writers haven't explored.

Should You Take Notes or Record Your Interviews?

We recommend taking notes and recording interviews with a digital voice recorder, which has many advantages over old-fashioned cassette recorders. Digital recorders cost between $35 and $100 and hold up to 144 hours of conversations. Here are some other advantages:

1   You have an accurate and legal record of precisely what the interviewee said.
2   Digital recorders fit easily in a shirt pocket or purse.
3   You can copy and listen to interviews from your computer while you transcribe them.
4   Audio files can be e-mailed to editors or fact-checkers.
5   You can "fast forward" or "rewind" interviews more quickly than on a cassette recorder.
6   You can keep permanent archives of all of your interviews on your computer.
7   You can download MP3 and iPod music files on many digital recorders.

SIDEBAR 3

The main advantage of recorded interviews is accuracy. No one can write as fast as people talk since most people speak about 170 words per minute. Therefore, writers end up filling in the blanks of their notes with re-created quotes of what they think their subjects probably said. Here are some disadvantages of relying solely on note-taking:

1 You probably miss writing some key words or colorful phrases.
2 You slow down the interview by asking your interviewee to pause or repeat statements.
3 You can't think about follow-up questions because you are busy writing.
4 You can't look the interviewee in the eye and pay attention to body language.

You can use a digital voice recorder to record cell phone conversations with a "wireless phone recorder controller" that you can purchase for about $20. Similar units are available for landline telephones.

INSIGHTS VS. INFORMATION

An interview is a conversation with a purpose. It's not a casual visit that meanders from one topic to another without an obvious direction. But what direction should it take? As an interviewer, you hope to leave an interview with enough insights and information to turn out a good feature story. If you plan to write a profile of a person, you want to tune into the person's character and personality. You want his opinions and feelings. If you are gathering material for an article about a timely issue, you're looking for statistics, facts and explanations. You also are hoping to gather an interviewee's unique perspective on the issue.

Well-known interviewers such as CNN's talk show host Larry King know the importance of keeping the focus on the person answering the questions and not on the person asking the questions. The word "interview" is misleading because "inter" means "between" and "view" means "thoughts" or "ideas." That suggests an exchange of thoughts and ideas between two people. But that definition doesn't work in feature writing because readers aren't interested in a writer's thoughts and ideas. Readers care about the interviewee. In his book *Anything Goes*, King writes that "The show has never been about what I think and feel; it's about how the major players in an issue think and feel. That's why it works."[3]

Whether you're a beginning writer or a veteran, you will likely take the same steps in preparing for and conducting a successful interview. In addition to considering the tips offered earlier, you must decide on the "voices" that deserve a place in your story. You also must think on your feet as you implement your plan for your question-and-answer session.

IDENTIFYING THE "VOICE OF AUTHORITY"

If your assignment is to produce a profile article, your central interview is going to be the person you are profiling. That "voice" will dominate. Secondary interviews, sometimes called support interviews, will be interviews with sources who can offer different perspectives—a best friend, spouse, employer, co-worker, roommate or parent (see Chapter 14). If your goal is an article that probes an issue or tracks a trend, your list of likely interviewees will include at least one voice of authority, plus persons who have differing opinions on the issue, and one or two persons who are caught up in the trend (see Chapter 18).

Topical features on issues and trends generally have two types of sources: the expert and the participant (sometimes called the expert and the actor). The expert is the voice of authority who has career or educational credentials in the subject you are investigating. The participant or actor is someone who has first-hand experience in the subject you are writing about. The questions that you put to the participants will be more open-ended than those you direct to your authority sources. Participants will often add colorful anecdotes and quotes to your story while the experts give it the voices of authority and enhance credibility.

The expert is a good interview to schedule first. This person commands respect and can offer credible insights and information because of experience, education, position or title. Examples: If you are researching obesity in children, your expert may be a pediatrician or a nutritionist; your participant will be a child or parent of a child who has successfully overcome obesity. If your assignment is to investigate alcohol abuse among college students, your expert might be a psychologist or an addictions counselor;

your participant will be a college student who is willing to talk about his or her experience with alcohol abuse. You might ask the addictions counselor, "What are five or six indicators of substance abuse?" You might ask the student, "Describe for me the moment when you realized that you had crossed the line between social drinker and problem drinker."

The more impressive your source's credentials, the more credible your article will be. A hierarchy exists. A doctor has more clout than a nurse; a professor's comments pack more punch than an instructor's observations; the president of a company gets more attention than a department manager. Readers often are skeptical, so you need to provide information from sources with impact.

In addition to the voice of authority, other interviewees will help explore the issue from a variety of angles. For the article about obesity in children, you'll want to hear from teenagers who are teased by peers because of their appearance. For the alcohol-abuse story, you'll want to hear from students who have observed excessive drinking and can provide anecdotes that move the story beyond statistics, advice and warnings.

GET READY, GET SET

One of the dangers of interviewing sources with impressive credentials is that you may feel intimidated when you sit down and begin the question-and-answer process. Control is everything. As an interviewer you should control the direction the interview takes and the information the interview produces; you also need the confidence to cut off responses that ramble, and you should doggedly restate questions that the interviewee wants to avoid. The best way to show who's in charge is by exhibiting professionalism the moment you pick up the telephone and request an appointment. Identify yourself, explain your writing project, tell your source how he or she fits into your research, and estimate the amount of time you need. Usually an hour is enough for an in-depth interview; a half hour works well for a secondary interview. Instead of asking, "Would you be willing to talk with me?" ask, "When would be convenient for us to meet?"

As you prepare for the session, make use of every available resource. Do a crash course in the topic that you plan to cover and the people you plan to interview. In addition to doing online research, remember that every hospital, university and business of any size has a public relations staff whose job is to deal with media requests. These people operate under different names. In the entertainment industry, they're called publicists; in the military, they're public-affairs officers; in the business world they're corporate-communications specialists. Whatever the job description, a PR person often is a writer's best friend. One of America's most gifted interviewers, *The Washington Post*'s Bob Woodward once rated PR people as "generally excellent" when it comes to getting writers the information they need to write a story. They're also valuable in setting up interviews and providing background on the person you are interviewing.

OFF TO A STRONG START

Just as the lead sentence in a story either grabs a reader's attention or causes him to yawn, so does the first question in an interview either capture the interviewee's interest or prompt him to nod off. You want to appear friendly but not casual, confident but not cocky, assertive but not pushy. Your opening question needs to be original and stimulating. It should show that you've done your homework, and you're not going to waste time with questions that you could have answered by doing a little research.

Example: A local homemaker has announced plans to run for the state legislature. Thinking she would make an interesting subject for a story about the changing face of American politics, you set up an interview with her. Which of these questions is most likely to send the message that, as an interviewer, you know what you're doing?

- Have you ever run for office before?
- Almost 52 percent of the voters in our state are female, yet only 14 of the 100 members of the House of Representatives are women. In your opinion, what are the reasons for the imbalance?

The first question is weak in three ways. First, the interviewee can answer it with a yes/no response. Second, you could have found out the information by reading her campaign brochure. Third, her reply isn't likely to yield an interesting or insightful comment. The second question shows that you've taken time to log onto your state's Web site and have done a gender count. As a reward, you will probably get a thoughtful reply that you can work into your feature and, simultaneously, you will earn the respect of the candidate. She knows she can't shift into automatic pilot and merely repeat the facts from her official biography. She's going to have to frame her comments carefully because her words may influence the way voters feel about her.

As important as it is to avoid an opening question that lulls your interviewee to sleep, so should you avoid making him angry. Save the negative questions until the final few minutes, after you've established a rapport. Even then, be careful not to phrase the questions in such a way that he feels you've turned against him. A good way to distance yourself from a delicate question is to precede it with a phrase like, "Some of your critics say . . ." or "Some people say . . ." and end with "How do you respond to that criticism?" Example: If you are interviewing an athlete who has just signed a multi-million-dollar contract, don't ask, "Why do you think you're worth this much money when teachers, police officers and firefighters can barely scrape by on their salaries?" Instead: "Some critics say that professional athletes are overpaid. How do you respond to that kind of comment?"

BUT WHAT IF . . .?

As an interviewer, you have to anticipate and successfully react to unexpected events. Although no one can prepare you for all the interesting (and sometimes bizarre) situations you may experience before, during or after an interview, some of these situations are predictable. Listed below are a dozen scenarios that you are likely to encounter in your writing career. Put yourself in the situations, consider your options, and decide how you would handle them.

1   You're assigned to interview a very busy executive. His assistant agrees to arrange the meeting but says that her boss prefers that you fax your questions in advance. It will save time, says she, and he'll have the opportunity to pull together information from his files that might help you write the story.
    What are the pros and cons of such an arrangement? Should you say yes?
2   You've called a local attorney and requested an interview to discuss a legal issue that you plan to cover in a Sunday feature. Before he schedules an appointment, he asks how much he'll be paid for the interview. Time is money, he says, and he typically makes several hundred dollars an hour.
    What's your response? Should you ever pay someone for an interview?

3   Five minutes into an interview your interviewee is called out of the room. You depress the "pause" button on your digital recorder and proceed to review your notes. She comes back and the interview continues. She gives you great information, and just as the session winds down you notice that you never released the pause button. You have about 10 minutes before your time is up.

How should you use those remaining minutes? Should you admit your mistake and start over?

4   You're interviewing someone who obviously is nervous about being quoted in print. When you set your recorder in front of her, she freezes.

What can you say to help her relax so she will give you the information that you need?

5   You are set to interview a person who has been well coached by his public relations staff. You know that he has a list of talking points that he will keep dredging up regardless of the questions that you ask.

How can you cause him to leave his script and answer your questions with spontaneity?

6   You're set to interview a person who has been at the center of some controversy at some point in his life. You've jotted down a long list of questions, and you know some of them are very sensitive and personal.

How do you handle the interview so he doesn't walk out?

7   Your editor wants a profile article of about 2,500 words. The problem is that circumstances require you to conduct the interview on the telephone, and the person gives you short, clipped answers. You don't have the benefit of describing his body language or the setting. You only have words . . . and not enough of them.

What kind of additional research can you do to salvage the story?

8   You've identified a key source to interview for a feature story you're researching. You call her, she agrees and then asks two quick questions: Where shall we meet, and how much time will you need? The success of your story might hinge on your responses.

What do you say?

9   You're having a great conversation with a source who is giving you colorful quotes and strong anecdotes. The trouble is, your interviewee keeps saying, "By the way, that was off the record." The material that is on the record is predictable and boring.

What do you do?

10   At the end of a very successful interview your interviewee thanks you and says, "When will I be able to read this before you turn it in to your editor?"
     How do you respond?

11   You've just had a great question-and-answer session with a very quotable source. You want to stay on his good side because you might want to feature him in future articles.
     What are some things you can do to build a strong professional relationship?

12   Three days have passed since you conducted a very candid interview. You get a call from the interviewee who has had second thoughts about a couple of the comments she made. She asks you to please not include them since they could cause her a great deal of trouble. You haven't written the story yet, so it's not as if she's asking you to edit something that is part of your story.
     What do you do?

TIME TO SWITCH ROLES

Interviewing sources is only part of a feature writer's job—the part that casts you in the role of researcher and reporter. Now you have to switch roles and become the writer. This means that you need to figure out what you're going to do with the material you've gathered during your interviews. You're certainly not going to use every comment uttered by every source. Which quotations are strong enough to warrant inclusion in your article? Are you going to use partial quotations? Are you going to use indirect quotations? Are you going to paraphrase some of the comments that you've collected? Are you going to tighten or "clean up" any of your interviewee's answers? If the person you've interviewed occasionally makes a grammatical error, should you fix it? If the person has the habit of saying "you know" too often, can you delete that phrase?

Here's what we suggest: After you've completed an interview, go through your notes (or transcript, if you've taped the conversation) and underline or highlight those comments that are likely to spark an emotional reaction from readers. Look for words that might surprise, amuse, anger or shock your readers. Look for ideas, opinions and insights. These highlighted sentences or parts of sentences will probably make the strongest quotations. If you have to cut through a lot of rambling words to get to the core of an interviewee's comment, consider using a partial quotation. Pull out the heart of the statement, put quotation marks around those words, and paraphrase the rest of the sentence. Likewise, if you understand a key point that your interviewee made but he didn't articulate it very well, consider paraphrasing it.

Some editors believe the best way to write the first draft is without using any of your notes. This forces you to put down on paper only those fresh ideas that are on top of your memory. Writing from memory helps you see the forest; then you can go back and take care of the trees. It helps you write with a conversational style. If you remember these ideas off the top of your head, they are probably going to be the same comments and ideas that readers find most interesting and compelling. Then you can go back, verify quotes and fill in missing comments from your notes.

Aim for a 50–50 balance between direct quotes and paraphrases of what your subject says in your article. Don't try to quote everything or paraphrase everything. The more articulate your subject, the more you can use direct quotes. If your interviewee is less articulate, you will need to use more paraphrasing. In general, too many quotes make it more difficult for the reader to comprehend the information. Do the reader a favor by paraphrasing some of it. The box, below, presents some guidelines about when to quote and when to paraphrase.

When to Quote	When to Paraphrase
Use direct quotes when the comments:	**Paraphrase when the comments:**
1 give a concise, revealing anecdote	1 offer biographical or factual information
2 cluster words in a colorful or entertaining manner	2 present numbers or statistical data
3 establish an emotional connection with the reader	3 are long or redundant and you can re-write them using fewer words
4 emphasize a significant point or display the subject's expertise	4 give information that is already public knowledge (which you may not include at all)
5 reveal the subject's personality, character or values in a unique way	5 offer dull but essential information to the story

Here are some examples of certain words that should never be encased in quotation marks.

- Empty comments: "It's a pleasure to be here," said the speaker.
- Clichés: The scientist said he likes to think "out of the box."
- Statistical information: "I am married and have two sons," said Smith.
- Obvious observations: "Whichever team has the most points at the end of the game will win," said the coach.

It's not a good idea to include quotations from two different sources in the same paragraph. This confuses readers. Instead, give each source a separate paragraph.

Publications often have policies regarding "cleaning up" quotations. Most editors don't object to a writer deleting an occasional "you know" phrase or correcting a minor slip in grammar. The important point is that a writer should never tamper with the meaning of an interviewee's comment. If you are uncertain about the meaning, you should contact your source and ask for clarification.

And this brings up two final suggestions. First, a good next-to-the-last question to put to an interviewee is this: "Have I missed anything that you feel is important?" Second, the last question before you turn off your recorder or close your notebook is: "Where can I reach you by phone in the next few days in case I need to clarify or double check your comments?"

SIDEBAR 4

He Said, She Said: Words with an Attitude

Before you begin to integrate quotations into a story, you'll need to decide if you are going to write your attributions in present tense or past tense. Examples: "My first celebrity interview didn't go well," *admits* the journalist (present tense). "My first celebrity interview didn't go well," *admitted* the journalist (past tense). Whatever your decision, be consistent throughout the article.

Some words of attribution carry little if any "baggage." They don't influence the reader's perception of the speaker or add any color to the speaker's comment. Among them are:

Said	Mentioned
Commented	Added
Responded	Remarked
Stated	Observed
Explained	Noted
Clarified	Pointed out

Other words have an attitude. They either suggest the emotional state of the speaker or offer clues to the speaker's personality. Some people call these "loaded words" because they are loaded with unspoken meaning. A few examples are:

Insisted	Swore
Argued	Proposed
Blurted	Whispered
Stressed	Shouted
Asserted	Whined
Revealed	Begged
Affirmed	Cried
Confided	Grumbled

Note: The only words that a person can legitimately "hiss" are those with a string of "s" sounds. ("Stop being so silly," she hissed.) Avoid attributions such as laughed, giggled, gulped, sniffed and smiled. Remember, it's impossible to "smile" words or to sniff and speak at the same time. (Try it!) Wrong: "Let's go out," she giggled. Right: "Let's go out," she said with a giggle. Above all, don't allow your sources to "share" words. It suggests that your interviewee is dealing out words: one for you, one for me. ("Skiing is my favorite form of exercise," she shared.)

ENDNOTES

[1] Interview with Holly G. Miller, June 11, 2008.
[2] Jack Huber and Dean Diggins, *Interviewing the World's Top Interviewers* (New York: Shapolsky Publishers, 1993), 128.
[3] Larry King and Pat Piper, *Anything Goes* (New York: Warner Books, 2000), 114.

PART II

SELLING FEATURE AND MAGAZINE ARTICLES

Successful feature writers shape articles to fit readers. After they've completed their research but *before* they begin crafting paragraphs, they consider the demographics of their audience. For freelancers, this involves studying the markets and creating query letters that reflect the interests and needs of a publication's readers.

6

FINDING THE RIGHT MARKET

Your takeaway . . .

Many feature writers experience rejection because they submit their manuscripts to the wrong publications. Writing articles and marketing articles are two different skills, and you need to master both. This chapter introduces you to Web sites and other resources that are available to help you tune into the marketplace, pick up on editorial "clues" and determine the most likely home for your articles. It all begins with analyzing a publication's contents and identifying its target audience.

A good way for feature writers to build their reputations, expand their portfolios and attract the attention of editors is to accumulate published clips early in their careers. Rather than explain to an editor what you *think* you can do, it's better to show an editor what you've already done. Clips prove your writing ability.

The bulk of this book concentrates on teaching the skills needed to create interesting and informative feature articles. In this chapter and the one that follows, we want to shift the emphasis and discuss how to market the words that you write. Specifically, how do feature writers sell articles to publications on a freelance basis? We feel this is an important question to answer for at least four reasons.

- Freelance bylines sometimes lead to full-time jobs. Certainly a benefit of being published is the ability to tuck a tear sheet into the envelope that contains your résumé. Clips set you a notch above those who don't have them.
- If you work in public relations, part of your job may involve writing and placing articles about your client or employer. A media-relations

specialist needs to know how to approach editors and convince them that a feature idea is newsworthy.

- Staff members of local newspapers occasionally write articles that may interest readers beyond their immediate circulation area. The idea of earning a byline in a national publication is appealing, but these writers need help in knowing where to look and how to identify likely markets for their stories.
- Persons who have worked full-time for media organizations may decide to leave their salaried jobs and try their hands at freelancing. They want to know how to make the transition from one side of the editor's desk to the other.

DISCOVERING AVAILABLE RESOURCES

Hundreds of resources are available to freelance writers hoping to break into print. In fact, an entire industry has emerged to serve people who want to sell their words to newspapers and magazines. Products include reference books that list the names and addresses of publications; monthly and bimonthly writers' magazines that offer tips on how and where to sell freelance articles; critique services that edit manuscripts for a fee; writers' workshops that schedule marketing sessions led by editors; newsletters and blogs that keep subscribers up to date on changes in the publishing industry; and writing-related Web sites that sponsor chat rooms where writers swap tips about potential markets.

We can't begin to cover all the places where you can go to tap into marketing advice. The number of products expands and contracts daily as Web sites and newsletters come and go. All we can do is to introduce you to a few major print and electronic resources and then let you take it from there. We also want to suggest several ways that you can evaluate a publication on your own to determine if it is a good place to send your queries, proposals and manuscripts.

A logical launch point for any discussion of marketing is www. writersmarket.com, a searchable database that is available by paid subscription and is updated every business day. It includes contact names and information on some 6,000 market listings. These range from book publishers to consumer magazines, from trade journals to regional publications and more. The roots of the online resource wind back to 1921 when the first edition of *Writer's Market* hit the bookstores. Still published annually, the 1,200-page *Writer's Market*—like its electronic counterpart—gives you the names and addresses of publications and indicates the editors to whom you should send your query letters. Both the print and the online products let you know if a magazine accepts e-mail submissions, how long you are likely to wait for a response from an editor, whether a publication expects photos to accompany the words and what the pay scale is.

As an example, if you look up *Mother Jones* magazine, you find that freelancers write about 80 percent of its content. That's encouraging. More good news: Writers who are fortunate enough to sell articles to this publication are paid about $1 a word on publication, and their articles have a potential audience of 210,000 readers. If you think you have a story suitable for *Mother Jones*, you need to know the kind of proposal that the editors prefer to see. By checking the *Writer's Market* listing against the guidelines published on www.motherjones.com, you learn the staff is looking for "revelatory journalism" and hard-hitting investigative articles. The guidelines specify that each query letter should include a fully fleshed-out idea and clips of the writer's previously published work.

The value of the electronic version of *Writer's Market*, of course, is its capacity to stay current. From month to month, the overseers of writersmarket.com are likely to make hundreds of changes to their listings. Editors are a mobile bunch; they switch jobs, titles and responsibilities frequently. The editorial needs of publications also shift. It's possible that information gleaned from any printed market guide is out of date by the time you read it. You don't want to pitch an idea to an editor who no longer works at a magazine. Worse yet, you don't want to send a proposal to a magazine that has ceased publication. Electronic resources alert you to magazines that have failed as well as start-up publications that are in the early stages of building their stables of freelancers.

The simplest way to make sure you're pitching the right article to the right editor is by making a telephone call to the magazine. Call the number listed in *Writer's Market* and explain to the receptionist, "I'm writing an article about X topic and would like to know which editor I should send it to." At smaller magazines you may even get to talk to the editor who can give you advice and suggestions.

Similar to *Writer's Market* is *The Writer's Handbook*, which offers marketing information on thousands of entries in a variety of categories. Both books are available in the reference areas of most libraries and major bookstores. The parent company of *Writer's Market*—F + W Media, Inc.—

publishes *Writer's Digest* magazine, one of three major writing magazines. The others are *The Writer* and *Writers' Journal*. All three magazines include marketing information in every issue. They usually cluster potential markets by categories. One month they might focus on publications geared to teens; another month they might choose to highlight men's muscle magazines. Each listing gives an editor's name and tells what he or she wants to see. The magazines also publicize (and sometimes sponsor) writing competitions. The annual *Writer's Digest* contest typically draws close to 16,000 entries in 10 categories.

For persons interested in writing for religious or inspirational publications, the *Christian Writers' Market Guide*, updated and released each January, offers contact information for 695 print periodicals and 133 online publications. Sally Stuart is the author of the guide and overseer of the Web site at www.stuartmarket.com. She also updates marketing information in her monthly column in *The Christian Communicator* magazine and discusses marketing trends and techniques in *The Christian Communicator*'s sister publication, the bimonthly *Advanced Christian Writer*.[1] Freelance writers can mine valuable nuggets of marketing advice by reading Stuart's blog at www.stuartmarket.blogspot.com. These resources are particularly helpful because many writers are unaware of the number of inspirational publications that exist. Most of the magazines have small staffs, are not sold on newsstands and are available only by subscription or as giveaways by churches. Stuart's Web site includes links to many of the magazines listed in her guide. This enables potential contributors to follow the links that lead to specific marketing advice from the publications' staffs.

COLLECTING WRITERS' GUIDELINES

The writers' guidelines that magazines distribute directly to writers requesting them may help more than anything else. These guidelines, available at no charge, describe the kinds of materials the editors are interested in seeing, the preferred length of articles and typical payment that contributors can expect. Some editors go into great detail and offer separate guidelines for different types of submissions—travel article guidelines, fiction guidelines, photography guidelines, etc. Freelancers sometimes can find guidelines posted on the publications' Web sites, although they are frequently buried in odd places. A quick way to locate the Web sites of some 3,500 magazines in dozens of categories is to go to Yahoo.com and look for the "news and media" link (Yahoo.com/news_and_media). From there, click on the magazine that interests you. Our best advice, after you get to the publication's Web site, is to go to the very bottom of the page and look for words such as "contact us," "press center" or "media." Sometimes the information you find there isn't encouraging. Major publications like *The New Yorker* flatly state, "We cannot consider unsolicited nonfiction . . ." Lesser-known magazines, such as the bimonthly *Angels on Earth*, offer detailed guidelines although the editors admit "we receive thousands of manuscripts each month." The market-savvy freelancer doesn't waste time and energy sending material to publications that have policies that clearly discourage submissions.

Some publications will share their future editorial calendars with writers. This is especially true of magazines that select themes for their issues and actively solicit articles that support the themes. As an example, a bimonthly national women's magazine once announced on its Web site that the theme for its upcoming January–February issue would be "career women, including at-home careers." The same publication planned to examine health-related topics in its March–April issue and wanted feature articles about mentoring and parenting for its May–June issue. Recalling that most magazine staffs work on a lead time of four to six months (see Chapter 17), the smart freelance writer studies the editorial calendar and then pitches an idea about a home-based business in July for the January issue, proposes a wellness story in September for the March issue and offers a parenting article in November for the May issue.

Editorial calendars serve as tools for a publication's advertising staff. The calendars give potential advertisers an idea of the content of each issue of the magazine. Based in part on that information, an advertiser decides whether or not to buy space. Sometimes the calendars are very general. As an example, *Rolling Stone*'s 2008 publishing calendar specified themes such as sports, Grammy awards and spring fashion. This is of little help to writers. However, other magazines offer details of their upcoming contents. *Road and Travel Magazine* lists its themes—green issue, pet issue, boomer issue—and includes a list of specific articles they plan to publish. The editors invite writers to "feel free to contact RTM with potential stories" and remind them that the magazine has a two-month lead time.

ANALYZING MARKETS—ON YOUR OWN

Besides visiting Web sites, accessing guidelines and tracking down editorial calendars, a writer can learn a lot about a magazine by analyzing back issues. When done carefully, this analysis alerts the writer to the kinds of articles that editors are likely to buy. It also can indicate whether or not the publication welcomes freelance submissions from newcomers. The writer who does not research a publication runs the risk of creating a query letter that is clearly inappropriate. Ron Kovach, senior editor of *The Writer* magazine, warns that a query can "show that the writer has not taken the time to learn anything about the magazine." He characterizes this faux pas as "a very big turnoff."

Part of a writer's challenge is to figure out the demographics of the publication's readers, pick up on new directions that the editors are pursuing and determine if the magazine is mostly staff written. As you conduct your analysis, you will want to take note of how often a publication revisits a topic and if it recently has covered the topic you want to propose. All this information, plus the tips you glean from reference books, Web sites, guidelines and calendars, should help you figure out if your unsolicited material has a chance of earning a place in a future issue. Good market research can greatly reduce the number of rejection letters that a freelancer receives.

Get to know the readers

Magazine staffs know a lot about their readers. They know the gender breakdown: male vs. female. They know how many subscribers live in each of the 50 states. They know their readers' average age, marital status, income and education levels. They know if their readers are predominantly conservative or liberal in their politics. They know what kinds of products their readers buy, where they are likely to travel on vacation and if they prefer to drive or fly to those destinations.

This demographic information, as we mentioned in Chapter 1, is essential when a publication's sales representatives call on potential advertisers. Companies make advertising decisions based on circulation figures, magazine content and demographic data. It's not good enough to know that a magazine has a million readers. Potential advertisers ask, "Of those million readers, how many are likely to purchase our products?" Example: A magazine read by young families is a good place to schedule ads for station wagons and vans, whereas a magazine read by upscale singles is a likely match for sports car manufacturers. Companies that sell cosmetics are more apt to buy space in magazines read almost entirely by women than in a magazine with an even split between male and female readers. Companies that produce computers want exposure in business publications; companies that make running shoes earmark a chunk of their annual advertising budget for fitness magazines.

The same demographic information that helps advertisers identify publications with the right audiences for their products helps writers identify publications with the right audiences for their articles. Young couples might like to read an article that offers tips on buying a first home, whereas upscale singles might welcome guidance on shopping for a condo. Writers can tune into the demographics of a publication by studying its cover, reading its letters to the editor and taking note of its advertising pages.

Here's how it works. Say you have an idea for a feature article and you want to pitch it to a magazine that you often read. Even if you feel you know the publication well, sit down with a recent issue, skim through it and take notes on these elements.

- **Cover:** Look at the face and study the cover lines. What kind of reader would find this celebrity and these articles appealing? Ask yourself if your article idea would interest that reader. Would the topic of your proposed article make an appropriate cover line for this publication?
- **Letters to the editor:** People typically don't sit down and dash off notes or pound out e-mails unless they feel strongly about a topic. Do the letters alert you to topics that anger, offend, please or rally the publication's readers? Ask yourself if your article idea would spark a similar favorable or unfavorable emotion.
- **Advertising pages:** Try to discern and describe the consumer who is the target for the advertisements. Remember that certain ad pages—the back cover for one—cost more than others. Ask yourself if your article idea would appeal to that targeted consumer.

Take note of editor's notes

Somewhere toward the front of a magazine you're likely to find a standing column written by the publication's editor. These columns usually occupy a single page or less and have accurate but often unimaginative names such as "Editor's Letter" (*Woman's Touch*), "Editor's Note" (*Home & Away*) or

"The Editor's Desk" (*Newsweek*). They are easy to overlook because they're usually wedged between major advertising pages or placed near the more interesting table of contents. But don't be tempted to turn the page and move on. Writers trying to tune into a publication's editorial needs should view these standing columns as required reading. They contain all sorts of clues. They explain new directions the publication is taking, announce staff changes, and offer hints about the magazine's point of view and its position on issues.

As an example, a few years ago *Runner's World* promised its readers that its editors were in the process of planning major changes to the magazine. Months later the familiar "Editor's Letter" carried the title "A Brave New Runner's World" and detailed exactly what those changes were.[2] Beginning with that issue, wrote the editor-in-chief, articles would include more tips about training, health, fitness, food and nutrition. Also, the magazine was planning profiles of non-celebrity runners who were doing interesting things. Smart writers paid attention to the note and scurried to produce articles related to training, fitness and diet. They looked for interesting, non-celebrity runners who would make good subjects for profile articles.

Staff changes mentioned in editor's notes are important for a couple of reasons. First, they give you the names of the editors to whom you should address your query letters and article proposals. Second, they might tip you off to changes ahead for the publication. Often publishers expect their newly appointed editors to shake up the content and bring freshness to the magazine. When the managing editor of *Money* wrote his last editor's note before moving to *Time,* he welcomed his successor and mentioned the career path of the new editor. The smart freelance writer would review articles the newly named editor had written. These articles might offer insights as to the type of material the editor would like to see from contributing writers.

As you read the editor's note, pay attention to the tone of the writing. Is it conversational or formal? Breezy? Precise? Any attempt at humor? To what kind of reader does it seem directed? Is your style of writing compatible with the editor's style?

Pick up on masthead clues

You can pick up on valuable clues by reading the fine print of a publication's masthead. First, how large is the staff? A small staff might mean that the magazine depends on freelance writers for much of its content. That's a good sign. It also might mean that the editors are very busy and may be slow in responding to your query letters. Bad sign.

Look at the titles of the various editors listed on the masthead. Sometimes a magazine with a large staff is very exact in its areas of responsibility. Rather than assigning all nonfiction material to an articles editor, it might break down this general category and divide submissions according to specialties. Depending on the topic of your manuscript, your submission might find its way to the desk of a lifestyle editor, beauty editor, new products editor, legal affairs editor, special projects editor, etc. Addressing your material to the right person in the first place will cut down on response time and display professionalism on your part.

Some publications won't consider submissions from writers they don't know. Instead, they rely on a group of regular contributors for their content. These writers often are listed on the masthead as "contributing editors." By comparing the masthead with the table of contents, you can figure out if the publication welcomes submissions from newcomers. If the bylines on published articles are the same as the names on the masthead, this is not a good market for an unknown writer.

One more item to check before you move on: Usually somewhere on the masthead you will find a sentence or two relating to unsolicited freelance submissions. Typically this information is at the bottom of the masthead and takes the form of a disclaimer. It states that the publication assumes no responsibility for unsolicited articles and photos. That doesn't necessarily mean that the editors aren't willing to look at material from new writers; it merely protects them from financial claims if the material is lost.

Study the table of contents

You'll want to survey several issues of the magazine to identify recurring features or departments. Publications frequently ease new writers into their circle of contributors by first buying short items that fit into standing departments. We will talk more about these foot-in-the-door opportunities in Chapter 13.

Most magazines have predictable content. They follow an editorial formula that they know their readers like. For example, each issue might contain two personality profiles, one major and one minor travel piece, three diet and fitness stories, a roundup of film and book reviews, a couple of advice columns and several how-to articles. Because this lineup varies little from month to month, you can almost predict what submissions the editors are likely to consider.

Read sample articles

As part of your analysis, you'll want to read and critique several articles from different sections of the magazine. Ten questions to answer as you read each feature are:

1   What is the length of the article?
2   What kind of lead does the author use?
3   Does the story have any accompanying sidebars?
4   Is the topic aimed at readers of a certain age group, gender or background?
5   Which one of these words best describes the writer's tone—conversational, formal, sassy, breezy, condescending, authoritative, preachy?
6   Does the author write in first person (I, me, my, our), second person (you, your) or third person (he, she, they, their)?
7   How many sources are quoted?
8   Any anecdotes?
9   Does the article fit into a particular category—how-to, calendar-related, profile, roundup or personal essay?
10   Is the vocabulary easy or difficult?

After you've read a variety of articles, look for characteristics that are present in all the stories. These probably reflect the preferences of the editors and the readers. Ask yourself: Are the articles about the same length? If not, what is the range? Do the articles contain a lot of quotations from expert sources? Do most of the articles have sidebars? Is there a prevailing tone to the writing?

Much like a person, a well-edited magazine has a distinct personality, a unique voice, an established point of view and a certain style. These traits usually resemble the personality, voice, point of view and style of the publication's readers. Even magazines in the same genre—fashion, health, home décor, travel—differ from each other. The challenge for the freelance writer is to identify the characteristics the magazine and its audience share and to offer material that is compatible. We often say successful writers are like chameleons; they have the ability to produce articles that blend perfectly into the magazines that publish their work.

Finally, as you analyze the content of a magazine, notice changes in its appearance. A new design can signal a new direction. As an example, late in 2003, *Prevention* designed a new look and introduced new features aimed squarely at its fastest-growing segment of readers—females under 50. The magazine's circulation has skyrocketed in recent years, a fact that its editor links to Americans' fascination with healthy living. Knowing *Prevention* is making an effort to reach out to women by offering articles about nutrition and fitness trends should help the freelancer who is trying to break into that market.[3]

NEW KIDS ON THE BLOCK

Sometimes it's impossible to read and evaluate content and design because the magazine's editors haven't released their first issue yet. Each year brings the introduction of many new publications to the marketplace. Not all survive. Because start-up staffs often are small, these new magazines are excellent places to send query letters. Getting in on the ground floor has its benefits. But how can a writer get a handle on content without first seeing and reading an issue or two?

The answer is in the mail. To generate excitement for a new publication, its promotional staff usually initiates a mass mailing to describe the product and offer a reduced rate for "charter subscribers." A detailed letter often outlines exactly what the magazine will contain. Sometimes a sample of the magazine—a "premiere issue"—follows. As an example, the editor of *Backyard Living* announced the publication's launch in 2004 with a letter that promised articles about gardening and landscaping, outdoor entertaining and do-it-yourself projects. He also promised "humorous stories from your fellow readers" and more than 100 full-color pictures in each issue. Upon receiving this promotional letter, a freelance writer could easily read between the lines and surmise the editor is likely to consider proposals for how-to articles written in a friendly tone and accompanied by strong photos. This evaluation would be right on target. The premiere issue of *Backyard Living* devoted two pages to an explanation of how readers can submit photos and stories about porch and patio living, barbecue grilling and backyard projects. "You can help us write future issues," invited the headline.

PERSISTENCE PAYS

Even with all the marketing aids available to them, freelance writers receive many more letters of rejection than letters of assignment. Having the right idea and pitching it to the right publication at the right time requires skill, hard work and a bit of good luck. Too many writers, new to the profession, try their hands at freelancing then give up after one or two rejections. A wiser strategy is to remember that writing is a business, and like all businesses it has its share of setbacks. Each publication—and there are thousands out there—represents an opportunity. For the writer in search of a market, persistence pays. Never give up.

SIDEBAR 1

How to "Nationalize" a Story

Many writers fail to sell their work to national publications because the articles that they submit are too local in scope. For example, a story about a college basketball team that devotes several hours a week to tutoring underprivileged kids may earn rave reviews from readers of the school's newspaper. Offer the same article to a national magazine and you can expect a rejection. Why? The story is of limited interest because it involves just one campus.

Don't be discouraged. Often a writer can "nationalize" an article by doing a limited amount of additional research. Let's continue with the example of the basketball team and see how nationalization works.

- **Determine if it is a trend.** Perhaps what is happening on the local campus is also happening at other schools. Send e-mails to athletic directors at a sampling of universities across the country and ask if they encourage athletes to do community service. If a sizable number of the ADs answers "yes," you've documented a national trend. Your story's readership has just expanded.

- **Do the math.** Based on your e-mail survey, create some statistics that verify the trend. Your assertion that a trend exists will acquire credibility when you write, "Of the 20 schools surveyed, more than half support programs to involve athletes in volunteer activities."
- **Look for quotable sources.** When you write a local story, you interview local sources. When you write a national story, you solicit comments far beyond your home area. Go back to your survey and identify one or two out-of-state athletic directors whose observations will have clout with national readers. Conduct brief interviews. An additional quote from a NCAA official will round out your research.
- **Piggyback on something in the news.** Look for ways to make your story timely. When you pitch your article to an editor, point out that sports pages too often focus on athletes in trouble. Your article offers a refreshing change from these negative headlines.

Transforming a local story into a national story doesn't involve as much work as you might think. In the case of the student athletes, most of the article is going to deal with what's happening at the nearby campus. The difference is that the writer is going to use the local example to illustrate a national trend. Statistics and quotes from national sources will help create a larger context within which the local story unfolds.

ENDNOTES

[1] *The Christian Communicator* and *Advanced Christian Writer* are available only by subscription from their parent company, Christian Writers' Institute in Nashville, Tenn.
[2] David Willey, "A Brave New Runner's World," *Runner's World*, April 2004, 12.
[3] Peter Johnson, "Prevention Is Healthy," *USA Today*, Dec. 4, 2003, 4D.

7

QUERY LETTERS THAT SELL

Your takeaway . . .

A successful query letter accomplishes two goals. First, it pitches an article idea that is so right for a publication that the editor can't possibly reject it. Second, it convinces the editor that the would-be contributor has the ability to turn the idea into a publishable article. This chapter offers help in achieving both goals. It also answers pesky questions such as, "Can I e-mail my query or does it have to go by snail mail?"

Entire books explain what a query letter is and what it's supposed to do. We can summarize both topics in two sentences. Definition? A query is a one-page, single-spaced pitch letter that a freelance writer sends to an editor. Purpose? It pitches an article idea and provides tangible proof of the writer's journalistic skills. In short, a letter of inquiry—which is where the word "query" comes from—asks the editor two questions: How do you like this idea? Do you think I have the talent to pull it off?

The stakes are high. If the letter doesn't capture the editor's interest and calm all doubts about the writer's ability, the result is no assignment, no byline and no article. For that reason, queries fall into two categories—winners and losers. There is no middle ground. A "winner" means that the editor says "yes" and invites the writer to submit the article. A query that is a "loser" results in a rejection letter, most often a form letter straight from the office photocopy machine. Occasionally the rejection includes a short list of labeled boxes that the editor can check to indicate why the staff rejected the query. These responses are usually generic—"this manuscript does not meet our current needs"—and offer little guidance for the writer trying to tune into a magazine's needs.

If a publication's editors like the query but aren't familiar with the writer, they may ask the writer to submit the article on speculation. Translation: The editors have no obligation to buy the article if it isn't as good as the query letter indicates. Beginning writers should be willing to work "on spec" until they have established their credentials in the marketplace.

If the editors like the query and have worked previously with the writer, they often will send the writer a contract that specifies a deadline, number of words needed and the amount of money they will pay for the finished article. Unlike working on speculation, the writer is assured of payment. That doesn't mean the writer is assured of publication, however. If the resulting article fails to meet editors' expectations, the writer may need to revise the submission. Occasionally editors decide not to use the article at all and, according to the contract, are obligated to pay the writer a kill fee. Translation: The writer will earn at least a portion of the amount originally specified in the contract. This typically ranges from 20 to 100 percent of the total agreed-to fee.

IN PURSUIT OF PERFECTION

Queries cannot be marginal, passable or even pretty good. They have to be flawless in presentation and terrific in content. Most are not, which explains why the majority are rejected. Occasionally editors will reject a query letter without reading a single sentence. One of our favorite stories tells of a writer who used tiny manicure scissors to clip words from various publications to fashion a query letter that resembled a ransom note. The freelancer must have spent hours finding the right words and then snipping and pasting them onto a piece of stationery. By contrast, the editor, a friend of ours, needed only a moment to reject the gimmicky submission. In another case, an editor rejected a query letter from a medical writer without even opening the envelope. The letter was addressed to Ms. Patricia Johnson. The editor's name: Mr. Patrick Johnson. The editor wasn't unduly sensitive about his name; he rejected the query because he doubted the writer's attention to detail. If the author couldn't get gender right, could the magazine trust him to get the facts straight in a medical story?

Many editors never meet their contributing writers face to face. The only way they judge competency is, first, by the appearance of the writer's correspondence and, second, by the content of the correspondence. Let's take a closer look at each of these key elements.

First impressions are important. Flawless presentation means attractive stationery and single-spaced text that is formatted in flush-left and ragged-right paragraphs. Paper and envelopes should match; the type font should be simple and professional; the letterhead should not be cluttered with silly graphics—quill pens, inkpots, computer monitors—or quotations from famous authors. Some writers try to underscore their previous article sales by including lists of publications in small print on the left-hand side of the query letter. Be careful; it's a fine line between looking professional and appearing pretentious.

The computer gives the writer the ability to design appealing packages that are extensions of the sender's personality. It also tempts writers to experiment with fonts that are difficult to read and graphics that distract from the content. There is no excuse for a less-than-perfect-looking query. They should be businesslike in appearance and creative in content. They also should be addressed to specific editors. Beginning a query with an anonymous "Dear Editor" means that no one is likely to respond. Do whatever you must to learn the name of the editor who evaluates query letters. This usually is as easy as checking the magazine's Web site, its masthead or making a quick telephone call.

What's the big idea? Assuming a query passes the appearance test, the editor begins to evaluate the creativity of the idea and the skills of the writer. Knowing if an idea is right for a magazine is the easy part. Editors understand their readers and can gauge reader interest in any given topic. Editors also know how recently their publication has featured a topic, and they typically won't revisit the subject for about three years. The exception is the occasional "update" when a major change occurs or a new angle surfaces. Also, certain evergreen topics are of sufficient interest to warrant regular exposure in some magazines. These include fitness, fashion and health tips in women's magazines, money management advice in business publications and stories about high-profile personalities in entertainment weeklies.

As an editor evaluates the idea, he's also looking for clues to the writer's ability. A typo or misspelled word raises questions of accuracy. A writer who includes clichés in a query is likely to include more clichés in an article. If run-on sentences, endlessly long paragraphs and difficult vocabulary fill a query, they will more likely weaken an article. The query serves as a preview of things to come—good and bad.

"As an editor, I liked to envision writers with their sweatshirt sleeves rolled to the elbow as they write their letters with the kids asleep, the dog snoring and all lights out next door," says Hank Nuwer, former magazine editor, and author of *How to Write Like an Expert About Anything*.[1] "Good letters encourage a sense of a writer at work. Letters that are too formal, banal and cliché-ridden make me think of grad students sweating blood to write dissertation proposals. Which would I rather read? Hey, what do you think?"

Formatting a Query Letter

Most business letters and query letters are written in a block format. That means:

- Put your return address, contact information and date in the upper-right hand corner of the letter.
- Write the editor's name and address followed by two line spaces.
- Write the salutation (i.e. Dear Mr. Smith:) followed by a colon.
- Insert a double space after the salutation and before the first paragraph.
- Do not indent the first line of the paragraph.
- Use single-space paragraphs and insert a double space between each paragraph.
- End the letter with the closure "Sincerely" or "Yours truly" followed by a comma.
- Leave four spaces for your hand-written signature followed by your typed name.

SIDEBAR 1

ESSENTIAL COMPONENTS OF A QUERY

Most successful queries contain five components, strategically arranged for maximum impact. Unfortunately, many beginning writers confuse the order, put the least important element first and are disappointed when their letters fail to yield favorable responses. Here are the components that we recommend, listed according to their correct placement within the query:

1   compelling lead paragraph
2   summary of the topic
3   statement of timeliness
4   nuts and bolts information
5   writer's credentials

Crafting the lead paragraph

Just as the lead paragraph of an article has to grab a reader's attention, so does the introductory paragraph in a query letter have to spark an editor's interest. For this reason, many successful queries begin with anecdotes—true stories, not hypothetical ones—that plunge readers into the topics that the writers are proposing. As an example, a query that pitched an article about identity theft began with this anecdote:

> Shon Bolden of Hillsboro, Ore., is a 23-year-old tire store worker who attends college part time. About four years ago, he tried to change his bank account to another bank, but the new bank refused the transaction. When he asked why, the bank said it ran his Social Security number through a credit bureau and found 14 people were using his Social Security number. Later he started receiving bills for items he never purchased. Shon discovered that his financial identity had been stolen. Identity thieves had opened accounts in his name at about a dozen retail stores and had run up big bills.

Besides engaging the editor's attention, this opening paragraph hints at the tone of the future article. The editor can assume that the author will deliver a manuscript written in the same conversational tone as the query letter that proposed it. Whether the opening paragraph of a pitch letter is an anecdote, a provocative statement, an insightful quotation or a question, it frequently re-emerges as the article's opening paragraph.

Summarizing a timely topic

Assuming that the first paragraph of the query succeeds in hooking the editor's attention, the second paragraph should summarize the article's topic and underscore its timeliness. It often resembles the "nutgraf" or billboard paragraph we describe in Chapter 8. Continuing with the example of the identity theft article, the billboard paragraph might state: "Shon is one of half a million Americans each year who are victims of identity theft—the country's fastest-growing crime. He is one of several persons who testified before the House Banking and Financial Services Committee last October."

In addition to explaining what the article is about, this billboard paragraph provides the third essential element in our list. It establishes the timeliness of the story by alerting readers to the fact that they could be at risk *right now* because identity theft is the country's fastest-growing crime. Suddenly the issue becomes personal; the author moves past the description of a single crime victim and makes the point that what happened to that victim could happen to anyone.

The same 1-2-3 formula—compelling lead, topic summary and statement of timeliness—that works for a hard-hitting article about identity theft is equally successful in a query that pitches a less serious subject. For example, suppose you decide to propose an article for a women's magazine about couples who choose to take separate vacations. You identify a publication that might be interested in such a story and you begin your query letter with this introductory paragraph: "Bob and Lynne Gray recently celebrated their 10th wedding anniversary by taking the vacation of their dreams. He headed for a camping trip in Michigan's remote Upper Peninsula; she opted for a week at a spa in Southern California."

Because the topic that you are proposing is much bigger than a profile of an otherwise compatible couple who choose to go their separate ways, the second paragraph places the anecdote in a larger context. It summarizes the topic and establishes its timeliness. "The Grays aren't alone. In the past three years nearly a quarter of all U.S. travelers have taken solo vacations. Although 53 percent are men, women are rapidly playing catch-up. To capitalize on this travel trend, Web sites, magazines and tour companies are designing trips and creating products that cater to the destination whims of female adventurers."

Nuts and bolts information

After crafting the necessary paragraphs that build interest, summarize the topic and establish timeliness, the writer next must outline the nuts and bolts of the proposal. This involves answering several pertinent questions: How many words will the article contain? Will it include any sidebars? What kinds of photos are available? When will a draft be ready? Who are the sources of information? Whom do you plan to interview and quote? At this point you are not displaying your creativity; instead, you're merely imparting vital information.

Writer's credentials

What most effective query letters have in common is that the word "I"— referring to the writer—does not appear until the end of the correspondence. A query should never begin with a statement about the writer. That information is the least important element of the letter. The writer should place his credentials toward the end, and, if he runs out of space, he can omit them entirely. By the time an editor reads the body of a pitch letter, he knows if the proposed idea suits the magazine's audience and if the letter's author has the skills to deliver the goods.

Among the most appropriate writer's credentials to include are those that link the author to the topic. For example, if you are pitching the article about identity theft and you were once victimized, that fact is worth mentioning. If you and your mate typically head in opposite directions for your vacations, you are a likely candidate for the solo travel assignment. Recapping your academic degrees will have little impact. Explaining that you once had a poem published in your high school newspaper will impress no one.

Remember that a query letter is a sales letter. As such, you should feel comfortable including anything that will enhance the chances of making a sale. A clipping of a recently published article—not your high school poetry—is a good way to establish credibility. If you are a writer who also takes photographs, you might want to include a sample of your work or direct the editor to your Web site where your work is posted.

A business card attached to the query could lead to a future assignment. Editors sometimes reject a query because the idea isn't right for their publication but they like the writer's style. They file the business card with a notation on the back. The next time they need an article by an author from a certain geographic area, they flip through their cache of business cards.

WHAT NOT TO INCLUDE IN A QUERY

Your academic degrees aren't the only thing to omit from a query. Although some writers always state in a pitch letter the kind of rights they are willing to sell, we think that discussion is better delayed until after the editor expresses interest in the article. Most publications are willing to negotiate rights at the point when the editor offers a contract to the author. Introducing the topic into the conversation at the query level seems as inappropriate as typing your Social Security number on a submission in anticipation of payment. Save it for later.

When the time is right, you will need a basic understanding of copyright law. Selling an article to a publisher means relinquishing partial rights in exchange for payment. Generally speaking, the more you are paid, the more rights you give up. Beginning feature writers deal with three kinds of rights—first rights, reprint rights and all rights. (We offer an explanation in the "Selling Your Rights" sidebar included in this chapter.)

Another pet peeve of many editors is a paragraph of gushy praise for the magazine. Avoid sentences such as, "I just love your publication and read it from cover to cover as soon as it arrives each month." The editor will know that you read the magazine "from cover to cover" if your query letter proposes an article that is exactly right for the publication's readers. By contrast, few things frustrate editors more than proposals that indicate the writers never took time to review the publication. A favorite war story of Ohio writer Bob Hostetler dates back to his three years as editor of *The Young Soldier*, a Salvation Army publication geared to youth. "In the Salvation Army, adult members are called 'soldiers,' and children are called 'junior soldiers,'" explains Hostetler, now a freelance author of more than a dozen books.

> Anyone familiar with the Salvation Army or with the magazine would know this. Still, every so often I would receive a query letter proposing an article for *The Young Soldier* about how to disassemble and assemble an M-16 rifle or about the newest developments in tank warfare. Obviously those writers had no idea what I did from 8:30 to 4:30 every day.[2]

Whereas freelance writers should never exaggerate their credentials in a query letter, neither should they tell negative tales on themselves. Lines that a writer should not include in a query are: "I don't know anything about this topic but thought it might be fun to learn," or "I've never published an article before" or "I just retired from my real job and have decided to become a writer."

Selling Your Rights

Most magazines are registered with the U.S. Copyright Office as single collective entities. The individual articles that appear in the magazine are not copyrighted individually in the authors' names. Magazines typically purchase partial rights to each article from freelance writers. Before your work appears in print and before you cash the magazine's check, you should have a clear understanding of the rights you are selling. Keep all correspondence that states whether the publication has purchased first rights, reprint rights, electronic rights or all rights.

First rights

Publications most typically purchase "first rights" or "first serial rights" from freelance writers. "Serial" is a librarian's term for any periodical published as part of a series, on a regular timetable, such as daily, weekly or monthly. By selling first serial rights, you give the magazine the first opportunity to publish the article. After the article is published, you retain the right to sell reprint rights to other publishers as many times as you want.

Reprint rights

While the formal term is "second serial rights," it's usually called reprint rights and means exactly what it says. Many print and online publications purchase reprint rights if the original publication's readership doesn't overlap with their own. Only the highest-circulation periodicals insist on buying editorial material that has never appeared elsewhere. Usually payment for reprint rights varies from 10 to 50 percent of the magazine's payment schedule for first rights.

All rights

If you sell all rights, you give the publisher full copyright owner-ship for reproduction and distribution. You should avoid selling all rights unless the publisher insists and the payment is suffi-ciently high. All rights means the publisher can publish the article in its magazine, put it on its Web site or publish portions in another magazine it owns or in a subsequent book or CD-ROM with a collection of articles. Unfortunately for writers, an increas-ing number of large publishers want to purchase all rights because it gives them the freedom to use the material in a variety of print and electronic formats.

WHEN TO QUERY

Some beginning writers go to all the trouble of researching and writing their articles before they submit query letters to see if any editor is inter-ested in the topics. This makes little sense. The writer-editor relationship often involves a dialogue as an article takes shape. The dialogue begins but doesn't end with the query letter. Frequently an editor will say "yes" to a proposal and then will offer suggestions as to length and angle. The editor may request that the submission take the form of a how-to article or a profile with a sidebar. The writer who has completed the project has to start over.

Most veteran writers submit their query letters at two points in the writing process.

1   They have an idea and have decided on a slant. **Query.**
2   They have an idea, have chosen the slant and have conducted their interviews. **Query.**

The advantage of sending a query at the first point in the process is that you have invested little time and energy. If no editor expresses interest in the idea, you've lost nothing. You file the idea for the future and move on to another project.

The advantage of sending a query at the second point, after you've done your interviews, is that the query will have more substance. You can include a comment from one of your sources. You can create an anecdote based on your research. If your spadework has caused your enthusiasm to surge, that excitement will spill over into the query and may be contagious enough to affect the editor. You'll have a good idea of how long the article should be, and you can pitch any ideas that you have regarding sidebar possibilities. The only disadvantage to querying at this point is that you have invested several hours in doing research. If no editor asks to see the finished article, that time is lost. However, if the topic isn't time-dated, you may be able to revisit it in the future.

SNAIL MAIL VS. E-MAIL QUERIES

Should you or shouldn't you? Only editors can answer the question of whether a writer should fax a query, send it by e-mail or let the U.S. Post Office do the honors. As we indicated in Chapter 6, the writers' guidelines of a publication usually state if electronic submissions are acceptable. E-mail queries work well in three instances: if the idea you are proposing is time-dated and you need an immediate reply from an editor; if you and the editor have a long-standing professional relationship; or if the magazine has stated that its editors prefer e-mail rather than other types of correspondence. Throughout the publishing industry, e-mail correspondence is gaining widespread acceptance.

An e-mail query has the same two jobs to perform as a traditional query. It has to propose a great idea and convince the editor that the writer can deliver an equally great manuscript. The query is often shorter, but the author should include enough details to help the editor make the right decision.

Here's a sample of a query that pitches an article to an editor of a national general-interest magazine. Sending it by e-mail is permissible because the writer needs to find a buyer for the idea before the topic loses its timeliness. Also, she has written previous articles for the editor, is on a first-name basis with him and doesn't have to convince him of her skills. The major challenge is to ignite his enthusiasm for the topic she is proposing.

Dear Ted:

The city is magnificent in spite of itself. With scaffolds encasing its monuments and clean-up crews scaling its spires, St. Petersburg, Russia, is withstanding another siege—this one, a massive makeover in preparation for the city's 300th anniversary celebration. The party will peak on May 27.

   The perception persists that what's left of the old Soviet Union surely must be gloomy if not dangerous. A few assurances: Russia is safe, and Big Brother won't hassle anyone who aims a point-and-shoot camera at a government building. English is widely understood, and most places accept U.S. dollars as readily as rubles. American money goes far here, but shoppers aren't tempted to part with much of it. Antique stores offer icons and other remnants of the monarchy, but the buzz is that buyers have to relinquish all treasures at the border. The safest purchases are the most predictable—fake fur hats, T-shirts and an endless supply of nesting dolls. Among the most bizarre set of dolls are those that depict Russian leaders and include Gorbachev with his signature head splotch, a woozy Yeltsin and a nondescript Putin. A favorite T-shirt reveals a profile of Lenin and the word "McLenin's" superimposed over the familiar Golden Arches of McDonald's. The back of the shirt carries the old communist symbol, the red star, and the message: "The Party Is Over."

   But residents of St. Petersburg hope the party is just beginning as they roll out the red carpet for tourists who want to celebrate the upcoming anniversary. What these visitors are likely to see is the subject of an article I'd like to write for the spring issue of your magazine. May I send you a draft on speculation? Great photos accompany the 2,000-word story that I have in mind.

Whether or not the editor agrees to consider an article about St. Petersburg won't depend on the writer's ability to deliver a good story. He is familiar with her work and her e-mail confirms her skill. However, that doesn't mean that he will say "yes" to her proposal. Editors reject article proposals for reasons that go beyond the ability of the writer or the value of the idea. Here are the top four reasons for rejection:

1   The magazine has a backlog of articles to publish before its editors buy new material.
2   Another writer is under assignment to produce an article on the same topic.
3   The article isn't right for the magazine's readers.
4   The magazine published a similar article a few months ago.

P.S. TRY AGAIN

Writers who bypass the query and send their completed articles to publications often are in for a long wait. Unsolicited submissions typically end up in the slush pile where they might spend several months before anyone looks at them. Editors evaluate query letters; they forward the slush to a first reader who is likely to open each envelope and, simultaneously, reach for a printed rejection slip. Professional writers submit queries; beginners send manuscripts.

There are exceptions. In a few instances, even the professionals send completed articles. This is the case when a writer is dealing with a newspaper or magazine that states in its guidelines that it prefers manuscripts to queries. Editors of daily publications in particular often don't have time to engage in back-and-forth correspondence with freelance writers. They want to see the finished product. Magazine editors who usually prefer queries to manuscripts will make an exception for articles that are very short—two or three pages—or those that fall into the category of humor. Since it is difficult to describe what is funny, they like to judge for themselves.

Although rejection letters are part of every writer's life, some such letters are easier to take than others. Occasionally an editor will scrawl a postscript on the bottom of the dreaded rejection note. A personal comment—"great idea, but not right for us"—is meant to encourage the writer to keep trying. The unwritten message is: "Don't give up."

SAMPLE QUERY LETTER

The following letter achieves the two goals of every query. First, the proposed idea is timely because it's a pocketbook issue—the high cost of fuel—and is linked to the environment; second, the author leaves no doubt that he is a skilled writer who can handle the assignment. Notice the use of bullets. These break up the gray text, draw attention to compelling facts and suggest the type of information that the resulting article will contain. In addition to hooking the editor on the topic, the writer estimates the word count and offers details on his research plans. Although his writing credentials are impressive, he distills them to one sentence and places it at the end of the letter.

Editor's name
Indianapolis Monthly
Address

Dear Ms.   :

Indiana's coal resources could help solve the nation's looming energy crisis and boost the state's economy.

But at what price?

Indianapolis Monthly readers benefit from Indiana's coal resources whether they know it or not. This hard-hitting business story makes sure they know it.

Thanks to Indiana coal, the state has nearly the lowest energy costs in the country, including retail electricity prices nearly 20 percent below the national retail rate. With blackouts in western states underscoring the weakness of the nation's power grid, and a White House administration pushing for reliance on domestic energy resources, *IM* readers need to view the state's coal industry as less of an interesting throwback and more of a potential, high-profile export.

Just as the Saudis sit atop much of the world's supply of bubblin' crude, Indiana lies smack above another type of black gold.

Consider these facts:

• One-sixth of the state, or about 6,500 square miles, is coal-rich. Eighteen billion tons of recoverable, unmined coal lie within our borders. This prime mining land covers west-central and southwestern Indiana, stretching from north of Terre Haute down to the Ohio River, forming a giant wedge.
• The energy contained within this acreage equals 75 percent of the nation's tapped oil reserves, 65 percent of its natural gas reserves and nearly three times its entire power requirements, according to former coal miner Rep. Russell Stilwell (D-Boonville)—one of more than 20 top sources interviewed for this balanced investigative story.

Indiana as an integral part of the next OPEC? It's a thrilling prospect for taxpayers in a state whose legislature struggles to make ends meet. New coal dollars could mean thousands of jobs. But instead of popping champagne corks, some observers are opening aspirin bottles. After all, even coal-touting Paul J. Ehret, deputy director of the Indiana Department of Natural Resources who now tours the state to ask communities to warm to the idea of coal, admits it is "not the cleanest" industry. Air pollution from coal-burning electric plants and run-off and dust from active, aging and abandoned mines that dot the landscape have all been targeted as environmental problems.

My proposed 6,000-word comprehensive piece for *Indianapolis Monthly* won't be just the facts, ma'am. Using literary journalism techniques, this article will show, not tell, *IM* readers how Indiana's dirty little secret provides both economic growth for the state and a plethora of environmental and health problems that our grandchildren's grandchildren still won't entirely undo.

This is a three-month investigation that will take me to the coal mines, to the legislative and DNR offices, and to the homes of anti-coal activists, scientists, geologists and energy experts. Balancing the Indiana opinions will be plenty of opinions from national experts and enforcement personnel from the Environmental Protection Agency.

Interested? Let's sit down at your conference table and discuss expenses and a reasonable fee for this potentially award-winning story that in turn can be mined to the fullest for quoting by other state media.

My credits as a reporter specializing in environment and education stories include the *New York Times Sunday Magazine, Harper's, Canadian Equinox* and *The Nation.*

Sincerely,

Hank Nuwer[3]

ENDNOTES

[1] Hank Nuwer, *How to Write Like an Expert About Anything* (Cincinnati, Ohio: Writer's Digest Books, 1995).
[2] Workshop lecture, May 21, 2004.
[3] Used by permission.

PART III

WRITING FEATURE AND MAGAZINE ARTICLES

Because feature writers have more time to research and create their articles, readers expect a certain level of literary quality. Successful magazine writers have the skills of a news reporter and gifts of a storyteller. They know how to craft a gotcha lead, sprinkle anecdotes throughout their text, add action to rev up the pace and humor to tone down the drama.

8

HOOKS, INTROS AND LEADS

Your takeaway . . .

If the opening paragraphs of a feature story don't grab readers'
interest, the content of the article—regardless of its importance—
may remain forever unread. An article's introduction has four
jobs to accomplish: attract attention, introduce the topic, set the
tone and establish the point of view. To add to the writer's challenge, the best leads occupy limited space. This chapter suggests
several ways to launch a story successfully.

Organizing a feature story is a lot like solving a complex jigsaw puzzle. By
the time you sit down in front of your computer screen you've gathered
an assortment of bits and pieces of information, many of them disjointed,
that you now must assemble into a seamless "picture" for your readers.
Where do you begin? Which note or quote do you pull from your stash of
research and use to create that all-important paragraph that will lead into
the content? Which piece do you set aside to serve as the perfect wrap-up
to your article?

Many journalists agree that the most difficult part of writing articles is
creating leads that attract readers and endings that satisfy them. One of our
colleagues underscores the importance of strong beginnings and appropriate conclusions with this comparison. He says that feature articles, like
airplanes, are most vulnerable to crash during takeoff and landing. His
point: An article can contain great information, but if the opening paragraph (the "takeoff") doesn't grab and hold readers' interest, they may turn
the page and move on. The ending of an article, like the landing of an air-
plane, should be smooth rather than abrupt, fast-paced rather than prolonged. Like pilots who know their destinations before taking off, writers
should identify their endings before beginning their articles. Otherwise
they risk getting lost, taking detours or wandering in circles as they try to
decide how and when to stop.

COMING TO TERMS WITH LEADS

Writers use three terms—often interchangeably—to describe the opening paragraphs of feature articles. Each term has an appropriate meaning. The "lead" is a fitting description because an effective first paragraph *leads* readers into the story. The "hook" is an accurate term because a strong opening paragraph *hooks* readers' attention and nudges them to continue. The "introduction" is a logical label because writers use the initial paragraphs to *introduce* their topics and establish the tone and point of view of their articles. If a writer is going to tell a story from his own point of view, as in a personal essay, the word "I" is likely to appear somewhere in the lead. If the tone of the article is going to be conversational rather than academic, that attitude is going to be evident from the first sentence.

Writers often labor for hours over their introductory paragraphs. They fine-tune, add, delete and exchange words until they are satisfied. They scrutinize their notes in search of effective hooks. They experiment with anecdotes, provocative quotations and surprising facts that may have surfaced during the research phase. Some writers tell us that they can't move forward with their articles until they have the leads precisely as they want them. Other writers prefer to forge ahead, complete their rough drafts and then return to their opening paragraphs to do the fine-tuning, the adding, deleting and exchanging of words. Whichever process works best for you is the process you should follow.

Taken together, leads and endings serve as the bookends of articles. They hold everything in place. Once you have created the lead paragraph and the closing paragraph you have established your boundaries. The next challenge is to arrange the remaining content in logical order. Not easy, of course, but the lead paragraph should give you a direction and the closing paragraph should give you a destination.

BEYOND THE SUMMARY LEAD

Unlike reporters who cover breaking news events and get to the point quickly, feature writers have the luxury of setting up their articles with well-crafted and engaging opening paragraphs. This doesn't mean that they never rely on the familiar no-frills summary lead that answers basic questions—who, what, where, when, why and how. It simply means that they have the flexibility to experiment with leisurely approaches.

Summary leads have taken a lot of criticism in recent years. They were the predictable way of getting into a story for so long that a backlash was inevitable. "Boring!" claim their critics. Maybe so, but what summary leads lack in creativity, they make up for in information. Here are two examples of summary leads that appeared in articles relating to the skyrocketing price of gasoline during the summer of 2008. The first lead introduced a news story published in *Rolling Stone*: "Four-dollar-a-gallon gas prices are eating away at the summer-concert business, with top festivals and tours taking unexpected box-office hits over the past few months."[1]

This 29-word opening sentence contains, in a nutshell, the essence of the article. It answers the six basic questions. Who? Gasoline. What? Is eating into profits. Where? On the concert circuit. When? This summer. How? By reducing attendance. Why? Because prices have soared to $4 per gallon. Depending on their level of interest, readers can stop reading after the lead sentence or can continue to learn details of rock artists who were playing to capacity crowds and those performers who were canceling bookings.

A similar summary lead worked equally well to introduce a round-up feature also linked to rising fuel costs. *The Wall Street Journal* began an article about inexpensive vacation opportunities this way: "Four-dollar-a-gallon gasoline, airline woes and unsteady financial markets add up to a summer of discontent for the travel industry. But it's turning into a summer of discounts for travelers."[2]

Unlike the *Rolling Stone* lead, this one doesn't answer the "how" question. To learn *how* gas prices have created discounts for travelers, readers must continue reading. The lead succeeds because it sets up the content of the article and piques reader interest.

Some feature writers, bogged down by writer's block, create summary leads as a way to get a few words on their computer screens and achieve some momentum. After their articles begin to take shape, they often go back to their summary statements and top them off with more creative leads. However, they don't delete the summary paragraphs. Instead, they keep them as their second or third paragraphs, often called billboard paragraphs or "nutgrafs." Such paragraphs, which we refer to several times throughout this book, tell readers, in a nutshell, what the story is about. Many editors expect every article to contain a nutgraf or billboard paragraph, which usually comes immediately after the lead.

LEADS THAT SUCCEED

In our opinion, few rules are unbendable when it comes to feature writing. A gifted writer can make almost anything work. For that reason, we encourage students to experiment with a variety of lead paragraphs and then decide which ones they like best. Factors to consider include:

- The publication—Many newspapers and magazines prefer short articles limited to a page that don't require much time to read. In these cases the editors are likely to depend on the old workhorse summary lead.
- The topic—How-to articles usually get to the point quickly because readers are anxious to access the advice and care little about the creative introductions. Often profiles and articles that probe complex issues lend themselves to more leisurely treatment.
- The audience—Demographic data such as age, profession and education levels sometimes influence readers' preference of writing styles. Persons who read for entertainment may enjoy descriptive opening paragraphs; persons who read for information may prefer a straightforward approach.

Of the many options available, we've chosen to describe six leads that work well regardless of the publication, topic or audience. We accompany each description with one or two examples to serve as models.

Scenario lead

By accurately recreating a place, the scenario lead allows readers to "see" the backdrop against which the story unfolds. The key to making a scenario lead work is to avoid too much description. Don't include every detail; use a light hand in sketching the environment. Let the reader's imagination take over from there and fill in the gaps.

In the following *Sports Illustrated* lead, the author invited his readers to experience the moment when avid but skeptical Oregon State basketball fans met their school's new coach for the first time. Notice the mention of the weather, the size of the venue and the flag.

> On a drizzly afternoon in early May, Craig Robinson addressed about 100 Oregon State boosters in a large banquet room in Portland. He stepped to

a podium next to an American flag and opened with a playful joke about the height of the school's athletic director, 5'7" Bob De Carolis, the man who hired him in April to coach OSU's basketball team.[3]

Shock lead

Lead paragraphs that contain a shock element are likely to grab and hold readers' attention at least for a little while. They succeed if, in the course of doing research, the writer uncovers a truly surprising bit of information. Chances are the information that surprised the writer also will surprise the readers. Sometimes, as in the case of the first example, the lead sentence is relatively short. The humorous tone, established at the outset, continued throughout the article, as the author gave an overview of new electronic gadgets available to consumers. "Shortly before Valentine's Day, a study was released claiming that 47 percent of men in Britain would give up sex in return for a big-screen plasma television. As with all matters relating to technology, numbers are key: precisely how long were these men prepared to go without sex? And how large a screen?"[4]

Sometimes a writer combines categories of leads as Wendy Brenner did for her introduction to a feature article for *The Oxford American*. The story was a finalist in a National Magazine Awards competition. Part shock and part anecdote, the opening paragraph is humorous and memorable. Notice the understated, casual tone.

> One day in 1971 in Wilmington, N.C., 14-year-old Dean Ripa was at home performing surgery on a cottonmouth snake, and it bit him. This was unfortunate for a couple of reasons. He knew enough about snakes to know he would probably not die, but he did need a ride to the hospital, which meant his parents were going to find out about the 50 snakes he was keeping in their spare room: rattlesnakes, the water moccasins he'd caught in local swamps, even several cobras he had purchased via mail-order—he had a king cobra years before he had his driver's license.[5]

Blind lead

A blind lead raises readers' curiosity by omitting a key piece of information. The omission causes readers to continue reading until their curiosity is satisfied. The lead is "blind" because it doesn't identify by name the persons who are the subjects of the articles. That important fact remains a mystery until the second or third paragraph solves it. In the following example, a feature article about President Ronald Reagan's former aides who planned his funeral far in advance of his death, the "they" of the story were not identified by name until the fourth paragraph.

> As Washington hotshots in their 20s and 30s, they pulled all-nighters, crisscrossing the globe to build the crowds and choreograph the most enduring moments of Ronald Reagan's presidency.... Then they went their separate ways.... But over the years, Mr. Reagan's advance men—pioneers in the stagecraft revolutionized by the actor-turned-politician—stayed in touch, quietly planning their boss's grand finale under the code name "Operation Serenade."[6]

Direct or indirect quote lead

A quotation can serve as an effective lead if a speaker says something noteworthy that sums up the article's main idea. A variation on the quote lead is the indirect quote lead. This works well if you want to capture the essence of what someone said but you don't want to use the speaker's exact words. We offer examples of both options. First, a direct quote from a fitness expert succeeded because his comment would surprise readers who hold different opinions. Thus it combined the shock/surprise and direct quote categories. "'Unless you're training for a marathon, bike race, or triathlon,' says Rodolpho 'Rudy' Reyes, 'Cardio is an inefficient waste of a guy's time.'"[7]

For a profile article about one of the world's best-selling romance novelists, a magazine writer opened with an indirect quotation and ended the paragraph with a direct quote. This lead contains elements of the scenario, indirect quote and direct quote leads.

> The trouble with writing at home, says author Janette Oke over the din of her dishwasher, is the ever-present lure of housework. It's always there, tugging her away from her computer, beckoning her from her research and causing her to leave her characters fending for themselves, mid-plot, somewhere out on the Canadian prairie. "Once a housewife, always a housewife," she adds with a shrug that lets you know she wouldn't have it any other way, thank you.[8]

Direct-address lead

The direct-address lead invites the reader to participate in the story. How? The writer speaks directly to the reader by using the word "you" as part of the opening paragraph. The resulting lead is much like a conversation between writer and reader. In the following example, the article's author has assumed that he and the readers share a common interest: running.

> If you live where there are four real seasons, then you already know that the year contains four absolutely must-run days. The runs on these days are of the cut school, skip work and get a sitter for the kids variety. In summer, it's when you get to run through a misty rain. In fall, it's the first day with a bite to it, when you think about buying a new pair of tights.[9]

Anecdote lead

Anecdotes excel as leads when they illustrate a major point of an article. Readers love vivid little stories that demonstrate rather than dictate the important facts of a feature. In writing about the desegregation of a southern high school, journalist Josh Peter captured the story's essence with an insightful opening anecdote. The series of articles, published in *The Times-Picayune* (New Orleans), was a finalist in the "diversity" category of the annual "Best Newspaper Writing" competition sponsored by the American Society of Newspaper Editors. Notice how the opening three sentence fragments set the scene for the action that unfolds in the locker room.

> Friday night. Homecoming. An hour before kickoff.
>   In the darkened locker room, hushed but for the sound of cleats scraping the concrete floor, one voice pierced the quiet.
>   "Juicy!"
>   Jarid Caesar called over teammate Anthony "Juicy" Trosclair, captain of the Riverside Academy football team, to hear the song he listens to before each game.
>   There they sat, side by side on a wooden locker-room bench: Trosclair, the white defensive lineman, and Caesar, the black running back, each pressing a headphone against one ear and nodding to the beat.
>   It was a moment once unthinkable at this small private school in Reserve.[10]

MISTAKES TO AVOID

The same characteristics that can cause introductory paragraphs to succeed also can cause them to fail. For example, including details is commendable, up to a point. Too much data can bog down a lead paragraph and turn it into a catchall. Some editors call this a "luggage lead" because the writer tosses in all sorts of random items. Rambling on and on, it may contain dates, ages and other specifics that the author would be wise to save and weave in later. Example: "Linda Brown, 45-year-old wife of John Brown and mother of Sue, 8, Jay, 6, and Bill, 2, launched a campaign in December to clean up the three-mile stretch of beach that edges her family's property on Long Island that is littered with trash from weekend campers who failed to observe the 'no trespassing' signs that Linda posted in July." (Huh?)

Touches of humor are always welcome, but sometimes writers try too hard to be cute and elicit groans instead of chuckles from readers. A profile article about cartoonist Jim Davis, creator of Garfield, is a case in point. Example: "Forget the nine-lives theory. Garfield, the fat cat in the orange and black glad wags, the one with the droopy lids, the thoughts that bite and the paws that refresh, is within a whisker of turning nine."[11] (Ugh!)

Giving human characteristics to inanimate objects is an overworked strategy that can create funny pictures in readers' minds. Example: "If walls could talk, these would speak of five generations of a farm family trying to survive the tantrums of Mother Nature." The problem here is that readers know that walls can't talk and although Mother Nature is capable of some wild weather, she doesn't throw tantrums.

Beginning an article with a question can engage readers, but asking a barrage of questions usually wilts them. Example: "Do you have a teenager who is approaching dating age? Are you worried by all the stories you've heard about kids making bad choices when they're out with friends? Are you wondering what you might do about it? Are you willing to carve out some quality time to address the issue?" (As a reader, are you tempted to turn the page?)

Many beginning writers, assigned to cover events, rely on chronological lead paragraphs that make their stories resemble the minutes of a meeting. Example:

> The concert began at 8:10 p.m., after the arena's maintenance crew fixed a problem with the sound system. The audience applauded the four back-up

musicians when they came on stage, warmed up and then played a medley from their recent CD. The cheers grew louder as the lead singer of the group took her place in front of the microphone at 8:45 p.m. She cleared her throat and nodded to the drummer. He gave the countdown to the first song.

Perhaps the most objectionable introduction of all is the hypothetical lead that is the product of the writer's imagination rather than the result of his research skills. Feature writing, like news writing, is based on truth. A hypothetical lead is fiction and has no place in the media. Don't resort to concocting scenarios or creating imaginary or composite people. Say you are assigned to write an article about university students who spend a lot of time and money on campus but never complete their education. Hypothetical lead: "A college student, undecided about his career goal, might change majors five times before leaving school without a degree." Instead, you find a real person who faced the dilemma that your article explores. Lead based on research: "Joe Smith, a sophomore at UCLA, changed majors five times before leaving campus last June without a degree." (See the difference?)

ENDINGS THAT SATISFY READERS

Bringing an article in for a smooth "landing" is more of a challenge for the feature writer than for the news reporter. The traditional inverted pyramid organization is still acceptable for a news story. The reporter clusters the most important facts of a story in the opening paragraph. Subsequent paragraphs flesh out details in descending order of importance. The rationale for this kind of organization is that a reader can stop reading at any point and still know the highlights of the story. Or, an editor, pressed for space, can cut the article from the bottom without fear of discarding important information.

The feature article requires more thought and planning. A good article can "crash" in its closing paragraph if the author makes one of these mistakes:

- repeats information in an effort to re-emphasize a previously stated point
- supplies conclusions that the writer wants the reader to draw from the article

- leaves key questions unanswered
- allows the story to dribble off or fade away without a sense of closure

Often the best way to identify an ending for an article is to revisit the lead paragraph. Many writers bring their stories full circle by returning to a question they raised in the lead, by quoting the same person who was quoted in the introduction, or by supplying the ending to an anecdote that served as the article's hook. For example, we know a writer who researched a story about how microchips, embedded in animal collars, have greatly reduced the frequency of lost pets. The story began with an anecdote about a dog owner whose German shepherd went missing. The owner ran a lost-and-found ad in the newspaper for two weeks before someone spotted the pet and alerted its owner. The anecdote served as an introduction to the article that then explored the development, availability and effectiveness of microchips. The last paragraph of the story circled back to the pet owner for a wrap-up comment that articulated his intention to purchase one of the chips for his dog's collar.

IDENTIFYING THE BOOKENDS

If three writers tackled identical assignments and interviewed the same sources, they would likely come up with three different articles with three different leads and endings. There is no single "right" way to start a story, organize its major points and bring it to a conclusion.

As you scan your notes and transcripts, try to identify several possible leads and potential endings. Don't stop with just one lead or one ending; give yourself a range of choices. From these choices, select the lead that you like best and type it onto your computer screen. Next, select the ending that seems most appropriate and type that paragraph onto your screen. With your "bookends" in place, you can return to your notes and determine how best to arrange the material between the bookends.

If getting started is a struggle for you, try constructing a basic summary lead. You can always go back and improve on it. Creative writers recognize that they have several options and they allow themselves plenty of time to experiment before completing their final drafts.

ENDNOTES

[1] Steve Knopper, "Gas Prices, Economy Shake Sales for Summer Tours," *Rolling Stone*, July 10–24, 2008, 18.

[2] Candace Jackson, "Getting Away for Less," *The Wall Street Journal*, July 19–24, 2008, W4.

[3] George Dohrmann, "The Unlikely Candidate," *Sports Illustrated*, June 9, 2008, 60.

[4] Patricia Marx, "Tech Stuff," *The New Yorker*, March 10, 2008, 82.

[5] Wendy Brenner, "Love and Death in the Cape Fear Serpentarium," in *The Best American Magazine Writing* (New York: Columbia University Press, 2006), 267. (This article originally was published in *The Oxford American* and was later, as a finalist in The National Magazine Awards competition, included in *The Best American Magazine Writing 2006* anthology.)

[6] Jacob M. Schlesinger, "Operation Serenade: Laying Groundwork for Reagan's Funeral," *The Wall Street Journal*, June 10, 2004, 1.

[7] Grant Davis, "Cardio Is Back," *Men's Journal*, Aug. 2008, 73–76.

[8] Holly G. Miller, "Janette Oke: The Prairie's Own Companion," *Ink*, Dec.-Jan. 1994/1995, 20.

[9] John Bingham, "Opening Day," *Runner's World*, April 2004, 66.

[10] Josh Peter, "About Face, Part One," in *2005 Best Newspaper Writing* (Washington, D.C.: The Poynter Institute for Media Studies and CQ Press, 2006), 187.

[11] Holly G. Miller, "Jim Davis: He's Got the World by the Tail," *The Saturday Evening Post*, Nov. 1984, 52.

9

ACTION-FILLED WRITING

Your takeaway . . .

Interesting writing contains action, which originates with people who bring change to their surroundings. This chapter teaches you how to use the tools and techniques that create action-filled writing. You will learn how to use and apply these principles:

- write about people doing things
- write using action verbs
- write with active voice
- write with concrete words
- write to create suspense

The movie *Indiana Jones and the Kingdom of the Crystal Skull* begins in the desert Southwest in 1957 during the height of the Cold War between the United States and the Soviet Union. Indiana Jones and his sidekick, Mac, just barely escaped a clash with Soviet intelligence agents on a remote airfield. After Prof. Jones returns home to his job at Marshall College, the dean tells him that his controversial activities have made him suspicious and that the government has pressured the university to fire him. Soon after that Jones meets an archaeologist who seeks his help in making what is possibly the most spectacular archaeological find in history—the Crystal Skull of Akator. So Jones decides to leave the college and travel with the archaeologist to the remote mountains of Peru to search for the treasure. But they quickly realize that Soviet agents are following and trying to beat them to the hidden site of the Crystal Skull.

This plot summary of the latest *Indiana Jones* movie illustrates the similarities between action-filled movies and action-filled writing. Compare that summary with this lead paragraph from an article about Peru in the *American Anthropologist*:

Much has been written about the maritime foundations of Andean coastal civilization. One topic archeologists have focused on is the role of marine resources in early Peruvian prehistory. This debate involves questions about the extent to which marine resources were utilized relative to terrestrial animals and/or plants and whether marine resources could support sedentary Preceramic Period coastal populations. Early sites are found associated with the shoreline, river valleys and vegetative communities known as *lomas*. . . . Eventually more permanent settlements were possible in lomas, in part because marine resources were now exploited in addition to lomas ones . . .[1]

Which of these two examples do you find more interesting? The answer is obvious—most everyone would rather find out about the adventures of *Indiana Jones*. This comparison shouldn't be interpreted as demeaning the importance of academic research and scholarly writing. But the styles of writing differ dramatically.

How many times have you started watching a movie but just couldn't get interested? The pace seems slow and the plot takes too long to develop. You begin to wonder if you missed something. However, don't underestimate your viewing sophistication. It's probably just another boring movie.

This chapter will explain the similar elements in action-filled movies and action-filled writing. Action scenes and strong characters propel a movie and hold viewers' attention until the end. "Every viewer knows how boring a talky or purely scenic movie can be; it's the action that makes it interesting," said Benton Patterson in *Write for the Reader*.[2] Action scenes and strong characters also propel good writing and hold the readers' attention until the end.

Feature writing applies specific principles to make writing more lively and interesting. It doesn't matter whether you're telling a dramatic story, explaining a current issue or a recent scientific breakthrough. Colorful, action-packed writing of all genres has certain characteristics. Let's look at these ideas in more detail.

WRITE ABOUT PEOPLE DOING THINGS

In the early 1970s, the editors of *Time* magazine discovered through audience research that the "People" department was the magazine's most-read section. This department contained brief news about celebrity marriages and divorces, controversies and other human-interest tidbits. That discovery led to the company's launch of *People* magazine in 1974, which grew to become the country's most profitable magazine.

The moral of the story? People like to read about people.

Behind every new product, controversy, piece of legislation, economic situation, scientific breakthrough or sociological trend are people. Use people to tell these stories because people invent products, create controversy, introduce laws, buy and sell stocks, discover cures and popularize a new fad or hit song. The bright, informative or entertaining story must bring those people into the spotlight because readers are more interested in people than in things, concepts or ideas.

Nick Paumgarten wrote a *New Yorker* story, "Up and Then Down: The Lives of Elevators," about the worldwide growth of the elevator industry. Filled with facts, statistics, trends and the history of elevators, he could have been boring. But Paumgarten brought the topic to life by weaving it around the saga of Nicholas White, a 34-year-old man trapped for 41 hours inside a stalled New York City elevator.[3]

Anecdotes like this are important for three reasons. First, they take a general topic and demonstrate it to the reader through a specific situation, therefore making it easier to grasp. They create a real-life example of an abstract concept. Second, anecdotes show people doing things so readers can see them, empathize with them and imagine themselves in the same situation. And third, anecdotes not only make articles more interesting, but add credibility and believability. Readers will more readily believe your ideas or arguments if they can visualize them occurring in a specific setting with real-life people. We will say more about anecdotes in Chapter 10.

Think about "people doing things" in a more theoretical framework. All types of writing consist of four basic building blocks: narrative, dialogue, description and exposition. One definition of narrative is "people doing things" and one definition of dialogue is "people saying things." Exposition means "explaining stuff" and description means "describing stuff." Would you rather read about people or stuff? While that's an oversimplification, it explains why narrative and dialogue are so crucial.

Narrative moves the story from Point A to Point B and finally to Point Z. Dialogue brings characters to life through their speech. Compare narrative and dialogue with a car's engine and frame. They give it the power to race down the highway. Think of description and exposition like the body, chrome and trim. They make the car attractive and eye-pleasing, but they aren't essential to get you from Point A to Point B.

For examples of these building blocks, we have chosen excerpts from the *New Yorker* story, "Up and Then Down: The Lives of Elevators."

First, narrative describes things happening; it tells a story; it's always moving from Point A to Point B. The more narrative you include in your writing, the more it will hold readers because it creates movement and propels the action forward. For example:

> The longest smoke break of Nicholas White's life began at around eleven o'clock on a Friday night in October, 1999. White, a thirty-four-year-old production manager at *BusinessWeek*, working late on a special supplement, had just watched the Braves beat the Mets on a television in the office pantry. Now he wanted a cigarette. He told a colleague he'd be right back and, leaving behind his jacket, headed downstairs [on the elevator].[4]

Second, dialogue introduces people into a story, and people always make a story more interesting. Dialogue recreates conversation with two or more people. For example:

> The time passed in a kind of degraded fever dream. On the videotape, he lies motionless for hours at a time, face down on the floor.
> A voice woke him up: "Is there someone in there?"
>
> "Yes."
>
> "What are you doing in there?"
>
> White tried to explain; the voice in the intercom seemed to assume that he was an intruder. "Get me ... out of here!" White shrieked. Duly persuaded, the guard asked him if he wanted anything. White ... asked for a beer.[5]

Third, description means what it says. It paints a word picture of the environment in which these events happen. The best stories create an experience of the senses. A reader doesn't only learn something from a good feature story; he feels, sees and hears it. While description can enhance some scenes, keep it brief because too much can bore the reader. The elevator story contained few examples of "description" because the story was mostly narrative, dialogue and exposition. But this paragraph describes the way that passengers typically arrange themselves in an elevator: "Passengers seem to know instinctively how to arrange themselves in an elevator. Two strangers will gravitate to the back corners, a third will stand by the door ... until a fourth comes in, at which point passengers three and four will spread toward the front corners, making room in the center for a fifth."[6]

Fourth, exposition explains with facts. It illuminates concepts, ideas and background information. Like description, you should keep exposition paragraphs brief and weave them throughout the story. For example:

> In New York City, home to 55,000 elevators, there are 11 billion elevator trips a year—30 million every day—and yet hardly more than two dozen passengers get banged up enough to seek medication attention. The Otis Elevator Company, the world's oldest and biggest elevator manufacturer, claims that its products carry the equivalent of the world's population every five days.[7]

Narrative shows people doing things while exposition conveys facts and concepts. The *Indiana Jones* plot at the beginning of this chapter has 100 percent narrative, while the *American Anthropologist* example is 100 percent exposition. Narration is specific and concrete while exposition is usually more abstract, which makes it more difficult to conceptualize.

WRITE WITH ACTION VERBS

The best writers strive to use action verbs in every sentence. Using action verbs will generate more reader involvement in your writing than any other single technique. For example, *People* magazine began its cover story of Tim Russert, the popular host of NBC's "Meet the Press" who died at age 58 of a heart attack, with this lead:

> The Big Guy, as his son liked to call him, had to do something he hated— leave his family. On June 12, Tim Russert wrapped up a hectic three-day vacation in Rome and prepared to say goodbye to his wife, Maureen, and their son Luke. They had seen the Pope, dined with a cardinal, swept through the Sistine Chapel, but now it was time for Russert to fly back to Washington, D.C., ahead of his family to tape *Meet the Press*, the Sunday morning show he had hosted since 1991.[8]

Notice the action verbs: *do, liked, hated, leave, wrapped, prepared, seen, dined, swept, fly, tape* and *hosted*. Note these action verbs in the *Indiana Jones* example: *begins, escapes, returns, tells, made, pressured, fire, meets, seeks, decides, leaves, travels, search, follow, beat.*

All verbs perform one of three writing functions:

1 display concrete action performed by the subject (action verbs)
   examples: crash, eat, jump, race, breathe, scream, die
2 express the subject's feelings or attitudes (state-of-being verbs)
   examples: believe, hope, feel, have, expect, consider, think, realize
3 link the subject to an object with a form of "to be" (linking verbs)
   examples: be, is, are, was, were, will be

Avoid the more boring verbs "is," "are," "was," "were" and other forms of "to be" because they don't describe anybody doing anything. Here are some examples of weak verb phrases followed by revised versions with an action verb:

- they are different—they *differ*
- used in combination with—*combined*
- their conclusion was—*they concluded*
- came up with—*created*
- made an adjustment to—*adjusted to*

Avoiding a dead construction is another way of ensuring that you use action verbs. Here are some examples of dead constructions: "there is," "there are," "there was," "there will be," "it is," "it was" and "it will be." These constructions display no life and convey no action. The pronouns "there" and "it" are on life support—used only because the author can't find a more colorful noun. The linking verbs—various forms of "to be"—lead your writing to the graveyard and the reader to the next page.

Twenty-Six Action Verbs

accelerate	join	simplify
bargain	kick	translate
convert	laugh	upgrade
decide	manage	verify
eat	nudge	win
forecast	organize	x-ray
greet	persuade	yell
hurry	quote	zip
invest	reject	

SIDEBAR 1

SIDEBAR 2

How to Replace Dead Constructions with Strong Nouns and Action Verbs

Poor	There will be a meeting of the Equestrian Club next Wednesday night.
Improved	The Equestrian Club will meet next Wednesday night.
Poor	There is no finer writer in American literature than Ernest Hemingway.
Improved	Ernest Hemingway deserves more accolades than any other American writer.
Poor	It is imperative that all Photography Club members attend the next meeting.
Improved	All Photography Club members must attend the next meeting.
Poor	There were tears in her eyes as she accepted the "Outstanding Editor" award.
Improved	Tears came to her eyes when she accepted the "Outstanding Editor" award.
Poor	It was a dark and stormy night.
Improved	The skies thundered while rainstorms filled the moonless night.

This rule has no exceptions: You can always improve a sentence beginning with a "dead construction" by rewriting it. Sidebar 2 displays some examples of "dead constructions" followed by recast sentences with an improved action verb structure.

Write in active voice

The *Indiana Jones* plot contains 15 active-voice verbs and not a single passive-voice verb. The *American Anthropologist* example contains four passive-voice verbs—"has been written," "were utilized," "are found associated," "were now exploited"—two linking ("to be") verbs and only three action verbs.

What's the difference between an action verb and an active-voice verb? "Voice" determines the *relationship* between the subject of the sentence and its object or objects. The verb's tense describes *when* the action occurs. The verb's voice describes whether the subject of the sentence is the actor (active) or the subject is acted upon by its direct object (passive). Look again at this passive-voice example: "Early sites are found associated with the shoreline, river valleys and vegetative communities known as *lomas*." "Sites," the subject of the sentence, is "acted upon" by the shoreline, river valleys and vegetative communities.

"Use active voice and not passive voice." You will hear this rule over and over again from teachers and editors for the rest of your career. Active voice creates better writing than passive voice for three reasons:

1   Active-voice sentences emphasize *who* performs the action.
2   Active-voice sentences use *fewer words* than passive sentences.
3   Active-voice sentences *clarify* the "who did what to whom" relationship.

The Difference Between Active and Passive Voice

Don't confuse voice with tense. Try to avoid using any verbs that look like those in the right column.

	Active voice	Passive voice
Present tense	see	is seen
	designs	is designed
Present perfect tense	have seen	have been seen
	has designed	has been designed
Past tense	saw	was seen
	designed	was designed
Past perfect tense	had seen	had been seen
	had designed	had been designed
Future tense	will see	will be seen
	will design	will be designed
Future perfect tense	will have seen	will have been seen
	will have designed	will have been designed

SIDEBAR 3

WRITE WITH CONCRETE WORDS

"Concrete" is a strong and durable building material used in sidewalks, streets and buildings. When used in writing, it means "specific"—the opposite of "vague" or "abstract" words. But using concrete words will also make your writing more strong and durable.

Don't say the person went to college; say the person went to Kent State. Don't write about "crime in America." Write about Greenville's rise in murder rates last year. If a dog comes snarling up to the screen door, tell the reader whether it was a German shepherd or a collie. Here are more examples of how to make abstract words more concrete:

1 Abstract: music
   Concrete: rhythm and blues, heavy metal, hip-hop
2 Abstract: bad weather
   Concrete: thunderstorm, rain and sleet, overcast
3 Abstract: flower
   Concrete: lily, sunflower, zinnia

Here are some examples of replacing an abstract sentence with a concrete sentence:

Abstract: The audience enjoyed the concert.
Concrete: The audience gave the performers two standing ovations.
Abstract: He makes a fortune from performing at concerts.
Concrete: He's earned $16 million from concert performances last year.
Abstract: Mary had a lousy day, and everything went wrong.
Concrete: Mary had a flat tire and lost her purse today.

Learn to fill your articles with colorful, specific details, and editors will love you. Give readers visual, auditory, olfactory, gustatory and tactile descriptions that will captivate their imaginations.

WRITE TO CREATE SUSPENSE

Writing with suspense means keeping the reader wondering how the end of the story will turn out. Mystery novels and movies begin with suspense. An unsuspecting person discovers a body, reports it to police and—

presto—there's the plot. You begin wondering "Who did it?" while the investigator spends the rest of the time following clues and interviewing suspects. The story ends when the suspect is arrested, convicted or sent to jail. The good guys win and the bad guy loses.

That's great for mystery novels, but how do you create suspense in an article about elevators? Paumgarten does it in "The Lives of Elevators" by making the reader wonder whether Nicholas White will escape from his stalled elevator. Not until the last page of the 10-page story do you learn the outcome. Although he was safely rescued, he went on to quit his job at *BusinessWeek* and spent the next four years suing the building's management and the elevator-maintenance company for $25 million. He eventually settled out of court for an undisclosed sum, but "it was a low number, hardly six figures,"[9] Paumgarten reports.

Jon Franklin in his famous book *Writing for Story* defines the origin of suspense as the complication. "A complication is any problem encountered by any human being; it's an event that triggers a situation that complicates our lives, which is where it got its name," he says.[10]

In *A Beautiful Mind*, Sylvia Nasar tells the story of John Nash, a Princeton University professor who spent years in and out of hospitals struggling with paranoid schizophrenia before going on to earn the Nobel Prize in mathematics in 1994. The book, which also became a movie, exemplified all of the characteristics of action-packed writing.[11] Focusing on Nash and his wife, Nasar created suspense by detailing the uncertain outcome of his illness, their divorce and eventual reunion, and his remarkable recovery. As the dramatic narrative unfolds, she reports the conversations that occurred between Nash and his intimate circle of family members, professional colleagues and doctors. Her writing bristles with action verbs, active voice, narrative and dialogue.

While not every story is as action-filled as *A Beautiful Mind* or an *Indiana Jones* movie, you can make any story more interesting by injecting people, action verbs, active voice, concrete words and some suspense. In conclusion, get moving!

ENDNOTES

[1]   Elizabeth J. Reitz, "Faunal Remains From Paloma, an Archaic Site in Peru," *American Anthropologist*, New Series, 90, 2 (June 1988), 310–322.

[2] Benton Rain Patterson, *Write for the Reader: A Practical Guide to Feature Writing* (Ames: Iowa State University Press, 1986), 15.

[3] Nick Paumgarten, "Up and Then Down: The Lives of Elevators," *The New Yorker*, April 21, 2008, 106–115.

[4] Ibid., 106.

[5] Ibid., 115.

[6] Ibid., 112.

[7] Ibid., 107.

[8] "A Good Life, Tim Russert 1950–2008," *People*, June 20, 2008, 46–51.

[9] Nick Paumgarten, "Up and Then Down: The Lives of Elevators," 114.

[10] Jon Franklin, *Writing for Story: Craft Secrets of Dramatic Nonfiction* (New York: Penguin Books, 1986), 72.

[11] Sylvia Nasar, *A Beautiful Mind* (New York: Simon & Schuster, 1998).

10

THE ART OF THE ANECDOTE

Your takeaway . . .

Readers remember anecdotes—little stories that illustrate big ideas—long after they've forgotten statistics and facts. Anecdotes work well as leads and endings. You also can scatter them throughout your articles to clarify and humanize data. Some of the best anecdotes surface during the interview process when the interviewer presses his interviewee for specific details about a key moment or event. This chapter shows you how to shape little stories into memorable illustrations.

The story goes this way: Two pals, Jack Canfield and Mark Victor Hansen, assembled a book of more than 100 heartwarming anecdotes that they felt certain would lift the spirits of readers. They offered their collection to 140 publishers, none of whom shared their enthusiasm for the project. Undaunted, the authors visited a booksellers' convention in California and convinced an editor from a small Florida press to read a few pages on his flight home. The editor opened the package in an airport lounge and soon had tears streaming down his cheeks. The result? Hansen and Canfield had a deal, *Chicken Soup for the Soul* had a publisher and America had a best-seller. With 112 million copies of their books now in print (170 titles, 41 languages), the authors have ladled chicken soup for the woman's soul, the baseball fan's soul, the bride's soul, the Canadian's soul, the writer's soul and the list goes on and on.

We retell this familiar success story for two reasons. First, the phenomenal sales of the *Chicken Soup* series prove that readers love little stories, especially those that are dramatic, inspiring or humorous. Second, the story about Canfield and Hansen is an example of an anecdote. It's an anecdote about anecdotes.

CREATING A SCENE

Most editors will tell you that the best feature articles are those that connect with readers' emotions, which makes a feature story memorable. "Editors see tons of 'sermonic' articles," says Mary Ann O'Roark, a former editor at *Seventeen, McCall's* and *Guideposts.* "In those articles, the writer says, 'Here's my wisdom, and I impart it to you.'" The result is a "stuffy lineup of information," explains O'Roark. Instead, "editors want good stories prepared in ways that engage readers. An article must entertain before it can educate and enlighten."[1]

One way that a writer can create engaging and entertaining articles is by learning to identify, write and place anecdotes. These tightly written ministories are delicious little morsels that one editor describes as the "chocolate chips" of articles. They are as much at home in speeches, sermons, comedy monologues and books as they are in feature stories. They work well as leads, endings or illustrations scattered throughout a manuscript. They humanize dry data. Example: An article about a major medical breakthrough may contain all sorts of important information, but the article becomes memorable when the author inserts an anecdote about a patient whose life is saved because of the medical breakthrough.

People want to read about other people. Long after readers forget the surprising statistics, compelling details or key points of a story, they remember the colorful anecdotes that showed rather than told the significance of the key points.

TECHNIQUES OF STORYTELLING

Fiction writers are skilled at creating memorable anecdotes. They know the techniques of building drama, painting word pictures and describing characters so realistically that readers understand and care what happens to the characters. For this reason, book publishers occasionally hire novelists to serve as writers or ghostwriters for nonfiction books. The publishers want their nonfiction books to have the same color, impact and readability as a good novel. That's not to say that they want the writer to fudge on facts or embellish the truth. Absolutely not. Accuracy is the top concern of all writers of nonfiction, even novelists recruited for nonfiction projects.

What fiction writers bring to nonfiction assignments is something that goes beyond the essential ABCs—accuracy, brevity and clarity—of good journalism. They have mastered the art of storytelling. They know how to use little stories to illustrate big ideas. They have the ability to describe real people and actual events in compelling ways. They recognize when a piece of writing is starting to lose momentum, and they understand how to pick up the pace by inserting a poignant or humorous true story. They have the skill to add dabs of color to what might have been a black and white documentary.

CHARACTERISTICS OF ANECDOTES

You don't have to be a fiction writer to craft memorable anecdotes. Successful feature writers follow these six pieces of advice.

Keep them short

Anecdotes should never overshadow the points they support or the topics they illustrate. They should not be so long or so strong that they pull readers' attention away from the subject of the article. This means that writers, after creating anecdotes on their computer screens, read and reread the sentences aloud, zapping words and deleting punctuation as they go. They notice adverbs and adjectives and remove those whose presence they can't defend. After they have reduced the story to its bare bones, they edit the remains.

This search-and-destroy mission is a familiar process that skilled writers have followed for centuries. As an example: The Irish poet and playwright Oscar Wilde once arrived at a party complaining of exhaustion. His host asked why he was so tired. "All day I worked on one of my poems," explained Wilde. "In the morning I took a comma out, and in the afternoon I put it back in."

Make them relevant

We include the 51-word anecdote about Oscar Wilde because it illustrates the point that the previous paragraph made—that good writers constantly tinker with their copy, even spending time debating the need for a comma. The Wilde story was relevant to the topic. We included the longer anecdote about *Chicken Soup for the Soul* at the beginning of this chapter because it introduced the discussion of anecdotes in general and underscored the idea that little stories are popular with readers. Again, it was relevant to the topic.

An anecdote must have a purpose; otherwise, it only adds clutter to an article. As we said in Chapter 8, anecdotes often make effective lead paragraphs. Used as a lead, an anecdote can fulfill three important purposes:

- It can provide a colorful introduction to the topic of the article by piquing readers' interest and luring readers into the article.
- It can create an emotional bond with readers by describing a familiar situation. This prompts the reader to respond, "I've been there; I've felt that same way."
- It can establish the tone of the article. If it's light and breezy, it signals an article that is going to be entertaining and fun to read.

Some anecdotal leads serve all three purposes. They introduce a topic, build a bond with readers and create a tone that will carry throughout the text. As an example, anyone whose favorite snack food is suddenly taken off the market can identify with this lead to a *Wall Street Journal* feature story:

> Robert Fliegel was craving a Hydrox. The 52-year-old computer consultant says he always liked the way the chocolate sandwich cookie, which he found crisper than Oreos, "stood up to the milk" when dunked.
>
> But Mr. Fliegel, who used to be able to devour an entire package of the crème-filled biscuits in a sitting, couldn't find them in any stores near his East Stroudsburg, Pa., home.
>
> Only when he went online a few months ago to try to order some did he learn the truth: Hydrox is dead.[2]

The last sentence—"Hydrox is dead"—serves as a bridge to the article's main point. The article isn't about Mr. Fliegel; instead, it explores how a product that has been around for almost 100 years can build a devoted fan base. When the product is no longer available, these fans mourn its demise and sometimes rally in an effort to reverse the marketing decision. They sign petitions, write letters and get results. In the case of the Hydrox cookie, the disgruntled consumers generated enough noise to convince Kellogg Co. to resurrect the product . . . at least for a little while.

Keep them real

A strategy that often strengthens the bond between writer and reader is including the word "you" in the lead anecdote. In our chapter about hooks and leads we called this the direct-address lead. By using "you," a writer reaches out as if to say, "Hey, reader, pay attention! I'm talking to *you!*" In the following example, the common bond between writer and reader works only if the reader is old enough to relate to the situation that the lead describes.

> You're downsizing. After so many years at the same address, you've decided to make your move. Florida, maybe. Or perhaps a smaller, more manageable place close to home with less lawn to mow and driveway to plow. Your friends recommend the laid-back life of a condo community. Sounds inviting. Whatever the choice, only one thing stands between you and your new digs. The attic.[3]

This lead introduced a how-to article that helped readers separate trash from treasure as they cleaned out attics and basements and prepared to relocate. It obviously is geared to older readers. The one-paragraph lead contains 64 words. Six of those words are a form of "you." Taken together, the sentences describe a problem that "you" faced—getting rid of a life's accumulation of stuff. Subsequent paragraphs resolve the problem and provide the end of the anecdote. To qualify as an anecdote, readers need to know the solution that "you" discovered.

The problem with the direct-address approach—and the reason we don't recommend it—is that it often results in a hypothetical anecdote that the writer invents rather than a situation that he reports. A similar lead, based on *real* people facing a *real* dilemma, can establish the same kind of bond.

> Susan and Don Shaw are downsizing. After so many years at the same address, they're making their move. Florida maybe. Or perhaps a smaller, more manageable place close to their Minneapolis home with less lawn to mow and driveway to plow. Their friends recommend the laid-back life of

a condo community. That sounds inviting, they admit. Whatever the choice, only one thing stands between them and their new digs. The attic.

Stress the specific

A powerful anecdote gives readers a tightly focused example that illustrates a general idea. It has one or two specific people doing specific things at a specific time and place. The more specific you are, the more impact the anecdote has. As an example, which of the following sentences do you prefer as the lead paragraph to an article about teen runaways?

- A Texas teenager ran away from home last winter because she was tired of her parents' arguments. She's still missing.
- Three days after Christmas, Meg Jones, 13, stuffed a pair of jeans and a T-shirt into her backpack and ran away from her parents' split level in a posh suburb of Houston. She couldn't tolerate their bickering any longer. They still haven't found her.

Whenever you add specific information to a story you also add words. This means you must make a decision: Should you be brief or should you be specific? The answer is that writers should be brief *and* specific. Most writers include a range of anecdotes in their articles. They want variety. One anecdote might be of the bare bones variety and contain only two or three sentences. Another may be more fully fleshed out and offer several details. The writer decides the degree of development that each anecdote deserves. If an article runs long, the writer looks for anecdotes to trim or delete. A good test to give a manuscript is to remove an anecdote and then read the manuscript from beginning to end. If the article flows well and is interesting, the anecdote was unnecessary.

Give them a beginning, a middle and an end

If an anecdote lacks all three elements, it doesn't qualify as a little story. As we indicated in Chapter 8, writers often create scenarios that serve as backdrops to their stories. These scenarios are colorful but they don't tell a complete story. Instead, they set the scene for a story. Here's an example of a scenario:

Long before the borrowed white limo delivered its very important passenger to the entrance of the Bowling Green, Ky., Holidome, word went forth to expect someone special. The clue was Room 168. Flowers had arrived at 11; a fruit basket followed at noon. By 12:30, green punch, wheat crackers and a cheese ball under plastic were arranged smorgasbord-style on the boguswood credenza.[4]

This opening paragraph gave readers a sense of how people in a small town prepared to welcome a celebrity guest, in this case, Miss America Sharlene Wells. It describes a place, complete with flowers and fruit. Until something happens to someone, it's not an anecdote. Later in the same article, the writer offers readers an anecdote:

A few days after winning the Miss America title in Atlantic City, Wells was interviewed and photographed by a words-and-pictures duo from *People* magazine. She had the sniffles, her eyes were bleary and, besides that, her feet hurt. The photographer assured her that the picture he wanted was the heads-and-shoulders variety—she had no reason to put on her shoes. She acquiesced, secured the crown to her blonde hair, arranged the folds of her reptile-patterned dress and assumed a regal pose.

Imagine her shock the next week when the picture was published full frame—her stocking feet revealing a full complement of Dr. Scholl's medicated disks. Ouch. The California designer Mr. Blackwell promptly named her to his infamous worst-dressed list and said she looked like an armadillo in corn pads. "Wasn't that cute?" she asks. "I learned never to trust a photographer."[5]

These paragraphs do more than create a scenario. They tell a cause-and-effect story. Something happened to Miss America and that "something" qualifies it as an anecdote. A photographer duped her into posing for a picture (cause). She was embarrassed after she saw the picture in print (effect). At the end of the anecdote she is a slightly different person because she has learned something from the experience.

In the case of a split anecdote, the beginning of the anecdote serves as the article's lead, and the end of the anecdote, separated by many paragraphs, concludes the article. Readers have to complete the entire article to find out what happened to the person introduced in the opening paragraph. Example: Suppose you are writing an article about the dangers of not wearing a seatbelt. You interview someone who was almost killed in an automobile accident, and you decide to use half of the story as your lead. It might sound like this:

> Bill Ryan never thought it would happen to him, but last Valentine's Day the unthinkable occurred. He hadn't snapped his seatbelt in place because he was only driving a few blocks to pick up his son after swim practice. He saw the van approach, clearly out of control. He heard the screech of brakes, felt himself lifted from the driver's seat and catapulted forward. Then everything went blank.

You stop short of telling readers the rest of Bill Ryan's story. Instead, you continue your article. You offer statistics about seatbelt usage and include comments and advice from various experts whom you interviewed. Not until the last paragraph of your article do you return to Bill Ryan and answer the questions that your lead raised.

> Ryan was one of the lucky ones. He limped out of the hospital—pins in both legs—four weeks after his car's head-on collision with the van. The doctors who patched him up say that with six months of physical therapy he'll be as good as new. He claims he'll be better than new because "Now I know how fragile life is, and I'll never put mine on the line again."

Place them strategically

You can overdo a good thing. If you have uncovered two great anecdotes that support the same point, don't use both. That's like assigning two people to do one person's job. Select the story you like the best and file the second for possible use in some future writing project. An overabundance of anecdotes can turn an article into a disjointed collection of random stories.

Deciding where to drop in an anecdote is a skill that all feature writers should cultivate. Too many writers, aware of the power of a good story, grab readers' attention with colorful anecdotal leads but then consider their jobs done. They follow the anecdotes with paragraph after paragraph of dry facts, which risks lulling their readers to sleep. Anecdotes, strategically placed throughout an article, can give readers a "time out" from information overload. A colorful illustration can offer a welcome pause in an article's narrative, insert the human element and underscore a point.

As an example, midway through an article about body language—"How to Read Between the Lines"—a magazine writer feared her article contained too much advice and was beginning to sound sermonic. She tucked in an anecdote to give readers a break and to illustrate the effectiveness of strong body language. The little story added humor and color as it described a meek secretary's confrontation with a gruff executive. To lead into the anecdote, the writer quickly explained the background of the story: A secretary had been asked by her boss to pull together a report. On the day it was due, her boss wasn't around and she needed someone to approve what she had written before she mailed it. This led to a face-to-face standoff with a man several rungs above her on the corporate ladder. The article's author let the secretary tell the story in her own words.

> "The executive looked at me and growled, 'What do you want?' I explained I was on a tight deadline and politely asked him to read my report to make sure it was correct. The man bellowed, 'I don't have time!' I marched across his office, planted my feet firmly in his carpet, and folded my arms as if to say, 'I'm here to stay.' He put his head down, shuffled his papers and tried to ignore me. But I never stopped staring at him. After a few minutes he looked up, grumbled, and reached for the article." Not until she had left his office with the wad of approved pages tucked under her arm did she begin to shake. "I couldn't believe my boldness," she said.[6]

The vivid scene, complete with "he-said-she-said" dialogue, makes a point and creates a bond with readers who identify with the secretary. The article's writer could have made the same point by simply stating, "strong body language has the capacity to empower a powerless person." Instead, the writer chose to use an anecdote to illustrate the fact and to add some zest to the article.

SEARCHING FOR ANECDOTES

The best anecdotes are those that you discover in the course of your interviews. This ensures that the colorful little stories that you include in your articles haven't appeared in dozens of other articles. Use these questions frequently when you interview people: "Could you give me an example of that?" "Can you tell me about a time when it happened to you?" "That" or "it" in these questions could refer to any statement or point your interviewee has made. In a pinch, you can always find memorable anecdotes in published collections or on Web sites such as www.anecdotage.com. These anecdotes typically deal with historical events and famous people. They may lack freshness. The anecdotes about Oscar Wilde and the *Chicken Soup* books, told earlier in this chapter, are examples of often-repeated stories.

Hal Karp, a contributing editor who writes frequently on auto safety for *Reader's Digest*, says that finding good anecdotes is difficult but essential. "I often spend two or three days or even a whole week trying to find one anecdote," he admits. Where does he look? He makes telephone calls to "points of contact" related to the type of anecdote he's seeking. "For example, if I'm looking for accident victims, I ask, 'Where are all the points of contact for an accident victim?' Victims come in contact with paramedics, police and emergency room doctors. So I start going down the list. I call fire departments, paramedics and law enforcement officers."[7]

The way you phrase your questions during interviews can determine your success in drawing out new and memorable anecdotes. Let's review four of the anecdotes included in this chapter and try to guess the questions that brought forth the stories.

Questions for Hydrox cookie fan Robert Fliegel

1   What, in your opinion, makes the Hydrox cookie better than its competition?
2   Describe your efforts to locate the cookies after they were taken off the grocery shelves.
3   How did you feel when you learned of the cookie's demise?

Questions for Miss America Sharlene Wells

1   What was the first mistake you made after winning the pageant?
2   Describe the interview that led to the embarrassing picture in *People* magazine.
3   Recreate the moment when you first saw the published photograph. How did you react?

Questions for accident victim Bill Ryan

1   Beginning with the time you got into your car, recount the drive that led up to the accident.

2   What went through your mind as you saw the van coming toward
    you?
3   Describe the scene when you first regained consciousness in the hospi-
    tal emergency room.

Questions for the secretary who confronted her supervisor

1   What circumstances led to your standoff with the corporate
    executive?
2   Recreate those few moments when you were at an impasse in his
    office.
3   What went through your mind as you stood your ground and waited
    for his response?

Most people speak in generalities. They gloss over major moments with
simple statements such as: "I was angry," "I was embarrassed" or "I was
scared." Beginning interviewers accept the generalities and move on to
their next questions. Sharp writers recognize the potential drama behind
such statements, zero in for details and don't stop asking questions until
they have the whole story, told in living color.

ENDNOTES

[1]   Lecture, July 29, 2004.
[2]   Christopher Rhoads, "The Hydrox Cookie Is Dead, and Fans Won't Get Over
      It," *The Wall Street Journal*, Jan. 19, 2008, 1.
[3]   Holly G. Miller, "Treasures in the Attic," *Columns*, Spring 2004, 7.
[4]   Holly G. Miller, "On the Road With Miss America," *The Saturday Evening Post*,
      May/June 1985, 42.
[5]   Ibid., 43.
[6]   Holly G. Miller, "How to Read Between the Lines," *Today's Christian Woman*,
      Oct.-Nov. 1991, 76–78.
[7]   David E. Sumner conducted this interview.

IMPROVING YOUR PIZZAZZ

Your takeaway . . .

Some writers are excellent reporters and create well-constructed stories. Their writing, however, lacks pizzazz, style and personality. This chapter tells you how to energize your writing by using rhythm, humor, viewpoint, voice and tone. Style results from an effective use of these qualities:

- rhythm—the music of writing
- humor—the fun of writing
- viewpoint—the perspective of writing
- voice—the personality of writing
- tone—the attitude of writing

Consider these words: client, patron and customer. Each means a person who buys something, but the connotation and tone of *what* the person buys differs. They could suggest legal services, works of art or soap. Mark Twain wrote in a letter to a friend in 1888, "The difference between the almost-right word and the right word is really a large matter—it's the difference between the lightning bug and the lightning."[1] Twain's memorable quotes pay tribute to his great writing style. Style is the quality that makes your writing fun to read. Stylish writing results from choosing the *right* word—not the *almost-right* word. Stylish writing also results from the appropriate use of rhythm, humor, viewpoint, voice and tone.

RHYTHM—THE MUSIC OF WRITING

Language has an inherent rhythm. You can recognize Spanish from its rapid-pace flow of words by its native speakers or French by its slower flow of words with their rising and falling intonations. English has its distinct rhythm; it's not a matter of whether—but how—you use rhythm when you write.

"Writers use music in many ways," according to Roy Peter Clark, a senior scholar at the Poynter Institute for Media Studies in St. Petersburg, Fla. These include:

- to establish a rhythm
- to create contrast
- to set a tone or a mood
- to strike a chord
- to end on a high note

Clark, author of *Writing Tools: 50 Essential Strategies for Every Writer*, is also a pianist who gives frequent workshops to professional journalists about how to incorporate musical qualities into their writing. He combines his lectures with live piano performances to illustrate how writers can use qualities like rhythm, tone, harmony and unity.

"Writing should appeal to as many of the readers' senses as possible," Clark says. "That means you can mention smells, sights, as well as sound, which appeals to our aural senses."[2]

Music taps into the deepest emotions of people. People prefer certain songs or musical genres because they capture how they feel, either consciously or unconsciously. You can mention a song and tap into those same emotions of your readers.

An interesting question to ask an interviewee is: What are your favorite songs? The answers can reveal something about the person's character, Clark says. "Years ago John McPhee wrote a book about Bill Bradley, not when he was a U.S. senator, but when he was an all-American basketball player at Princeton. One of the songs that Bradley listened to before every game was 'Climb Every Mountain' from 'The Sound of Music.' That revealed a lot about Bradley's character," Clark says, because it captures an inspired "I can do anything" kind of motivation.

Music can also establish contrast to reveal a dissonance between what people feel and the outward circumstances they face. "I would much rather read a story about a depressed, down-and-out guy going to Disney World and listening to 'Sing a Song' than read about him sitting in a bar listening to the blues," says Clark.

"We all know we sometimes feel sad on bright and sunny days and sometimes happy and cheerful on cold, rainy days. Sometimes you can talk about what people hum or listen to when it creates a contrast with their immediate environment," says Clark.

In one of his articles, Roy Peter Clark says music has special value to journalists for several reasons:[3]

- Because music is inspirational, it breathes life into the creative process.
- Because music is mood altering, it can speed you up, or slow you down, depending upon your need and the moment.
- Because music is an abstract art, it manages to evoke powerful emotions.
- Because we depend upon music for many of our most important writing metaphors: voice, audience, rhythm, cadence, tone. (These last three aren't parallel with the earlier ones.)
- Because musical preferences reflect character and culture.
- Because music crosses media platforms.

Clark says you can use musical metaphors to create endings for stories, such as these examples:

- the crescendo: building toward a powerful climax ("Try a Little Tenderness")
- the head-on collision: loud noise to silence ("Louie Louie")
- the fade-out: walking into the sunset ("Twist and Shout")
- the surprise re-start: you think it's over, but we have one more wrinkle ("Do You Love Me?")
- the bookends: it ends right where it began ("Three Blind Mice")

When Clark asked some journalists in one of his seminars about their favorite music, he received some interesting responses. Jonathan Dube of MSNBC.com said he likes "Start Me Up" by the Rolling Stones: "Listening to this song is like getting a shot of adrenaline in the arm—again and again and again. I can feel it moving through my body each time Keith Richards strokes his guitar, flooding me with bursts of energy," said Dube.

Reading your writing aloud helps you determine whether it is smooth and harmonious or choppy and off-key. Many of the nation's best-known writers do this. For example, Ellen Goodman, a Pulitzer Prize-winning columnist from *The Boston Globe*, says, "I think you have to listen to your own work. When I was working in the city room, everybody used to joke about me moving my lips while I was writing. I was putting it through my own ear. You have to really learn that. If there's a clang in your ear, then that's bad."[4]

Leonard Pitts, another Pulitzer Prize-winning columnist, says, "I think a great deal about rhythm. It's indispensable in good writing—creating that sense of propulsion, of ebb and flow and movement to different pulses."[5]

Three Practical Techniques to Improve Rhythm

- **Vary sentence and paragraph length.** Use a two-word sentence followed by a 22-word sentence; a short paragraph then a long paragraph. A writing style characterized by sameness in sentence length and structure produces a boring monotonous rhythm.
- **Use a variety of one-, two- and three-syllable words.** While choosing short and simple words is generally good advice, varying the length of words can also improve your pace and rhythm.
- **Create parallel structure.** Using parallel structure gives a poetic flow to writing and makes it appeal to the reader's inner ear. Use the same verb tense, phrase or clause structure. If you use three elements in a sentence, make sure all three are nouns, all three are verbs or all three are objects. Using "all three are nouns, all three are verbs or all three are objects" in the preceding sentence is an example of parallel structure.

SIDEBAR 1

HUMOR—THE FUN OF WRITING

If you can make people laugh, especially with your writing, then you have a wonderful gift. Humor involves poking fun at something—usually the foibles, flaws or inconsistencies of people. Sometimes it means pointing out the absurdity of situations or ideas that others take seriously. Dave Barry of *The Miami Herald* received a Pulitzer Prize for his widely syndicated humor column.

As a humor columnist, Barry can take liberties in style that nonfiction writers cannot, such as writing in first-person and creating fictitious facts for the sake of making a humorous point. Yet most of his columns illustrate some principles of humor that nonfiction writers can learn. In his book *Boogers Are My Beat: More Lies, But Some Actual Journalism!* Barry pokes fun at the ubiquitous service contracts that you're pressured to get whenever you buy home electronic equipment or home appliances.[6]

In "Quality! Craftsmanship! Service Contract!" Barry says he was visiting an electronics store to look for a telephone. "While I was looking at this phone, a previously invisible salesperson materialized next to me and said the words I have come to detest more than any others in the English language except 'prostate exam.' Those words are: 'You definitely should get the service agreement.'" Then he continues the conversation:

SALESPERSON: . . . so this is an excellent product. Totally reliable.
YOU: I'll take it!
SALESPERSON: It's going to break.
YOU: What?
SALESPERSON: There's this thing inside? The confabulator? You're lucky if that baby lasts you a week.
YOU: So you're saying it's not a good product?
SALESPERSON: No! It's top of the line! Totally dependable!
YOU: Well, okay, then, I guess I'll . . .
SALESPERSON: Of course if the refrenestator module blows, you're looking at a $263,000 repair, plus parts and labor. One customer had to sell a lung.

This column contains five common characteristics of funny stories and humorous writing: *truth, universality, surprise, exaggeration* and *absurdity*. Think about each one and think about how you can apply it to your writing.

Truth

The best humor originates from real-life situations. Good humor often involves poking fun at things that people do or say that annoy others. Every store that sells electronics or home appliances pushes customers to buy service agreements with their products. Other everyday topics Barry covers in his book include waiting on hold for customer service, talking on cell phones in public, *Cosmopolitan* cover lines and snoring wives.

Universality

Barry writes about a situation that everyone can relate to because almost everyone has felt pressured to purchase a service agreement. On the other hand, if you don't "get" a joke, it's usually because you haven't experienced the kind of situation it describes. The more common the experience, the more likely the humor will appeal to a wide audience.

Surprise

"Humor depends so much on timing and the order of the words. You have to use the ends of sentences and the ends of paragraphs as powerful points of emphasis," says Roy Peter Clark. For example, Dave Barry writes that while he was looking for a telephone, a salesperson suddenly appeared and said, "You definitely should get the service agreement." This punch line seems to come from out of nowhere. To use surprise effectively, say something that readers don't expect to hear or choose a word that offers a surprise ending to a mundane statement.

Exaggeration

A device used frequently by comedians is exaggerating the unintended outcome of a behavior or an action. "I love exaggeration; I use it a million times every day," Barry once told an interviewer. For example, "Of course if the refrenestator module blows, you're looking at a $263,000 repair, plus parts and labor."

Absurdity

This piece on service agreements contains some ridiculous absurdities, which Barry uses with exaggeration to make his point. After the quote about the $263,000 repair, you get this line, "One customer had to sell a lung." Of course, you've never heard of anyone selling a lung to pay for a telephone repair.

While we encourage you to sprinkle humor in your writing, we also encourage you to proceed with caution. What's funny to one group of people will insult and anger another group, particularly if it involves their ethnicity or religious beliefs. Profanity or bathroom humor often causes persons older than a teenager to roll their eyes in disgust.

Finally, you can always follow the advice of Roy Peter Clark if you don't have a natural sense of humor. "I am not a humorous person, and I am sometimes worried that my writing is too serious or too heavy," he says. "So if you can't write jokes, then quote a lot of people who are funny."

VIEWPOINT—THE PERSPECTIVE OF WRITING

First person? Second person? Third person? Most writers of most feature and magazine stories use third-person viewpoint. The writer is the narrator. The writer tells a story about other people and reports an objective set of facts and circumstances. The words "I" or "you" occur infrequently. For many reasons, the third-person viewpoint is also the safest route to go for beginning and advanced writers.

Beginning writers want to use first person because it seems easy. They think it requires less research and on-scene reporting. But it's actually the most difficult kind of writing to do successfully.

First-person viewpoint

"The number one mistake that most beginning writers make is to write in the first person automatically just because it feels comfortable when the fact is that the reader doesn't know you and doesn't care about you," says Art Spikol, a *Writer's Digest* columnist.[7] It creates the impression that the writer thinks himself more important and influential than he is. Readers are not interested in the personal experiences of unknown writers.

On the other hand, first-person viewpoint can enhance three types of articles. First, you can write about yourself if you are the most interesting character in the story. Writing about some types of dramatic, life-and-death experiences clearly lends itself to a first-person narrative. It can add a tone of warmth and familiarity if used appropriately. Readers are interested in hearing the first-person stories of people who have achieved great success or overcome dramatic obstacles. If you're not involved in the action, however, then keep yourself out of the story.

Second, when the article explains a topic of wide public interest, the writer can share on-the-scene insights not possible in third-person. When the first-person viewpoint appears in feature stories in magazines like *The New Yorker* or *Atlantic Monthly*, the writer's personal experiences are not the point. When it does appear, then it describes situations or incidents that the writer personally observed. The purpose of sharing these insights is not to draw attention to the writer, but to bring more light on the topic of wide public interest that he or she is discussing.

The third appropriate use of first-person is in service journalism or how-to articles whose purpose is to help readers with practical information. Writers can use first-person when they are experts or have significant experience with the topic they are writing about. Used this way, it can enhance both credibility and rapport with readers. However, the writer's credibility as an expert must be clear. You have to introduce yourself as an expert by mentioning either formal credentials or experiences that qualify you to write authoritatively about this topic by including your credentials as a separate author's bio at the end of the story.

When you choose to write a feature story in first-person viewpoint, then follow this advice. First, use it sparingly—not every paragraph—but perhaps once every three to six paragraphs.

Second, use it only when it originates from "on the spot" reporting. When used judiciously, a first-person approach can lend credibility to on-the-spot reporting and create more rapport between the reader and the writer. It demonstrates that you were there and know what you are talking about.

Third, use it consistently throughout the story. The writer's viewpoint can't appear suddenly at the end. It should be used consistently throughout the story. Also, don't use it in interviews to report, "I asked so-and-so" and "she told me." To readers, this type of attribution is annoying, cluttered and unnecessary. Instead of writing, "I asked so-and-so." you can write, "When asked about . . . so-and-so said . . ."

Second-person viewpoint

As we have written earlier, second-person writing using the "you" voice can create a personal relationship between the writer and the reader. It enables the writer to speak to the reader as one friend speaks to another friend. Second-person viewpoint is also effective in service journalism and "how-to" articles. It can be combined with first-person viewpoint when the writer is an expert on the topic.

The second-person viewpoint has two limitations, however. First, it can annoy readers when the writer uses it to create a false familiarity with the reader that doesn't exist. It's sort of like strangers and clerks who call you by your first name the first time they meet you. Don't assume you "know" the reader; don't assume you know exactly what readers like, dislike or what they have experienced.

Second-person viewpoints can annoy the reader if they describe a situation that some readers can't relate to. For example, what if an article starts with this lead: "When you're in a bar and a sloppily dressed guy comes over and offers to buy you a drink, what do you say?" Male and female readers who don't go to bars will be annoyed by this lead. You can't assume that readers have had a particular kind of experience unless you are writing for a magazine with a young female audience who enjoys going to bars.

A second disadvantage to second-person writing is the possibility of "talking down" or appearing presumptuous to the reader. Second-person works best when it comes across as one friend talking to another—not as an expert telling a beginner how to do something. If the writer conveys any hint of arrogance, then readers will detect it.

Third-person viewpoint

Third-person is the most common viewpoint in magazine and feature writing. It follows the typical "he," "she," "it" and "they" approach to reporting on the subjects you are writing about. It's also the best approach for beginning writers. If you do excellent research and reporting, then all you have to do is tell the reader what you discovered. Good, solid factual reporting can—and will—speak for itself.

VOICE—THE PERSONALITY OF WRITING

Voice refers to how writers reveal their personalities in their writing. Magazine editors, more than newspaper editors, like stories with voice and personality. Except for columnists, newspapers typically rely on an objective style of reporting in which the writer remains out of sight. Dave Barry has a strong voice in his funny stories, and it's likely his fans could recognize him even if the columns didn't carry a byline.

Voice is your way of putting yourself in your writing even when you don't write in first-person viewpoint. If style is the external way you dress up your writing—voice is the unseen force that drives your narrative and comes from deep within. The writer's voice cannot be separated from the writer's core beliefs. If you possess a clear sense of identity—who you are, what you believe and where you intend to go in life—then you will more likely display that same strong voice in your writing. Writers with strong beliefs about various issues have a greater chance of bringing their "voice" into their writing.

A strong voice can be achieved using first-person, second-person or third-person viewpoint. Some writers with a strong "voice" may never use the pronouns "I" or "me" in their writing. The best way of describing voice is by comparing it with music. Some artists have a unique, strong voice. As soon as you hear them on a radio or CD, you immediately recognize the voice. The enduring popularity of Bruce Springsteen or Stevie Wonder, for example, is a tribute to their clear, mellow voices recognized by almost everyone who hears their music.

Writers can have a unique voice, too. You can read an article and recognize who they are without seeing their bylines. Voice is your natural way of producing words. It's the power behind your words that evolves out of your unique way of seeing the world. It gives your writing a special strength, friendliness and credibility that sets it apart from weaker, boring stuff.

No one can teach you the use of voice. You have to develop it through a lifetime of experience. Here are some suggestions to point you in the right direction.

First, write in a conversational style. Some writers like to put it all out on the keyboard, go back, and do the editing and revising later. Don't worry about how your writing looks and sounds the first time around. Just write. Explain a topic the same way that you would explain it to a friend.

Second, trust your instinct. Don't write what "seems" appropriate or acceptable. Write exactly what you see, hear and feel. If you think an obscure detail is significant, then trust your instinct and report it. If your gut tells you that the angle your editor suggested is not the real story, then go with your gut and get the facts needed to report it. You can convince your editor later.

Third, displaying your interpretation in feature stories should be subtle and guided by common sense. Ask yourself, "How would the reasonable person react to this set of facts I've discovered?" Your interpretation can guide the way in which you organize the material and whom you choose to quote. If your article takes a position on a controversial issue, then reveal it in a manner consistent with the editorial policies of the publication for which you are writing.

TONE—THE ATTITUDE OF WRITING

Think of tone as the attitude with which you approach a topic. The tone may be humorous, satirical, light-hearted, heavy, sarcastic, whimsical, persuasive, argumentative, self-deprecating, disparaging or respectful.

Joe Treen, a former *People* magazine editor, says that consistency of tone is important: "You need to work around one single tone. You don't want to switch your tone around. As another editor once said to me, 'What gong do we want to be hitting here?' You only get to ring one 'gong' in a story."[8]

New York-based writer Judith Newman, author of *You Make Me Feel Like an Unnatural Woman*, advises writers to be careful with tone, especially sarcasm. "If magazines are infected with any disease, it's the disease of snarkiness and sarcasm for its own sake. Snarkiness means trying a little too hard to be hip without much thought behind it. If you're going to treat something skeptically, then really be thoughtful about it. It's easy to not treat people's concerns sensitively."[9]

If you're just starting your writing career, rhythm, humor, viewpoint, voice and tone may seem like too much to conquer all at once. And they are. Writers with decades of experience still struggle with learning them. At this point, conducting in-depth research and writing with clarity are the most important skills you can master. Eloquence and style will accrue with experience.

ENDNOTES

[1] Mark Twain to George Bainton, Oct. 15, 1888. Accessed at www.twainquotes.com, Aug. 20, 2008.

2 Telephone interview with David E. Sumner, July 21, 2008.
3 Roy Peter Clark, "Why Music Is of Special Value to Journalists," Nov. 27, 2001. Accessed at www.poynter.org, Aug. 20, 2008.
4 Interview with David E. Sumner, Boston, Mass., Dec. 18, 1997.
5 Interview with David E. Sumner, Bowie, Md., Dec. 19, 1997.
6 Excerpted from "Quality! Craftsmanship! Service Contract!" in Dave Barry, *Boogers Are My Beat: More Lies, But Some Actual Journalism!* (New York: Crown Publishers, 2003), 153.
7 Art Spikol, *Magazine Writing: The Inside Angle* (Cincinnati, Ohio: Writer's Digest Books, 1979), 109.
8 Telephone interview with David E. Sumner, Nov. 21, 2003.
9 Telephone interview with David E. Sumner, Dec. 11, 2003.

DON'T BOTCH THE BASICS

Your takeaway . . .

This section explains how to avoid the most common mistakes that beginning writers make. While some readers could benefit, others might not need it. Use it as a quick reference to check your work. It teaches you how to recognize and correct these mistakes: run-on sentences; sentence fragments; lack of noun-pronoun agreement; comma errors; unnecessary capitalization; and misuse of possessive nouns, pronouns, colons and semi-colons.

Dozens of editors say they automatically reject a query letter or a cover letter with a job application if it contains any grammar, punctuation or typographical errors. They conclude that if the writer is too careless to proofread the letter, then the sender is likely to display as much carelessness in researching and writing articles. The purpose of this chapter is to help you avoid these pitfalls that damage your writing career.

MOST COMMON MECHANICAL MISTAKES AMONG WRITERS

"Grammar is not just a pain in the ass; it's the pole you grab to get your thoughts up on their feet and walking," writes Stephen King.[1] Most students cringe at the idea of learning grammar in a writing course. Grammar isn't typically a serious problem among students in our feature and magazine writing classes. Yet some mistakes seem to occur again and again.

Visualize punctuation marks like road signs. The purpose of road signs is to prevent accidents. The purpose of punctuation marks is to avoid confusing the reader. Used properly, they create clarity. A period tells you to "Stop," and a comma tells you to "Slow Down." Colons and semi-colons tell readers to "Yield Right of Way." Don't think of using proper punctuation as having to memorize rules but as making your ideas more understandable to the reader.

Run-on sentences

Run-on sentences are the most common grammar mistakes among beginning writers. For example: "Students who don't know grammar write run-on sentences, they usually get a failing grade." The preceding type of "run-on sentence" is sometimes called a "comma splice" because a comma is used to "splice" two sentences. Here are three acceptable revisions:

- Writers who don't know grammar write run-on sentences, *and* they usually get failing grades. (add the conjunction "and")
- Writers who don't know grammar write run-on sentences; they usually get failing grades. (separate the sentences with a semi-colon)
- Writers who don't know grammar write run-on sentences. They usually get failing grades. (re-write as two separate sentences)

Sentence fragments

Every sentence requires a noun and a verb. The most frequent sentence fragments begin with subordinating conjunctions such as "although," "because" or "which." They're called "subordinating" because they create a clause that is subordinate to the main clause. Therefore, the subordinate clause isn't complete and can't stand by itself. Example: "[John passed the course] because he studied hard."

Pronoun agreement

If you use a singular noun, use a singular pronoun when you refer to it later. If you use plural nouns, use plural pronouns when you refer to them later. That's what pronoun agreement means. The most frequent problem comes from "collective nouns"—singular nouns that describe a group of people. For example, use "it" and not "they" when you refer to a company, university, name of a store, a magazine or an organization: "The popular magazine announced that it (not "they") will no longer accept cigarette ads" or "The downtown store is having its (not "their") annual sale."

Possessive nouns and pronouns

The most common misuse of possessive nouns and pronouns comes with confusing plural and possessive forms of many nouns and pronouns. For example:

- The committees (more than one committee) are meeting now.
- That committee's (singular possessive) assignment is difficult.
- Those committees' (plural possessive) tasks are varied.

Another common mistake results from confusing "its" (the possessive form of the pronoun) with "it's" (a contraction for "it is"). Normally you do form the possessive case by adding an "s" with an apostrophe, but with the word "it," the apostrophe forms the contraction for "it is."

Unnecessary capitalization

Beginning writers are more likely to capitalize a word that shouldn't be capitalized than fail to capitalize one that should be. The most common mistake occurs when referring to a collective noun that doesn't occur as part of a proper noun. For example, most writers know to write "University of Massachusetts" or "Edward Jones Company." But when you refer to them later, you should say "the university" or "the company" and not "the University" or "the Company." Both the Associated Press and Chicago style manuals follow this rule.

Proper use of colons and semi-colons

Colons introduce. Use a colon to introduce a list of items, names of people or a long quotation. Examples:

- He made big promises: no new taxes, more social services and less government spending.
- Smith had this to say about the changes: "I am in favor of progress, but these proposals will cost too much, take too long . . ."

Semi-colons separate. They divide two or more complete sentences that are related to each other in theme or content. A semi-colon can always be replaced by a period, but never by a comma. Example: "The day is long; the students are tired; it's time to go home."

Misusing commas—a special problem

Commas are the most frequently misused punctuation marks. In most cases, students use more than necessary. The reasons for the misuse are, first, that style manuals vary in designating how and when to use the comma. Second, in a few situations, not even English and journalism scholars agree on proper comma usage. Remember that commas have one purpose: slow down. Just as road signs tell drivers to slow down to avoid danger, commas tell readers to slow down to avoid confusion. Here are the most common rules about comma usage:

Do use a comma
- to separate items in a series
  Example: "The new dean enjoys sailing, cooking, stamp collecting and gardening."
  (*The Associated Press Stylebook* specifies no comma before the final item, while the Chicago, Turabian and other style manuals do use a comma before the final item.)
- after years or names of states or countries when they fall in the middle of a sentence
  Example: "He left school on May 13, 2008, to go to Chicago, Ill., to take a summer job."
- between complete sentences (two subjects with two verbs) separated by a conjunction
  Example: "The fire alarm went off for the third time, so the motel clerk called the fire department."
- to set off introductory clauses and phrases from the rest of the sentence

Example: "When the fire alarm went off for the third time, the motel clerk called the fire department."

- to set off non-restrictive clauses, phrases and modifiers from the rest of the sentence

  Non-restrictive clauses begin with "who" or "which." They add interesting information to the sentence, but aren't essential to its meaning.

  Example: "My two sisters, who are older than I, live in Alaska."

  Example: "The motel fire, which started around midnight, did not cause serious damage."

- to set off appositive phrases—phrases that follow and explain a noun

  Example: "John Smith, vice president for finance, said the company expects a shortfall."

- to set off quotes preceding or following the attribution verb "said"

  Example: "John Smith, vice president for finance, said, 'The company expects a shortfall.'"

Do not use a comma

- to set off restrictive clauses, phrases and modifiers from the rest of the sentence Restrictive clauses begin with "that" or "who" and restrict the meaning of the nouns they modify to a particular person or thing. Omitting a restrictive clause can confuse the sentence's meaning.

  Example: "Two sisters who sought refuge in a church suffered injuries when the tornado struck the building."

  Example: "The tornado also damaged two storage buildings that are owned by the Smith farm."

- to set off subordinate clauses and phrases that come at the end of the sentence

  Example: "The motel clerk called the fire department when the fire alarm went off for the third time."

- between compound verbs in a sentence with only one subject

  Example: "The motel clerk called the fire department and started notifying guests about the fire."

- to set off a month and a year when there is no specific day

  Example: "He graduated from Michigan State in May 1986 before entering the U.S. Army."

Here is the most simplified version of common usage: If the reader won't be confused without the comma, then leave it out. If the reader might get confused, then use it. If in doubt, then omit it. After all, who wants to see a 40 mph speed-limit sign on the wide-open highway?

STYLE MANUALS AND PROPER USAGE

"Rules of style" are matters of preference and somewhat flexible. You may have used the *AP Stylebook* or *Chicago Manual of Style*. Newspapers are primary users of the *AP Stylebook*, while magazines and book publishers often use the *Chicago Manual of Style*. Some publications create their own style manuals for their writers and editors.

Do you write "29" or "twenty-nine"? Do you add or omit the last comma in a series—such as "coffee, sugar and cream"? The *AP Stylebook* says "29" and no comma," while the *Chicago Manual* answers, "twenty-nine and use the comma." The Modern Language Association and American Psychological Association publish two other style manuals, which are used mostly for scholarly writing. So what's a poor writer to do with all this conflicting advice?

The answer is easy. Follow the style manual required by your teacher or editor. We have written this textbook following the *AP Stylebook* because it's most commonly used in journalism schools, writing classes and newspapers. That's why that last sentence didn't have a comma before "and newspapers."

ENDNOTE

[1] Stephen King, *On Writing: A Memoir of the Craft* (New York: Simon & Schuster, 2000), 121.

PART IV

DIFFERENT TYPES OF FEATURE AND MAGAZINE ARTICLES

Under the umbrella title of "features" are several categories of articles. Flexible writers gather research and then determine the right length, depth and format of their editorial packages. The same information might emerge as a profile, a narrative, a how-to or an issue-related article. It also can be fashioned one way for print, another way for the Web.

BLURBS, BRIEFS AND BRIGHTENERS

Your takeaway . . .

Tight focus and tight writing are the keys to producing successful short features (50–750 words). These quick-read items can take the form of a flexible list, a stand-alone anecdote that prompts a laugh or makes a point, a timely piece of advice, or a mini-profile that explores a single aspect of its subject. This chapter shows you how to find and develop "little" articles and distill them to their bones. These briefs often help new writers get their foot in the door of national publications.

Magazines that have interactive Web sites—and most of them do—give editors up-to-the-minute reports on the topics and issues that interest their readers. Staff members can monitor which articles that appear in the online versions of the publications attract the most "clicks" or "hits." This information is valuable as the editors plan future content. Frequently the most popular features are not the in-depth cover stories that occupy much of the magazine's pages but the colorful blurbs, briefs and brighteners that pepper the pages throughout the issue.

The length and range of fillers, shorts and one-pagers vary and include everything from 50 words for a quip or quote to 750 words for a mini-profile or a personal essay. Readers like shorts because they are quick to absorb and less intimidating; they offer variety, can be clipped and saved, and they play to the current preference for skip-and-skim media. Art directors and layout editors welcome short items because they add color and energy to a page. They can be clustered, boxed, set at an angle or dropped as an attention-getter onto an otherwise gray page. Editors value short items because they ensure flexibility. If a major feature article runs long, an editor can remove a short to accommodate the need for extra inches. If an advertiser decides at the last minute to cancel an ad, the editor can retrieve a self-contained short from a file and plug it into the open page without disrupting the rest of the publication.

PROVIDING THE LOCAL ANGLE

Unfortunately, many new writers overlook the opportunity to break into print with short, and often local, items. We know of an aspiring young travel journalist, bound for his first trip to Europe, who mailed a flurry of query letters to newspaper and magazine editors offering lengthy articles about every stop on his itinerary. Using a bulleted format sometimes called a gang query because it includes multiple story ideas, he tossed out three possible titles:

- "Barging through Burgundy"
- "Jack the Ripper's London"
- "Prague's Incredible Flea Markets"

The ideas were creative, yet all but one editor responded with a standard thanks-but-no-thanks rejection note. The lone encourager was a staff member at one of the giant New York-based travel magazines who scrawled across the bottom of the query: "Sorry, foreign assignments only go to our senior contributors." Then the editor added as an afterthought, "But I notice you're from Ohio. Anything going on out there?"

What the beginner didn't realize was that some national publications—not just travel magazines like this one—produce as many as four or five regional editions. The cover story and most main features in an issue don't vary, but a certain number of pages are dedicated to editorial material about people and places within a specific region. For example, magazines shipped to the West Coast might contain a one-page story about a small family winery in California's Anderson Valley; readers in the Southwest won't see the winery story but they'll be alerted to a new bed-and-breakfast inn near Santa Fe. Midwest subscribers won't have access to either the wine or the inn stories, but might read about an upcoming exhibit at the Rock and Roll Museum and Hall of Fame in Cleveland, Ohio.

Regional editions make sense for a couple of reasons. First, Americans are eager to learn about people close to home and about things they can do and see on a tank of gasoline. The publication that offers a steady stream of ideas for regional attractions is likely to build readership and retain subscribers in those locations. Second, advertisers are more apt to buy space in publications that feature stories linked to their service area. A small airline that schedules daily flights in and out of Key West, Fla., might be interested in placing an advertisement in a publication that features "The Cuban Cuisine of Key West."

Editors who operate from offices in New York City, Los Angeles or Chicago need to know what is new and interesting in out-of-the-way places around Key West, Fla; Santa Fe, N.M.; and yes, Cleveland, Ohio. They're interested in bright and brief articles that offer readers a variety of content choices. The editor who asked the Ohio freelancer, "Anything going on out there?" was dead serious. The smart writer should have taken the hint, forgotten about the barge in Burgundy and checked out the riverboat docked near Cincinnati.

WIDE, WIDE WORLD OF SHORTS

Short articles seldom require a query letter (we explained queries in Chapter 7) and they serve as foot-in-the-door features that eventually can lead to major assignments, internships or—best of all—permanent jobs. The student journalist who feeds a New York editor a constant stream of brief but bright items from Ohio, Oregon or North Carolina may earn a place in the publication's stable of trusted contributors. The editor lets the writer know about major stories slated for future publication and the writer responds with related shorts that help expand the articles into editorial packages.

Example: An editor plans a feature about a new crop of young entrepreneurs—recent college grads who take risks and start their own companies rather than join established corporations. A writer from Michigan hears about the project and offers a 500-word mini-profile of two sorority sisters who have launched a successful catering service out of a Detroit storefront. The article, "Tea for 200," adds an element of humor as well as geographic and gender diversity to the 3,000-word package that is dominated by males who have built businesses around their high-tech skills.

Before long, the back-and-forth communication between editor and writer results in a professional relationship that benefits both parties. The editor's network of writers grows, and the publication takes on a national flavor, thanks to fresh voices reporting stories from rural and suburban areas of the country. Who knows, the writer may even earn a place on the publication's masthead as a contributing editor or a regional correspondent. This may not translate into a salary (a token honorarium is sometimes the best a contributing editor can hope for), but it ensures that any story idea that the writer submits is seriously considered. It also means that when an editor has an important assignment to make, he will look first to his list of contributing editors. Before long that Ohio writer may get a firm assignment to barge through Burgundy, shadow Jack the Ripper around London or scout bargains at Prague's flea markets.

RELEVANT VS. RANDOM

By definition, shorts are interesting, informative and relevant nonfiction items of various lengths. Don't confuse them with fillers, which suggest items that have little purpose other than to take up space. (Out of habit, some editors use the terms interchangeably, but they know the difference.) Years ago, newspapers and some magazines often kept on hand a supply of random fillers to dust off and drop into a story that didn't quite fill the space allotted it. It was possible for a reader to finish a profile article about a Washington politician or a Hollywood celebrity and then be informed, "The capital of Nevada is Carson City" or "The average person uses 123 gallons of water a day."

Fortunately, the old-fashioned variety of fillers is rare these days. Editors no longer fear white space; in fact, they welcome "air" because it allows a story to "breathe." Also, technology now permits an editor to eliminate small amounts of unwanted air by slightly adjusting the space between lines and words.

Unlike fillers, shorts are a planned, not a random, part of a publication's content. They might take the form of humorous anecdotes of under 100 words such as you see in *Reader's Digest* or recipes, appropriate for a magazine such as *Woman's Day*. They might be brief inspirational stories that fit perfectly into the pages of *Guideposts*. They can be 300-word how-to articles—"Five Steps to a Great Mid-Career Résumé"—for an issue of a business magazine or the business pages of a daily newspaper. Or they might offer a quick compilation of shower gift ideas for the bride-to-be for the front page of almost any newspaper's feature section in June. They might occupy a box, a column or an entire page. All are tightly focused and self-contained, and they never include the line "continued on page . . ."

SHOPPING FOR SHORTS AND BRIEFS

The amount of research necessary to produce a marketable short varies. For the story about shower gifts for the bride-to-be, the writer might browse the specialty shops of a mall and visit the Web sites of high-end boutiques. As she "shops," she is taking notes on unusual items that a young couple would unlikely purchase for themselves. Two or three brief interviews with retail buyers about what's hot this season will provide insider tips from experts who have a handle on trendy merchandise.

Sometimes a single interview with an expert source provides enough information for two or three shorts. For example, a college journalist might research a profile article about a literature professor for the campus newspaper and come away with three ideas to pitch to larger publications. The professor mentions during the interview that many teenagers lose interest in recreational reading during their middle-school years. The journalist picks up on the comment and asks the professor to expand on it. The writer then poses several follow-up questions such as:

- What should parents look for when they buy books for their kids?
- How do contemporary books like the Harry Potter series compare with the "classics" like the revived Nancy Drew mysteries or the Narnia books that adults remember?
- How can you tell if a child is ready for a book that deals with serious themes?
- Are comic books bad for kids?

From this conversation come these three shorts:

1   "How to Keep Your Kids Reading This Summer"
2   "The Five Best Kids' Books of the Year"
3   "When Harry (Potter) Met Nancy (Drew)"

The same three story ideas also might spring from a report, issued by experts and reported in the media, saying that the reading skills of

American teenagers are rapidly diminishing. The sharp writer, always looking for breakthrough studies conducted by reputable researchers, clips the news story and contacts a credible expert—that same literature professor—for comments. The resulting interview doesn't have to be long because it is tightly focused on ways that parents can reverse a disturbing trend. Depending on the angle that the writer chooses to take, the shorts are appropriate for publications aimed at parents, grandparents, librarians and educators.

FLEXIBLE LIST ARTICLES

One of the article possibilities cited above—"The Five Best Kids' Books of the Year"—could be packaged as a list article. Editors at many newspapers and magazines welcome list articles because these features can be expanded or reduced as space allows. More important, list articles make great cover lines that motivate readers to buy magazines. "When we put lists on the cover, our newsstand sales go up," said *Men's Health* editor David Zinczenko in a televised interview about the power of lists.[1] In his blog, Zinczenko offers lists that inform readers on timely topics: the six worst foods to eat at the movies, the eight ultimate flat-belly summer foods and the six things your dad wants for father's day. "Lists are perfect for guys with short attention spans," jokes Zinczenko.

As an example of an evergreen (always in season) article, prolific freelance writer Dennis Hensley once created a list of tasks that an airline traveler can accomplish when stranded by an unplanned layover in an airport. He got the idea, as you might guess, when he was delayed for several hours by a canceled flight.The resulting article—which we include in this chapter—reaped multiple sales because it appealed to a broad audience. By changing examples within the article, he could aim it at men or women, college students, business travelers or family vacationers. Because the topic has long shelf life, the article could be tweaked, updated, shortened or lengthened for ongoing marketability. Hensley recalls that one publication that wasn't pressed for space printed "10 tasks that a traveler can accomplish during a layover." Another editor, with less available space, pruned the list to seven tasks.

List articles usually follow a two-part formula. First, you need an introductory paragraph that sets up the article by explaining the purpose of the list. Since these articles are straightforward, the introduction should be brief and to the point. Second, the list is presented in either a bulleted or a numbered format. Timely examples might include:

- 25 Christmas gift ideas under $25
- 10 New Year's resolutions you can keep
- the 8 highest-paying jobs for new college graduates
- the 5 best political Web sites this election year

Although list articles seem simple to write, most of them require research. If you want to write about "12 foods that sharpen your memory," you will need to do a great deal of background reading and then interview a medical doctor or nutritionist who has impressive credentials related to the topic. Your reward for the time that you invest in such an article is the likelihood that you will sell it many times to many publications. The wise writer who recognizes that an article might be marketable more than once takes care to sell only first rights to a publication. We discussed copyright questions in Chapter 7.

PERSONAL-EXPERIENCE SHORTS

Some editors solicit short items pulled from a writer's personal experience. These anecdotes are often either humorous or inspirational, but not complex enough to support a full-length feature. They have maximum impact on readers when the author distills the "message" rather than dilutes it with a lot of description and background information.

Good examples of inspirational shorts are the little stories contained in a standing column in *Guideposts* called "His Mysterious Ways." (Examples of these are posted on the magazine's Web site and range in length up to 750 words.) Each anecdote comes from the writer's personal experience, recounts an incident that cannot be explained by logic and has the capacity to raise gooseflesh on readers. At the center of each story is an unforeseen turn of events that skeptics would call "luck," and religious believers would call a "God thing." For example, an unpredicted shower drenches a burning house where young children are sleeping unattended. No one else in the neighborhood experiences the rain, and the pavement around the house remains perfectly dry.

As popular as "His Mysterious Ways" is with readers, the column almost didn't get off the ground. Editors at *Guideposts* kept rejecting "miracle stories" because they didn't fit into the magazine's mission to equip readers with practical tools to help them face and overcome life's inevitable obstacles. After all, a reader who struggles with a problem similar to the one recapped in the magazine cannot expect a duplicate miracle to provide a happy ending. Only after these "miracle" submissions continued to pour into their offices did the editors decide to group them under the common label of "His Mysterious Ways" and offer them as unexplainable stories of faith. That was years ago. Since then, the column has evolved into a mainstay of the magazine and typically tops the list of subscribers' favorite features.[2] Its popularity supports the notion that people like "short reads" that stir emotions.

RECYCLING ANECDOTES

One of the best places to look for shorts is within articles you've already written. Most stories contain anecdotes, and many anecdotes can stand on their own merit. The editors at *Reader's Digest* survey scores of magazines in search of stories within stories that meet the *Digest*'s high publication standards. For example, a 2,000-word profile of Garfield creator Jim Davis published in *The Saturday Evening Post* yielded a 100-word nugget about how Davis grew up on a farm and often was confined to his home because of asthma. His mother encouraged him to pass the time by sitting at a window and sketching the family's "outdoor" cats. The anecdote may have caught the eye of the *Digest* editors because it showed how a negative situation (asthma) could result in a positive outcome (fame as a cartoonist). Also, the little story would appeal to the *Digest*'s middle-aged readers who have been reading Garfield strips since the cat debuted on America's comic pages in 1978. The lesson here is that demographics are important, even when combing your copy for small, salable blurbs.

To enjoy a second life as a "short," an anecdote doesn't have to deal with celebrities. Some publications compile stories about non-celebrities under a title that clearly identifies the common element that unifies the content. *Reader's Digest* compartmentalizes 100-word stories into columns with labels such as "Off Base," which are anecdotes related to military life; "Life @ Work," which are career-related stories; "Laugh!" and "Quotes." The

Digest encourages contributors to submit their anecdotes to the editors by typing them directly onto the magazine's Web site.

Magazines typically solicit submissions about people who reflect their readers. A publication geared to runners will welcome blurbs about interesting people who share that passion. A magazine for career women may look for anecdotes that fit into a monthly feature called "Timeout" that offers ideas on how to reduce job stress. A magazine for teachers solicits brief stories about educators who have developed creative ways to deal with universal classroom challenges.

BEYOND THE BLURB

The longest short is the one-page story that usually contains no more than 500 to 750 words. The one-pager is a challenge to write because the author has to prune every unnecessary word from the text. This means that the article that emerges can have only one focus. If it's a profile, it zeros in on a lone aspect of the person's life; if it's an essay, it centers on a single key point. A one-page travel article would never try to embrace the entire city of Nashville but might transport readers to a historic pub in Music City where wannabe singers take turns at an open microphone.

Regardless of whether you want to submit 50-word jokes or 600-word articles to a publication, the steps that lead to success are the same.

- **Do your homework.** Survey several publications and determine if they use short items. Pay particular attention to the table of contents where you'll find a listing of departments and standing features. For example, *Newsweek* lists a standing feature called "My Turn," which tells you that the editors are obligated to come up with a first-person essay of 850 words every week. If you have a good story, you just might earn a byline. Tip: Review back issues to ensure these departments and features are present in every edition.
- **Analyze several short items.** What seems to be the preferred length? Are they clustered under a common title? Do they carry bylines? If so, do the bylines belong to regular contributors or members of the staff? In other words, does a newcomer have a chance of breaking into print?

- **Keep up on trends.** The best shorts are timely items. Often editors cluster nuggets that are linked to trends, new research, innovations and recently released statistics.
- **Keep your eye on the calendar.** Editors love to drop in seasonal shorts: "Three Causes of Holiday Depression" (December); "Quiz: How Compatible Are You?" (February/Valentine's Day); "A Checklist for Winterizing Your Garden" (September). We talk more about seasonal features in Chapter 17.
- **Be patient.** Remember that short items with long shelf life are always in demand. The problem is that editors aren't always sure when they will have just the right place for them. If an editor tells you he wants to hold your short for possible use in the future, be willing to wait.
- **Be resilient.** This is a competitive business. As an example, *Newsweek*'s "My Turn" editor says the magazine receives an average of 800 submissions each month and can print only one per week. Those odds aren't good. To help potential contributors, the magazine's Web site offers a variety of tips, including topics that the editors are most interested in seeing addressed.

Seven* Ways to Overcome "Terminal" Problems[3] (*or as Many Ways as Space Allows)

You're stuck on a two-hour layover between Dallas and Denver. What do you do when there's little time to do anything? You'd be surprised.

By Dennis E. Hensley

I travel a lot. I also wait a lot. I love the former, loathe the latter. But if I go any distance by plane or train these days, I find myself a victim of the one-to-four-hour layover.

Recently, for example, on a flight from Chicago to Fort Myers, Fla., I spent two and a half hours airborne and three and a half hours waiting in Atlanta for a connecting flight. Absurd, right? Nevertheless, it's a reality.

For someone like me, who takes the phrase "time is money" as his life's motto, wasting time sitting in terminals is akin to setting fire to five-dollar bills. No doubt you feel the same way.

SIDEBAR 1

No matter what business we are in, travel cannot be avoided. Out-of-state conventions, visits to the company's home office, conferences, seminars, business meetings and customer relations seem to keep us in the air or on the tracks more and more each year. With travel costs soaring, many of us find it necessary to seek out the discount rates; usually, these bargain fares only compound the number of layovers, stops and "dead hours."

I have come to grips with the problem by game-planning ahead of time ways in which I can use layover hours to my best advantage. Let me share with you several activities that you can do while waiting for your next flight departure.

1. **Go shopping.** As long as the terminal is overrun with kiosks and vendors anyway, you may as well make use of them to take care of several necessary tasks. Sure, you might pay a little more for the convenience, but the time you will save for yourself will justify the added expense. So, go ahead and buy presents to take home for the kids; get that haircut you need; have your shoes shined, and order ahead the rental car you'll need in your next town.

2. **Put together a fail-safe kit.** Even if you travel as little as five or six times a year, you still are a potential victim of misrouted luggage. As a guard against this, you should put together a small all-purpose kit, made up of functional items that you can purchase at any terminal's gift shop or newsstand. These items can be stashed in your carry-on bag or in your briefcase. I recommend such things as a tin of aspirin, toothbrush and toothpaste, comb, snacks and a razor. Even if your luggage arrives late, you can still freshen up in the terminal restroom or in your hotel room before that first meeting.

3. **Do your homework.** It's wrong to think the only kind of book you can read in a noisy terminal is a novel, since "light reading" doesn't demand strong attention. In truth, a professional magazine, a training manual or other work-related documents are easier to read. Why? Because they are the kinds of printed materials that you read with a highlighter in hand. You frequently stop to underline important points, make notes in the margins or circle key terms. It's sporadic reading and is perfect for a distracting environment. Save the novel for the quiet of your flight.

4. **Draft a business letter on your laptop.** We all have sticky problems we must deal with—an irate client who needs to be soothed, an associate in another office who needs to be queried, or a hard-to-reach prospect you desperately want to contact. The layover in the terminal gives you a chance to write such a letter carefully. Send it as an attachment via e-mail or save it until you're back at the office and can print it out for snail-mail delivery.

5. **Call clients.** Make use of all those minutes you have accumulated with your cell phone carrier to catch up on calls. A couple of cautions: Find a quiet corner so your conversation won't be interrupted by other passengers making calls; don't skim through your phone list and place unnecessary calls merely to kill time.

6. **Clean out your purse or wallet.** Here, at last, you've got time to rid your purse or billfold of outdated credit cards, slips of paper, a stash of pens that don't work and a collection of business cards from people you never call. After you've completed your chores, consider balancing your checkbook.

7. Play "what if" mind games. While seated in the terminal, use the time to challenge yourself with problems that may arise in the coming months. Strategize on possible solutions. If a job opens up in another department, should you apply? If you have the opportunity to relocate, should you do it? You need a new car; so what are the pros and cons of leasing rather than buying?

ENDNOTES

[1] Interview on CBS *Sunday Morning*, June 8, 2008.
[2] Van Varner, *His Mysterious Ways* (New York: Ballantine Books, 1988), xi.
[3] Copyright Dennis E. Hensley (used by permission).

IN FOCUS: THE WELL-BALANCED PROFILE

Your takeaway . . .

To succeed, a profile article should focus on what makes the person interesting to readers *right now*. This chapter includes suggestions on finding a timely slant and asking probing questions that result in answers that go beyond bland, "cheerleader" comments. You'll see the importance of conducting support interviews that round out your article. We also introduce you to the option of presenting the material in a question-and-answer format, a trend that is gaining popularity.

In *Almost Famous*, a semi-autobiographical film by journalist-turned-screenwriter Cameron Crowe, a teenager attaches himself to a rock group for the purpose of writing a profile article for *Rolling Stone* magazine. In the course of the story, 15-year-old "William" (played by actor Patrick Fugit) comes of age as a person and as a writer. The first draft of his article is shallow, full of hyperbole and reads like a news release generated by an overly enthusiastic publicist. The editors at *Rolling Stone* promptly reject it. His next attempt, an honest portrayal based on personal observations, several days of shadowing and a variety of interviews, earns praise and launches Cameron/William on a successful career. The published article acknowledges the band members' shortcomings but also captures their strengths. The musicians emerge as very real and likeable characters. William scores a byline and earns a sale.

AVOIDING THE "PORTRAIT"

If you've ever visited an art gallery you've probably encountered formal portraits of famous people—presidents, world leaders, members of royalty and high society—who smile (or glower) down at you from gilded frames. You recognize some of them, but barely. The portraits are likenesses of people on their very best days. Gone are the wrinkles, blemishes and other imperfections. The artist has thickened the hair, whitened the teeth, bobbed the noses, flattened the ears and trimmed the tummy. Misty colors and soft brushstrokes have embellished the gifts of nature and eliminated the ravages of time. If the subject of the portrait had a flaw, the artist has either ignored or downplayed it.

You ask: Were these people *really* as attractive in life as they appear on canvas? Answer: probably not. Wealthy folk throughout history have spent hundreds of thousands of dollars to have artists portray them as they *wished* they had looked in their prime.

What do these overly complimentary portraits have to do with you as a writer? Just this: Some feature editors are satisfied with profile articles that are written versions of see-no-evil portraits. Such articles are usually based on single interviews and superficial questions. The result is a shallow, overly complimentary likeness of the interviewee that contains no insights into the person's struggles or shortcomings that helped shape him. If a profiled person is a celebrity who has had a well-publicized problem that the publication must acknowledge or risk losing credibility, the writer downplays the problem with carefully chosen euphemisms. Inappropriate behavior becomes "playfulness," run-ins with the law shrink to "skirmish" status, multiple marriages emerge as "broken relationships" and periods of substance abuse are downgraded to times of "unwise lifestyle choices." If these esteemed icons smoked marijuana in their college days, they certainly didn't inhale.

Authors who write these profiles and editors who publish them don't intend to be dishonest or mislead readers. They merely subscribe to the old advice: If you can't say something nice about a person, don't say anything at all. They aren't in the business of probing beyond the superficial. The profiles that emerge put subjects on pedestals for readers to admire. These stories are most at home on the pages of fan magazines, religious publications, internal newsletters, company magazines and other sponsored periodicals.

Idealized profiles can be dangerous to a magazine, its readers and even to the personalities who serve as subjects for stories that gush. Here are three reasons why overwritten profiles are not as harmless as they seem:

- Readers are savvy enough to know that no one is perfect, and they question the honesty and ethics of a publication that perpetuates such a myth. The public will not take the magazine seriously and may categorize its writers as lightweights. If the publication is sponsored, the writers risk acquiring the label of "spin doctors."

- Readers who believe the pumped-up portraits that they read often feel in awe of the people who are profiled. These readers measure themselves against the featured personalities and, compared to perfection, they always come up short. A working mother feels guilty when she reads about the "super mom" who successfully balances home, career, family, friends and community service. The high-school student loses self-esteem when she reads about the teenage rock star who manages to get great grades, wears a size 4 and just signed a movie deal.

- People who fall off pedestals sometimes never recover from the injuries they sustain to their reputations. This is especially true of highly visible religious figures who too often are depicted in the religious press as practically flawless. If the personality slips and makes a human error, the secular world responds with a loud "Aha!" The "sin" may be as common as getting a divorce or as innocent as an inspirational vocalist "crossing over" to the pop charts. Whatever the problem, the blame rests less with the personality and more with the publication for holding the personality to an unattainable standard of perfection.

What Makes a Person Newsworthy?

Prominence: For a national magazine, the prominent person is likely a celebrity, a well-known politician, author or business executive. For a campus publication the prominent subject could be a professor, athlete or student government officer.

Perseverance: Readers love stories about persons who have overcome great odds to live out a dream or persevere in the face of adversity. Examples: A blind student graduates from law school with honors; a single mom juggles four jobs to complete her degree.

Oddity: Ideas might include the first female to play on the boys' soccer team or the student who earned a perfect score on the SAT and entered college at age 12. Example: *The Chronicle of Higher Education* published a profile about a man who had earned 11 degrees.

SIDEBAR 1

Achievement: Success stories are everywhere, and the reading public never tires of them. Examples: The singer who earns a recording contract; the business major who launches a company; the athlete who breaks a long-standing school record.

Experience: Interesting experiences come in two varieties. First is participating in a one-time event such as competing in an Olympic trial; second is an ongoing experience such as serving as a summer intern on Capitol Hill.

Vocation/Avocation: Persons with unusual jobs and hobbies might be fair fodder for profile articles. Examples: Interview a storm chaser, a documentary filmmaker, or a collector of antique juke-boxes and Coca Cola machines.

Anniversary: These stories often involve a person looking back on an event or an era. Examples: Profile a professor who recalls the changes he has witnessed on campus as he marks 30 years of teaching; or profile an eyewitness to the 9/11 disaster who is willing to talk about how the event changed his life.

"WARTS AND ALL" PHOTOGRAPH

As a writer, you aren't writing to please the person you write about; you are writing to inform your reader. For that reason, many editors stipulate they don't want "portrait" articles; they want "warts and all" profiles. This suggests a story that is a written version of a black-and-white news photograph that hasn't been manipulated on the computer screen. It's an honest representation of the person, flaws (warts) and all. This does not mean that you, the writer, must dig around in a subject's background trying to unearth controversy. Your goal is merely to present the profiled person as normal, real and worthy of readers' interest.

Striking the right balance between a person's positive and negative qualities requires skill. Just as the writer and editor want to avoid elevating the personality to sainthood, so do they want to avoid discrediting or embarrassing the person. The goal is honesty, but the transition from creating word portraits to crafting word photographs can be clumsy at first. The tendency is for writers to mention one human shortcoming and then tout five attributes to offset it. Some writers attempt to humanize their subjects by passing off a positive quality as a negative one. For example, "He admits to being overly generous with his family," or "She can't say 'no' to a good cause, especially if it involves children."

Tuning into a subject's "humanity" requires a serious investment of time. You cannot merely sit down with a person, run through a short list of questions and then expect to create an in-depth profile from the answers. You're going to have to use your power of observation and ask open-ended questions during the interview portion of your research.

Shadowing the person for a day allows you to immerse yourself in the person's world. It also reveals insights into the way he relates to co-workers, family, friends and even pets. Is he shy? Funny? Are people relaxed when they are in his company? Ride in his car with him. Does he drive too fast? Is he often late for appointments? Is he constantly on his cell phone? What kinds of music does he like? (Check out his CD collection in the car.) Take note of his personal space (home, office, dorm room). Is it messy? What pictures hang on the walls? Do you see any indication of a hobby—a motorcycle helmet, tennis racquet, computer games, guitar? As your recorder captures his words, your notebook becomes a receptacle of colorful but unspoken details.

Ten Questions to Reveal Personality

After you've established a rapport with your profile subject, ask a few questions that will reveal the person's deeper or more whimsical side. These should be used sparingly and sprinkled throughout your conversation.

1   Recall a major turning point in your life and how it affected you.
2   Walk me through a typical day.
3   Describe what, in the past year, has given you the most pleasure.
4   What was the best piece of advice you ever received?
5   If someone were making a film of your life, what part would you want to omit?
6   What have you learned from your biggest failure?
7   Just for fun, let's say someone gave you a great deal of money and told you that you had to splurge on something for yourself. What would you buy?

SIDEBAR 2

8   What tops your "bucket list" (list of things you want to accom-
    plish or experience before you die)?
9   What do you like/dislike most about yourself?
10 Fast forward a decade. Where are you? What are you doing?
    What do you hope to accomplish in the next year?

If your interview includes a meal in a restaurant, how does your interviewee treat the server? What does she eat? Is she watching her weight? Is
she a vegetarian? These are observations that you can explore in your conversation with her. If she's on a diet—and who isn't—she is on common
ground with many of your readers. If she admits to an addiction to chocolate, there's another connection.

ASSEMBLING THE PICTURE

Ideally you should shadow your subject before you sit down for your
"formal" interview. During the shadowing experience you engage in casual
conversation and take notes on topics you want to pursue when you
conduct your question-and-answer session. As you prepare your list of
questions, review the clues you've gathered during the shadowing experience. If you spotted a guitar in the corner of your subject's office and you
know that country music dominates the CD collection in his car, you can
ask about it. Your reward might be a great anecdote about how he once
spent a summer in Nashville trying to make it as a studio musician. By
including the story in your article you let readers know that your subject
has had lofty dreams and has experienced disappointments. With one
brief anecdote you succeed in humanizing him and making a link with
your readers.

Peter Jacobi, a consultant and contributor to numerous magazines, suggests that a good profile article is a combination of A-B-C-D factors. First,
it is an *authentic* portrayal of a person—honest in tone and accurate in
facts. Second, it provides a *bridge* between the reader and the profiled
person; the reader makes a link or finds common ground with the article's

subject. Third, the article presents a *challenge* because it can't cover every aspect of the person's life but should nudge the reader to continue to think about the information presented. Fourth, the profile should offer a sense of *discovery* as the reader gains new knowledge or appreciation after becoming acquainted with the profiled individual.[1]

Keep these factors in mind as you continue to gather information and schedule secondary interviews. Constantly review your notes and compile a list of unanswered questions. This list will help you determine additional people you need to consult as you attempt to create a well-balanced representation of your subject.

PURSUING DIFFERENT CAMERA ANGLES

One of the major differences between a "portrait" article and a warts-and-all "photograph" kind of story is the number of interviews that the writer conducts. Imagine watching a full-length motion picture that was shot from one angle with one camera that never zoomed in for close-ups or panned the room to show the person in the context of the environment. This would be the ultimate "talking head"—boring, one-dimensional and predictable.

An article based on a single interview with the profiled person can be equally tiresome and superficial. Readers see the individual from only one perspective—his own. Even if the person is candid, witty and wonderfully quotable, he can't make up for the absence of other viewpoints. The article may be good, but probably won't be as good as it could be if you included insights from other sources.

By conducting support interviews with a variety of people who know your subject, you move your camera back and forth and up and down. In short, you capture your subject from different angles. How many support interviews are enough? That depends on your time constraints, the availability of sources, the projected word count of your article and the number of personality traits you hope to explore. Beware: It's possible to talk with too many sources and end up with a collection of disjointed comments. Also, avoid support sources that give only "cheerleader quotes" such as "she's a wonderful friend" without any insights into your subject's character or personality.

SIDEBAR 3

How to Avoid Cheerleader Quotes

Asking a tightly focused follow-up question is the key to gathering information from a secondary source that goes beyond superficial "cheerleader" responses. As examples:

Interviewee's comment	Follow-up question
"He's a very good leader."	Describe a moment when he showed his leadership skills.
"She has a great personality."	Tell me your impression of her when you met for the first time. How did she win you over?
"She's an excellent student."	How do her study habits differ from those of other students?
"He's a lot of fun; you never know what he's going to do or say next."	Give me an example of something outrageous that he's done or said.

The point is, you should choose your interviewees carefully and strive for quality rather than quantity. If an interview subject fails to bring something fresh to the profile, you shouldn't feel any obligation to include the comments.

When identifying support interviews, you should go back to the idea of the roving camera. You'll probably want at least one close-up. The person's spouse or some other member of the family can best provide this angle. If you want a "view from the top," set up an interview with the person's boss. If you want to focus on the person's hobbies or interests, talk with her tennis partner, roommate or best friend.

Support interviews usually don't require a lot of time, and you sometimes can conduct them on the telephone. (We strongly discourage trading e-mails.) This doesn't mean support interviews aren't important or don't deserve careful planning. You don't want responses that are generic affirmations that could describe almost anyone. The best way to get past one-size-fits-all comments is with questions that invite anecdotal answers. (See our sidebar on avoiding cheerleader quotes.)

Some veteran profile writers like to conduct their support interviews first, then schedule their shadowing experience and, last of all, sit down for their in-depth, one-on-one sessions with their primary subjects. This makes sense and can save time. Conversations with secondary sources often uncover routine information that might have eaten up valuable minutes if you had to gather it during your in-depth interview. ("How long have you been married?" "Where did you go to college?" "How many children do you have?")

More important, secondary sources and the shadowing experience often result in great questions that you otherwise might miss. A best friend might tell you a funny story that you can recount to get a reaction from your primary interviewee. A wife might tick off several awards that her husband won, whereas the husband would be too modest to mention them. You can play one person's comments against another's and end up with a humorous he-said/she-said kind of anecdote.

ADDING COLOR TO THE PICTURE

As an example, let's say you are writing a profile of a prominent leader in your community. Before you sit down for your in-depth interview with him, you spend some time talking with his wife of many years. As part of your conversation you ask her to recall their first date. She supplies a colorful anecdote, complete with lots of details. Of course, the story is told from her point of view. A few days later you sit face to face with the husband, and you want to hear his side of the story. The dialogue might go something like this:

INTERVIEWER: Your wife tells me that your first date was a disaster because you neglected to warn her that you were taking her to a football game . . . in the rain. She says that she spent the first half wrapped in a plastic trash bag and the second half under the bleachers. True story?

INTERVIEWEE: Yeah; she thought we were going to see a play, but at the last minute a friend gave me tickets to the Bears' season opener. The weather was brutal. But it was a great game, and the Bears won in the fourth quarter.

Resulting article excerpt: Their relationship got off to an icy start when he swapped front-row theater tickets for a couple of passes to a Bears-49ers game. The soft drizzle turned into a Chicago-style downpour and caused her to seek refuge first in a plastic trash bag and then under the bleachers. "We couldn't leave," he explains, adding as justification: "The score was tied, third down and goal to go." The Bears got the win, she got the flu and he got the cold shoulder for two weeks. They now have season tickets . . . to the theater.

Obviously the resulting excerpt required a bit of extra research on the part of you, the interviewer. Since the couple's first date occurred many years ago, both the husband and wife were fuzzy in their recollection of the facts. You compensated for this by asking a lot of follow-up questions and then by visiting the library and finding on microfilm the *Chicago Tribune*'s account of the Bears' season opener. You scribbled down a few notes about the weather and the final play of the game and blended these details with the memories that your interviewees supplied. A great little story emerged.

FILE FOR THE FUTURE

If collecting strong comments and anecdotes from a variety of sources has a negative side, it's the fact that you can't include all the material in a single profile article. Most editors don't want a chronological rehashing of a person's life. Instead, they expect you to weave in just enough background to give context to the interesting and timely focus of your profile. This requires you to sift through your notes and transcripts (if you taped your interviews) and select the information that fits the article's focus and temporarily set aside the material that doesn't make the cut.

But don't throw anything away. Chances are you'll be able to fold your interviewee's "discarded" comments into any number of future stories.

Here's how it works: Say you research and write a profile about a student who just completed a summer internship in the White House press office. Although you include some background—she's a junior, majoring in political science and hopes to go to law school after graduation—the focus of your story is on the eight weeks that the student spent in the West Wing. The other material you gathered, such as the way she found out about the internship in the first place, doesn't fit the focus and never makes it to print.

Later, you tackle a how-to article assignment that offers tips on how to land dream jobs in a tight economy. Your primary interviewee is the director of the campus career center who emphasizes that internships attract a lot of attention on résumés. To answer the logical question about how students discover internship opportunities, you pull from your files the comments from the student who beat out the competition and spent a summer in the White House. Whereas she dominated the profile article, she now plays a supporting role in the how-to article and occupies only a paragraph or two. Her contribution is important, though, because she provides an anecdote that illustrates a key point.

PUTTING A FACE ON AN ISSUE

A profile is a great way to put a "face" on an important issue and cause readers to get involved and care about a topic they might otherwise dismiss. Many magazine and newspaper writers use this tactic in preparing in-depth articles about complex issues. For some journalists who do this, their rewards have been the lofty Pulitzer Prize for feature writing. (The full texts of Pulitzer-winning feature articles from 1995 to the present are available online at www.pulitzer.org. They also are compiled in an anthology produced by Iowa State Press.) Some examples:

* We've all heard the criticism that Americans live in such a fast-paced society that too few of us stop to smell the roses and enjoy the moment. *Washington Post* feature writer Gene Weingarten won a Pulitzer Prize in 2008 when he tested the validity of this statement by shadowing world-class violinist Joshua Bell. The good-natured Bell agreed to go incognito and give an impromptu performance for commuters during rush hour in Washington, D.C. Playing his $3.5 million violin, Bell filled a well-trafficked subway station with incredible music as Weingarten looked on, taking notes about commuters' reactions to the anonymous street musician. The resulting article proved a point even as it gave readers insights into one of the world's finest virtuosos.
* Illegal immigration was at the heart of a 30,000-word feature called "Enrique's Journey" that won the 2003 Pulitzer Prize for *Los Angeles Times* feature writer Sonia Nazario. The story, divided into chapters

because of its length, traces the life of Enrique from age 5 to adulthood. The author conducted scores of interviews to piece together Enrique's journey from Honduras to North Carolina. Readers "accompany" Enrique and, at the end, emerge with a better understanding of an international problem that has no simple solution.

Of course, not all profiles have the potential to explore complex issues and win Pulitzer Prizes. Some articles are meant merely to provide a quick snapshot of a person for the purpose of entertaining or informing readers.

FROM SNAPSHOT TO ALBUM

The New Yorker invented the term "profile" with its in-depth articles about 1920s personalities. When *The New Yorker* celebrated its 75th anniversary, the editor, David Remnick, collected some of the magazine's best profile articles and created a 530-page anthology called *Life Stories*. In his introduction, Remnick admitted that writing a great profile is difficult, and writing a profile suitable for *The New Yorker* sometimes requires months or even years to produce.[2] The problem is, of course, that not every writer— or publication—has the luxury of such open-ended assignments. Also, not every writer—or publication—is interested in producing comprehensive life stories. The result? "We are awash in pieces calling themselves profiles that are about the inner thoughts of some celebrity; more often than not they are based on half-hour interviews and the parameters set down by a vigilant publicist," notes Remnick.[3]

He may be right. But "quick takes" (we call them snapshots) are mainstays of some publications and are very popular with readers. Why else do magazines such as *People* and *Entertainment Weekly* boast large circulations? Why else are the inside front covers of *USA Weekend* and *Parade* among the best-read pages of those Sunday tabloids?

A snapshot profile can range from a one-paragraph blurb to an article that fills a single page. The story focuses on an interesting aspect of an interesting person's life. It might be little more than an update or an announcement or a breezy comment about a timely issue. In the case of a celebrity, it might result from a half-hour interview that a "vigilant publicist" has set up and monitored.

But all snapshots don't have to be lightweight efforts with limited journalistic value. A writer can assemble a series of snapshots into an "album" and publish the results as a round-up article. As an example, *Marriage Partnership* magazine won a first-place award from the Evangelical Press Association in 2003 for a round-up article called "Happily Even After." The writer, Paul Kortepeter, wrote short profiles (about 500 words each) on four married couples who had stayed together and were "happily even after" experiencing a variety of hardships.

Other round-up articles composed of several short profiles might be: Five entrepreneurs offer advice on how to start a home-based business; four female members of Congress explain what it's like to be "Ladies of the House."

Round-up articles can give comprehensive coverage to a topic by including various points of view from people who see the issue through a range of lenses.

CHOOSING THE RIGHT FORMAT

A profile article can take many shapes and forms, and the versatile and marketable writer is able to tune into a publication's style and produce the kind of profile that the editors and readers want. As different as portrait, photograph and snapshot profiles are, they should share two characteristics: accuracy and truthfulness.

That said, a writer has flexibility in deciding which quotations to integrate into the story, which characteristics to emphasize, how many details to include and what kind of tone to adopt. Those decisions will determine if the profile emerges as a quick take, a positive glimpse or an in-depth study. The writer, in consultation with the editor, also will decide whether the profile will take the form of a traditional article or if it will be packaged as a question-and-answer conversation.

Many newspaper and magazine editors are including one or more question-and-answer articles in each edition of their publications. As examples: A recent issue of *Newsweek* contained six Q & A articles based on interviews with a film star, a doctor, a politician, two business executives and an entrepreneur; a special section of *The Wall Street Journal* that dealt with "All Things Digital" featured eight Q & A articles in which *WSJ* staff members interviewed experts who ranged from Microsoft's Bill Gates to media mogul Rupert Murdock.[4]

An article that follows a Q & A format typically begins with a narrative paragraph (or several) that sets up the conversation. This introductory section serves a variety of purposes. It gives you, the writer, an opportunity to describe the backdrop against which the interview took place. You can weave in enough biographical information about your subject so readers will understand who the person is and what makes her an interesting subject for a profile article. You also set the tone for the interview—casual, chatty, formal, academic—by your choice of language and the "attitude" that comes forth in your questions.

The article that we offer as an example is a Q & A interview with Meredith Vieira, co-host of television's *Today* show. The opening paragraphs (about 350 words) accomplish at least three goals. First, they remind readers who Vieira is. Although she has been a TV presence for many years as part of such high-profile broadcasts as "60 Minutes," "The View" and the syndicated "Who Wants to Be a Millionaire," she is not as well known as Katie Couric, the person she replaced on *Today*. Second, the paragraphs fill in a lot of background that chronicles the run-up to her current job. Readers learn how the offer and her acceptance played out. Third, this introductory section establishes the tone of what will follow. By using slang ("At first I wrote it off . . .") and offering a behind-the-scenes look at Vieira's early-morning routine, the writer creates an informal tone. The purpose of the interview is to provide an update on her career and to let readers know how she has settled into her high-profile job.

As you read the article, pay attention to the questions that the interviewer asks and how these questions steer the conversation. They aren't random. They have direction, and they are designed to give readers a peek at Vieira when she isn't on camera.

MORNINGS WITH MEREDITH[5]

Replacing Katie Couric as Matt Lauer's sidekick on the "Today" show was a risky career move for veteran journalist Meredith Vieira. Would the public accept her? Would the ratings hold? Would she ever get used to the 3 a.m. wake-up call?

Meredith Vieira's alarm clock, strategically placed on husband Richard's side of the bed, blasts forth at 2:30 a.m. She allows herself 30 minutes of extra doze time before reluctantly padding downstairs to where Jasper, Felipe and Sweet Pea await their breakfast. "They're on my schedule," says Vieira, explaining the eating habits of the family's dog and cats. The "schedule" is dictated by Meredith's job as co-host of "Today," NBC's venerable morning news show now in its 56th year.

Replacing the popular Katie Couric as the program's co-anchor in 2006 was a risky career move for Vieira. She had been comfortably juggling her roles as host of "Who Wants to Be a Millionaire" and moderator of "The View" when rumors circulated about Couric's likely jump to CBS. Even before the gossip was confirmed, a network honcho had approached Vieira: Would she be interested in Couric's job? Would she at least consider the possibility?

"At first I wrote it off," she recalls. "I'm not a big morning person, and although I talk a good game, I'm scared of change. Besides, I didn't feel it would fit into my life." Her family disagreed. At their urging she met with the show's regulars—Matt Lauer, Al Roker and Ann Curry—and the chemistry seemed right. Heck, she and Lauer even discovered they have the same birthday. "Finally I got out of my fetal position and thought *I'll kick myself if I don't do this!* That was it. I knew I'd regret it if I didn't take the chance." The transition was seamless. Two years later, "Today" continues to enjoy a commanding lead over its chief competitor, "Good Morning America." The show hasn't missed a beat, and Vieira hasn't missed a wake-up call.

The Post recently sat down with Meredith on a Friday, at the end of another long workday. Since taking her place next to Lauer at the anchor desk that morning she had chatted with visiting celebrities, updated viewers on the race for the White House, tracked a band of violent storms in the Midwest, issued warnings about nursing homes predators, discussed a dip in the stock market . . . and the list goes on.

All this, and it was only 9 a.m.

For someone who claims she's not a morning person, you look and sound amazingly perky. So, let's back up to Jasper, Felipe, and Sweet Pea. Walk us through your day before you go on camera. What happens after you dish up the pet chow?

Vieira: It's funny . . . I still have this feeling of guilt if I don't leave my mark—the Mom Mark—on the house. At that hour of the morning it usually comes down to me tidying up a room or washing any dishes that are in the sink. I head out the door about 4:30 a.m., and since we're only

20 miles north of the city, I usually get to the studio around 5. Then the staff wanders in and we start the process of doing my hair, applying makeup, and gluing on my eyelashes so I look halfway decent. After I get dressed, the producers and researchers come in and we go through the rundown for the show. I already know what to expect, but there are often last-minute changes. I'll get a call from the control room saying they've dropped or added an interview. They try to have all the ducks in a row, but with news, you never know what's going to happen. Then Matt and I take turns doing the cross talks with our affiliates across the country. That's when a local news anchor says, "Let's go to New York now and see what's going to be on the 'Today' show." By 7 o'clock we're in our places and the train pulls out of the station.

Let's fast forward to 9 a.m. when your part of the show is over. How do you decompress?

Meredith: I come back here to the dressing room where I hang out. We often have news updates for the West Coast because it's three hours earlier out there. Sometimes I just sit, have a cup of coffee, read the newspapers or call friends. I always check in at home to make sure everybody got to school on time. That's it. At 10 o'clock I write my blog and then I try to get out of here.

Speaking of your blog, it seems that the demands on a high-profile journalist like yourself have really soared. In addition to your day job, you're expected to keep a blog for the fans, pop up occasionally on Leno's show, and choose a charity to champion. How do you make time for yourself?

Meredith: It's hard; but I think it's hard for any working mom to find time for herself. Even when we do, we often feel guilty because of the millions of things we could be doing for our families. Whenever I carve out time—whether it's taking a walk, reading a book or going to a movie—I always feel better for having done it. I think it's kind of dangerous not to do something for ourselves. We need to get away from it all and recharge ourselves emotionally.

Co-hosting America's most popular morning show is enough to inflate anyone's ego. What keeps you humble?

Meredith: I think I have stuff in perspective. I have a family that certainly keeps me humble. Being a celebrity is a very temporary thing, and if you take it too seriously no good can come of it. I started in this business as a reporter, which meant that my job was to record the stories of others. A lot of journalists have been turned into celebrities, but it certainly doesn't begin that way.

As an interviewer you have to know what's going on in the world, you need a heightened sense of curiosity, and you must be able to ask good questions. How did your parents instill these traits?

Meredith: I was probably always a curious kid. My brother, Jeff, and I started a neighborhood newspaper when we were about 12 or 14. We called it a newspaper but it was really just an opportunity to spy on people and report the gossip in town. I had forgotten about that until my parents reminded me of it after I got into the business. They thought journalism was in my blood even back then. Come to think of it, maybe there's a genetic component. My grandfather was editor of one of the first Portuguese-American newspapers on the East Coast. Also, my dad was always a curious guy. He was a doctor—a general practitioner—and would bring home a lot of stories about his medical practice. We used to have great conversations around the dinner table, back when families still ate as families.

As the only little girl seated around the dinner table, how did you hold your own with three big brothers?

Meredith: My mom was a very opinionated lady. Back then, gender mattered, and she was concerned that I take control of my life and never let the fact that I'm a female hold me back. She always said, "You can do whatever the guys do . . . and even more!" I'm sure that bothered my brothers to no end.

Throughout your career at "60 Minutes," "The View" and "Today" you've been part of an ensemble team of journalists. On camera the friendships seem very real. How genuine are they?

Meredith: The camera doesn't lie. The relationships and genuine affections are real; you can't fake them, at least not for long without people picking up on the stress. There's a natural chemistry that exists on the "Today" show. It's a very comfortable fit. The point of the broadcast is to help everybody shine as individuals and as a group. We're a family, and it's important that we operate as a family. I think that's what people want in the morning.

As the newest member of the family, did you ever doubt that it was going to work? Was there a moment when you heaved a sigh of relief and said, "Yes, this was a good decision"?

Meredith: Every day I wonder if this is going to work! Once you're a part of a show you feel such an obligation to succeed. I wanted to fit in as cohesively and smoothly as possible. That was my goal, and everybody made me feel at home from day one. The longer I do it, the greater my comfort level. Of course it was a big change for the audience, too. The blog was a decision of the network executives who saw it as a way for people to get to know me.

The transition to the new job was followed by a transition at home. Your oldest son, Ben, left for college and Gabe is shopping for a campus. That leaves daughter Lily at home. Are you suffering from out-of-the-nest syndrome yet?

Meredith: Not yet, but it will be interesting when Lily is gone in another three years. That will be a tricky dance. Richard and I have begun talking about what our next step will be . . . whether we'll move into the city or stay where we are. The family dynamics have changed since Ben left for school. We're getting used to it, but when he comes home for a visit it's always sad to say goodbye when he has to go back. Change isn't easy.

Career-wise, you've got a busy agenda in the coming weeks and months—a couple of national political conventions, the Olympics in China, and a presidential election in November. Do you ever think about the distant future? What will Meredith Vieira be doing in, say, five or 10 years?

Meredith: I don't think that far ahead, which is probably shortsighted of me. Let's see . . . I could see myself behind the camera creating documentaries, or I could see myself being totally out of this business, puttering around the house or being a pediatric clown. That's something I've done in the past, and was very fulfilled by it. We dressed up as clowns and visited children who were very ill in the hospital. I loved doing it. Really, all I want is to be content in my life and know that those people around me are happy and secure. The rest takes care of itself. One of the reasons I think I fell into the news business in the first place is because I have the attention span of a two-year-old child. I like a lot of things and can see myself floating from one thing to another and being totally satisfied. The great thing about the "Today" show is that within the two-hour time frame, that's exactly what I get to do.

ENDNOTES

[1] Peter Jacobi, *The Magazine Article* (Bloomington: Indiana University Press, 1991), 217.

[2] David Remnick, *Life Stories* (New York: Random House, 2000), ix.

[3] Ibid., xi.

[4] "Technology: The Journal Report," *The Wall Street Journal*, June 9, 2008, R section.

[5] Holly G. Miller, "Mornings with Meredith," *The Saturday Evening Post*, Aug. 2008, 48–51.

WRITING DRAMATIC STORIES

Your takeaway . . .

Everyone loves a good story. Magazines always look for inter-esting stories about everyday people and writers who can tell those stories. In this chapter, you will learn how to recognize, construct and write true-life stories. We explain the character-istics of a good story and practical tips on writing the story. You will also learn how to recognize the most common plots, including "failure to success," "victim to survivor," "danger to safety," "chaos to meaning," "saving the world" and "love con-quers all."

During spring break, Daniel Moreno, Brian Stanley and 23 other students from Westfield State College in Massachusetts sunned on the beaches and partied around Acapulco, Mexico. After returning to their hotel room late one night, Moreno and Stanley heard shattering glass. Rushing out on the fourth-floor balcony, they saw black smoke and realized the hotel was on fire. Joined by fellow student Drew Nalewanski, they spent the next hour banging on the doors of the hotel's 502 rooms, shouting "fire" to wake their fellow students and helping them all escape the fire. Although a few suffered smoke inhalation, no one was seriously injured. The three Massachusetts students returned home as local heroes.[1]

"Heroes: Close Call in a Hotel Fire," was published in *Reader's Digest* and offers a good example of a dramatic story. The story is reprinted at the end of this chapter. Popular with many types of magazines, these true stories tell how a central character or characters encounter a complicating situa-tion that they fight to overcome.

Don McKinney, a former editor with *McCall's* and *The Saturday Evening Post*, says these true-life dramas don't usually make national headlines.

"In most cases, they are things that happen to ordinary people, in out-of-the-way places and get reported on, if at all, in local newspapers. These are the stories you should be watching for, and when you learn of one . . . then fire off a query. Your chances of a sale are excellent."

McKinney says he published hundreds of these types of stories during his years as a magazine editor. "Some of these writers were inexperienced in writing for magazines, and their first tries were pretty shaggy. But because they had good stories to tell, we wanted very much to help them succeed. We gave them detailed rewrite instructions, talked to them a number of times about their problems and helped them through several rewrites."[2]

This genre of writing has historical roots in the 1960s when *Esquire*, *Harper's*, *The New Yorker* and *Rolling Stone* pioneered the "New Journalism." Later called "literary nonfiction," its distinguishing characteristic was the use of fiction techniques in nonfiction reporting. Led by Tom Wolfe, Hunter Thompson, Truman Capote, Gay Talese, Joan Didion and others, these writers took the stories about people and reported them using the fiction techniques of narrative, dialogue, description and scene-by-scene reporting.

For example, Tom Wolfe wrote *The Right Stuff*, which chronicled the story of the seven Mercury astronauts, who were the first Americans launched into space and a new frontier. Wolfe's story later became a movie by the same name, which won four Academy Awards in 1983. Pulitzer Prize-winning author Tracy Kidder took these storytelling techniques further with his books *Among School Children* and *Among Friends*. His first book chronicled a difficult year in the life a third-grade schoolteacher, while *Among Friends* told about the year-long tribulations of two men living in a Massachusetts nursing home.

The plot of a good story looks like this: You introduce a main character or characters possessing enough admirable qualities to attract the empathy of readers. You introduce a situation that throws an obstacle or conflict in the person's path. You give your character a possible solution and show him trying to reach that solution. This same type of structure forms the plot for thousands of movies and novels. If you want to learn how to write true-life stories, then watch movies based on real events. Or read novels and study carefully the techniques that the writers use. Most novels have a lot of action, dialogue and character development.

Here are more examples of titles of true-life dramas from some magazines:

"A Haven For Molly" (how a baby girl abandoned on a rock at birth found a happy home with a loving family)—*Good Housekeeping*

"Dr. Ben Carson: Top Surgeon's Life-And-Death Struggle With Prostate Cancer"—*Ebony*

"Captain Southworth's Decision" (a 30-year-old bachelor and army captain adopts a 9-year-old Iraqi boy and brings him back to the United States)—*Guideposts*

The dramatic story can have a chronological span ranging from hours to years. Jon Franklin, a two-time Pulitzer Prize feature writer, explains how to write these kinds of stories in his famous book *Writing for Story*. This book contains the two Pulitzer Prize-winning stories he wrote as a reporter for *The Baltimore Sun*. The first story, "Mrs. Kelly's Monster," occurs within a few hours while a doctor operates on Mrs. Kelly to remove a life-threatening brain tumor. His other prize-winning feature, "The Ballad of Ole Man Peters," spans more than 50 years as an elementary-school dropout fights to overcome his poverty and lack of education. Eventually Mr. Peters earns a master's degree, learns five languages and becomes a respected academic librarian.

CHARACTERISTICS OF A GOOD STORY

These characteristics help you recognize a good story and guide your questions when you build a story and interview people. First, a good story has a sympathetic main character or characters. Good stories are about people. Second, it has a plot. That means the main character confronts and overcomes an obstacle to achieve a desired goal. Third, it has a resolution, which means the main character solves the problem. And fourth, it occurs at a specific time and place. That means it begins and ends at specific times in specific places. Novelist Kurt Vonnegut offered these five rules for writing, which apply to the writing of true-life stories:

1　Use the time of a total stranger in such a way that he or she will not feel the time was wasted.
2　Give the reader at least one character he or she can root for.

3 Every character should want something, even if it is only a glass of water.
4 Every sentence must do one of two things—reveal character or advance the action.
5 Start as close to the end as possible.[3]

Main character

The best stories tell about something that happened to one or two people, not to a large group of people. The best stories also focus on sympathetic characters—people who are easy to like because of their admirable qualities. Good writers know how to develop their characters. They do interviews that bring out admirable qualities such as courage, honesty or persistence—and display these qualities in telling their stories. Skilled interviewers write questions that elicit quotes that reveal character. External characteristics—the things people do or the groups they belong to—also reveal character. Does that mean you can't write a good story about bad people? Not at all, but it's more difficult. Truman Capote, who had already written several novels, wrote his first nonfiction book *In Cold Blood*, which chronicled the murder of a Kansas farm family by two itinerant drifters. His best-selling book was one of the pioneers of the "New Journalism" and later became a movie. Capote spent hundreds of hours interviewing the two murderers during their five years on death row prior to their execution. His compelling character development in this story revealed their deranged lives and at least gave the reader some sense of why they did what they did.

A good story should also focus on a series of events in a person's life. It isn't a profile. *Guideposts* advises prospective contributors in its writers' guidelines:

- Don't try to tell an entire life story. Focus on one specific happening in a person's life. The emphasis should be on one individual. Bring in as few people as possible so that the reader's interest stays with the dominant character.
- Don't leave unanswered questions. Give enough facts so that the reader will know what happened. Use description and dialogue to let the reader feel as if he were there, seeing the characters, hearing them talk. Dramatize the situation, the conflicts, the struggle, and then tell how the person was changed for the better or the problem was solved.

The Difference Between a Profile and a Dramatic Story

Don't confuse writing a profile with writing a true dramatic story. Think about the differences this way:

Profile	Dramatic story
• focuses on a person	• focuses on events in a person's life
• mixed chronology of events	• specific beginning, middle and ending
• no particular structure	• chronological structure
• assorted quotes and experiences	• contains a plot and an outcome

Plot

The deepest, oldest conflicts are few and simple: We struggle against nature, against ourselves and against each other. No one enjoys a saccharine-sweet story that is all goodness and light because we know that's not the way life is. On the other hand, no one enjoys a story full of suffering and evil that ends in sadness. We look for realism but also hope for redemption. The conflict between the way things are and the way things ought to be often creates the most compelling and powerful stories.

Jon Franklin describes this problem or conflict that the central characters overcome as a "complication." Another word is simply "plot." The plot drives the story's action by motivating the central characters. The plot may be a problem, accident or illness, failure or inspirational challenge faced by the central character.

Whether it's called a plot or a complication, it's simply any problem encountered by any man, woman or child. To create a story with literary value, a problem must meet two criteria. First, it must be a basic problem that everyone can relate to. "Basic" in this sense means related to issues that everyone faces: love and hate, life and death, sickness and health, joy and sadness, deprivation and abundance. The reader must be able to say, "I can relate to that."

"You can write about someone who has a peculiar problem. Not everyone has to have that particular problem, but the reader must identify with the dilemma itself or what it does to the person's family," says New York-based writer Judith Newman.[4]

The second criterion for a good complication is that it must matter enough to the central character that he or she is willing to struggle and fight to overcome it. That means a major problem and not a minor annoyance.

Not having enough money to stay in a five-star hotel is a complication. But it's not a basic problem because it doesn't threaten you with starvation or death. But getting caught in a burning hotel in Acapulco late at night is pretty basic. It threatens you and others with serious injuries and death. And you must take significant action to overcome the danger and escape the threat it poses to you and your friends.

The bond between a mother and child is basic to humanity; a complication occurs when that bond is threatened by external forces. One popular movie told about a mother's successful rescue of her daughter from a Middle Eastern country. The mother's divorced husband kidnapped the girl and took her to his native country. The bond between mother and daughter was threatened, and the mother made a dramatic effort to rescue her daughter. The complication was both basic and significant.

Resolution

The problem must have a resolution, or it won't fly with readers. That sounds harsh because everyone knows that life presents many sad problems without seeming solutions. That's okay because it's life, but readers of articles and books expect resolutions. A "resolution" doesn't necessarily mean a perfect or happy solution. It simply means the central character figures out a way to deal with it. Sometimes the resolution means the central character simply accepts an unhappy situation in life and decides to move on to other things.

Time and place

Think of a good story as one with (a) geography and (b) a clock. "Geography" means it's anchored in a real place that you can find on a map. The events you describe occur in specific towns, states and countries. The dramatic story tells what the main character did as he or she grew up in Atlanta, went to college in Chicago and started her career in Miami. Having a "clock" means the story began at a particular time and ended at a particular time. The amount of time within a good story can range from a few hours to dozens of years.

COMMON PLOTS

The following six types of plot themes run the risk of over-simplification because life isn't always this neatly divided. They do, however, characterize the most common types of themes found in stories. All good plots serve to create suspense and make the reader wonder how the story will end. These themes, therefore, begin with the type of problem or complication and end with the type of resolution.

"Failure to success"

Failure and success are common themes to everyone. The only person who never fails is one who never tries. Failure-to-success stories involve aspects of life as diverse as weight loss, finances, education, careers, romance and marriage.

Example: In "The Art of Rebounding," *Men's Health* profiled Randy Pfund, who achieved his lifetime dream of becoming head coach of a professional basketball team. However, after two dismal losing seasons, he was fired as head coach of the Los Angeles Lakers. After spending time reassessing his life, he decided to try something different. He went into sports management and became a chief executive for the Miami Heat team. In the same article, *Men's Health* profiled four others who achieved success after failure: Deborah Norville, television news anchor; Michael Dukakis, former Massachusetts governor and candidate for president; Dan O'Brien, Olympic athlete; and Barry Minkow, who became pastor of a large San Diego church after founding a company and serving time in prison for business fraud.[5]

A variation on this theme may not begin with outright failure, but start with an ordinary person in an ordinary situation who achieves great success at a task or career.

"Victim to survivor"

A victim receives unfair suffering inflicted by either the negligence or the malevolent intent of others. Victims result from incidents of crime, ignorance or simple accidents. The best victim/survivor stories have specific causes that you can easily describe. It's better to write about a girl who survives an abusive father and alcoholic mother than one who survives a "deprived childhood." It's better to write about a man forced by poverty to quit school in the fifth grade than one who grew up with "limited educational opportunities."

Example: In a *Reader's Digest* story, Richard and Penni Domikis watched their house in Fredericksburg, Va., burn down one night. That evening only began their suffering, however, after they discovered that their insurance company refused to pay for the full cost of rebuilding. The insurance company claimed that an obscure amendment on their original policy meant it didn't have to pay full replacement costs. The couple fought back and won.[6]

"Danger to safety"

The most common types of "danger to safety" stories involve people who overcome injuries, illnesses, danger and natural disasters. "Lost in the wilderness" and "accident recovery" stories have formed plots for many articles, books and movies. The best healing and recovery stories come from those that defy predictions because the sufferer has a courageous, determined desire to get well and return to normal life. These stories tell not just what happened but how it happened because of the sufferer's inner resolve and courage.

"Chaos to meaning"

In "chaos to meaning" stories, change occurs inside the central character more than in his or her outward circumstances. These stories are more difficult to write because you have to describe psychological, emotional or spiritual changes. A "chaos to meaning" story might describe how a man or woman finds new meaning in life after losing a spouse to death or divorce. For example, in "The Tender Mercy of Cheryl Kane" (*Good House-keeping*), a Boston nurse "lost all zest for life . . . the pain was just excruciating" after her middle-aged husband died. Cheryl Kane found new meaning in life working in a street outreach program giving medical care to the homeless.[7]

"Saving the world"

These "one person can make a difference" stories have a positive, inspirational quality. In this type of problem-resolution, a motivated citizen confronts a social problem and organizes the resources to bring about a solution.

Example: *Reader's Digest*, *Clarity* and other magazines told the story of a Los Angeles woman who founded "The Garden," a cemetery for babies who were abandoned by their mothers in dumpsters and trash bins. Debi Faris lobbied the California legislature to pass a "safe haven" law that allows young mothers to give up their babies for adoption without fear of retribution. (We offer a reprinted version of this story in Chapter 19.)

Another example: *The New Yorker* told the remarkable story of Zell Kravinsky, who grew up as the son of a poor Russian immigrant. After starting out as an inner-city schoolteacher, he began investing in real estate and eventually earned millions of dollars. After he gave away almost his entire $45 million real-estate fortune to charity, he felt he needed to do still more for humanity. So he donated a kidney to a complete stranger—something only 134 other Americans had ever done.[8]

"Love conquers all"

These stories follow a separation-reunion theme and also have a positive, upbeat tone. They can tell the story of the separation and reunion of lovers, of siblings, parents and children or even long-lost friends. Dozens of stories have been published about adopted children who located their biological parents after a long search. Many newspapers and magazines have published features telling about couples who were high-school sweethearts and, after graduation, married someone else. Many years later, their marriages ended in death or divorce. Then the sweethearts found each other, often with the help of the Internet, and rekindled their romance and married.

TIPS ON TELLING THE STORIES

Build suspense

Predictability kills a good story. The problem that you introduce must make the reader wonder how the story will turn out. That's why good mystery novels are best-sellers. People love to get hooked with a "page turner" and will read past midnight waiting to see how it turns out. That's why the plots described earlier introduce an element of unpredictability by their nature. For example:

Failure: Will he succeed?

Victim: Will she survive?

Danger: Will he escape?

Chaos: Will she discover meaning?

Meg Grant is a former *Reader's Digest* editor who has edited some of its "Drama in Real Life" stories that appear in every issue. She says, "These stories have to be told in a dramatic way in the same way a fiction writer would. The piece has to be crafted to be suspenseful and not give it all away in the first couple of paragraphs. You have to take the reader on this journey."[9]

Chronicle the events

Your job as a writer is to skillfully lead the reader through the actions taken by the central character to confront and resolve the problem. These events can be physical or psychological. Psychological events are more difficult to describe than physical events. Meg Grant edited a *Reader's Digest* story about a kayaker who was lost in the ocean for three days. She says, "There was some question about whether there would be enough sustained action—because basically he sat on a kayak for three days. There wasn't a whole lot that happened. But there was the mental action, the hallucinations, that really carried the piece."

She adds, "Sometimes you have these things happen too fast, and you can't make that work either. You can have a helicopter crash and everything happens in an instant. That wouldn't work as a dramatic narrative because you have to have some time that elapses and some different things that happen."[10]

An important part of that story is the plot point. It's the moment when the central character recognizes what he has to do to solve the problem that he faces. In the story about the insurance company that wouldn't pay for rebuilding the couple's house, Richard and Penni Domikis recognized they needed to take legal action when the company refused to budge. After Debi Faris learned that the county cremated and dumped abandoned babies in a communal grave, she realized that she needed to raise money and find land to create a cemetery for them.

Develop character

Character development is what novelists do best. Most journalists need some practice. Character development means creating empathy in the reader for the characters you are writing about. Character development will result from several interviews preceded by good preparation. You must not only get your subject to describe what happened, you must ask questions that will bring out her motivating values and beliefs. You must ask her not only what she said and did, but what she thought and felt as these events happened.

Revealing character may involve these dimensions of a person's life:

- **Work habits:** What people do for a living may not reveal as much about them as their work habits. Look for such characteristics as ambition, carelessness or laziness.
- **Family relationships:** Whether a person is single, married or has children is basic information. The details of those relationships, however, are more revealing of character, such as whether they are close and intimate or aloof and estranged.
- **Social affiliations:** Affiliations reveal character because someone who belongs to the American Civil Liberties Union, the Sierra Club or the United Auto Workers may possess different values than someone who is a member of the Rotary Club or the American Rifle Association.
- **Religion:** A person's religious affiliation or lack of affiliation also hints about their values and beliefs. A Southern Baptist differs in outlook and values from a Mormon or a Muslim. A practicing Buddhist evokes a different image than someone who is a practicing Presbyterian.

- **Moral beliefs:** Nothing is more basic to character than a person's ethical beliefs and practices. You have to look at what people do, as opposed to what they say, to show their moral character. Anecdotes and stories that reveal honesty are always refreshing to read.

Character is developed through effective and frequent use of dialogue. Dialogue and quotations are not the same. Dialogue occurs when two people talk to each other. Monologue, which originates from one person, is what writers normally call "getting quotes." Good quotes are better than no quotes, but conversation between two people really brings a story to life. Conversation also brings out the character of the people whose story you are telling.

Meg Grant says that *Reader's Digest* editors are trying to emphasize more character development in these stories. "Sometimes the action in these stories received more emphasis than the character development. Part of what we're trying to do now is put the character back in and make the character important. The mental and emotional journey is part of the story." When a freelance writer proposes one of these stories, "We need to know that the writer can focus on one or two characters, get in their heads and sort of go through what they went through psychologically," she says.

Create the ending

Happy endings are more fun to read than sad endings. Can a true-life story have a sad ending? Many human stories do, and we could all tell a few of our own. The more relevant question is whether readers accept an unhappy ending. Can you publish a story that has an unhappy ending? You can, but it's tricky and you have to handle it skillfully.

Think about yourself. When are you willing to watch a movie with an unhappy ending? Some sad movies end with a sense of closure and resolution, but others simply end. You leave the theater feeling like something was missing.

Readers will accept an unhappy ending if it leaves them with a sense of closure, resolution and meaning. The central character learns from his mistakes and decides to move on. The parent accepts the death of a child killed by a drunken driver and finds new meaning in lobbying for stricter drunk-driving laws. The victim of an accident accepts her disability and discovers a new talent that allows her to earn a living.

Just as there is no one right lead, there is no one right ending. If it is a sad ending, the reader knows it could end no other way. Find some image, quote or anecdote that ties together the theme of the story and brings it to an emotionally satisfying ending. The ending should leave the reader feeling satisfied, inspired or moved.

Finally, you can't write a great story until you find a great story. No amount of careful editing or literary polish will make a mundane story fascinating. Reading newspapers for short stories you can build from is one way to find them. Watching local TV news is another good way. Meeting people, engaging in conversations and asking a lot of questions is the best way. If you hear a story that moves, inspires or touches your heart, then you've probably found a good one that others will want to read.

Ten Tips for Telling Stories

1 Interview the central character several times and do supporting interviews with several friends or family members. A one-interview or one-source story never succeeds.
2 People, not places or things, create a story. Develop interview questions that will bring out not only the action, but your subject's values, beliefs and emotions.
3 When you interview your sources, ask them to tell you what they thought and felt at the time; not just what they said and did.
4 Look for the problem, conflict or tension that will provoke readers' curiosity and keep readers involved with the story.
5 Record dialogue and quotations accurately by using a recorder. Buy one if you don't have one. A writer always needs one.
6 Create complex, multi-dimensional characters. Reveal the faults and weaknesses of your heroes and the admirable qualities of your villains. No one is all saint or all sinner.
7 Find the meaning or "take home" value for readers in your story. What is the point of the piece? Is there a moral engine that drives the story? Make it more than simply a factual chronology.
8 Record little details about a person and the physical surroundings you are writing about. However, use only those details

SIDEBAR 2

that reveal character and move the story along. Don't include this description just for the sake of exercising your literary talents.

9   Spend time with the people you are writing about where they live and work. Hang around. Don't just depend on interviews in a neutral place. Capture the mood and ambience of their lives.

10   Set your story in its wider context. For example, if a person suffers from a rare disease, then do some research to provide details and context. Research the facts, statistics, issues or history of the larger issue that your story involves.

HEROES: CLOSE CALL IN A HOTEL FIRE

By Joseph Tirella

It would be dawn in less than an hour. For a week straight, Daniel Moreno, Brian Stanley, and 23 other juniors and seniors from Westfield State College in Massachusetts had relaxed on white-sand beaches and club-hopped around Acapulco, Mexico. On their last night, Moreno and Stanley, who'd been friends and workout buddies for years, partied until after 4 a.m. Now, back in the room they shared at Best Western Playa Suites, they figured it was time to turn in.

But as Stanley's head hit the pillow, he heard glass shattering and bolted upright. From the balcony of their fourth-floor room, Moreno and Stanley saw black smoke pouring from the hotel's adjoining tower. "We watched one window blow out, and then another, and heard people shouting," says Stanley, 21. Students were throwing ropes made from twisted bedsheets off their balconies, and a couple of them were trying to climb down. "There was so much smoke, they couldn't see five feet in front of them," says Nalewanski, left, with Moreno and Stanley.

Moreno, also 21, ran out into the corridor and began pounding on doors and shouting, "Westfield!" and "Fire!"

"Some people thought we were joking," says Stanley, a criminal-justice major who is a volunteer firefighter in his hometown of Thomaston, Connecticut. "But after they saw the smoke, they didn't think it was funny anymore."

Almost all the hotel's 502 rooms were filled with college students from across the United States. "People were yelling, 'What the hell is going on?' and trying to get out," says Ryan Senecal, a 21-year-old junior who had a room on the second floor. "It was pure chaos." Because of the hour, the students were on their own; only a minimal staff was on duty. The smoke was attributed to a fire in a laundry chute, say authorities. And while a spokesperson for the hotel—which suffered smoke damage and was closed for several days—asserts that the fire alarm system had passed inspection just two weeks earlier, several students have insisted it was not working that night. "I pulled an alarm and nothing happened," says Drew Nalewanski, 22, a business management major.

As the smoke thickened, Moreno raced upstairs to where other Westfield students were rooming. "I thought of all their parents back home," he says. "It motivated me."

Meanwhile, Stanley was downstairs helping people get through the smoke-filled lobby. There he joined forces with Nalewanski, who comes from four generations of firefighters. Just back from his own night out, Nalewanski had come across the first group of students to get out, who were milling around outside the hotel's entrance. Many were wearing only shorts and T-shirts and were clutching their passports.

"Let's go," Nalewanski said. He and Stanley wet their shirts in the lobby bathroom and wrapped them around their mouths and noses so they could breathe. Then they charged up the stairs.

In the meantime, Moreno had made it up to the eighth floor before turning back. "Kids had no idea what was going on," he says. "I was screaming at the top of my lungs. I made sure I hit every door."

Nalewanski and Stanley found Moreno on the fourth floor, vomiting and struggling to breathe. After making sure he could get back down on his own, they continued upstairs, down the corridors on every floor, slamming their fists on every door.

Protected by their makeshift masks, the two fought their way to the top, then turned around and began their descent. By then, says Stanley, "there wasn't any air. My throat and lungs just burned."

In the end, while a few students were treated for smoke inhalation, no one was seriously hurt. Even more incredible, all the Westfield students made it back to Massachusetts later that same day.

The trio have become local heroes. But Stanley didn't crow to his friends. "I told a couple of them. Then I started getting calls from other people, asking, 'Why didn't you tell me?'" he says. "But I didn't think it was that big a deal."

Westfield president Evan Dobelle disagrees. "I have a great deal of pride in these young men and how they were able to react in such an emergency," he says.

How much danger were they in? "My roommate thought I was stuck inside," says Nalewanski. "They all thought we were dead."

Trying to describe how he found his courage that morning, Moreno says, "You run on adrenaline, and your instincts tell you it's the right thing to do. There were hundreds of people in the hotel. It was our obligation to help them."

ENDNOTES

[1] Joseph Tirella, "Heroes: Close Call in a Hotel Fire," *Reader's Digest*, July 2008. Reprinted with permission.

[2] Don McKinney, *Magazine Writing That Sells* (Cincinnati, Ohio: Writer's Digest Books, 1993), 104.

[3] Kurt Vonnegut, *Bagombo Snuff Box: Uncollected Short Fiction* (New York: G.P. Putnam's Sons, 1999), 9–10.

[4] Telephone interview with David E. Sumner, Dec. 11, 2003.

[5] Bruce Schoenfeld, "The Art of Rebounding," *Men's Health*, Jan.-Feb. 2003, 114–119.

[6] M. Robicheau, "Raked Over the Coals," *Reader's Digest*, Nov. 2002, 124–129.

[7] Elizabeth Gehrman, "The Tender Mercy of Cheryl Kane," *Good Housekeeping*, Jan. 2004, 79–83.

[8] Ian Parker, "The Gift," *The New Yorker*, Aug. 2, 2004, 54–63.

[9] Telephone interview with David E. Sumner, Nov. 29, 2003.

[10] Ibid.

16

HELP! WRITING THE HOW-TO FEATURE

Your takeaway . . .

"Service" articles help readers solve problems and achieve desired outcomes. Many how-to features follow a four-part formula that includes an introduction, segue, steps and conclusion. Sometimes writers package how-to advice in bullets, and sometimes they parcel it in paragraph form. Either way, the success of these articles depends on interviewing savvy experts and delivering their tips in simple language. This chapter offers advice on how to write how-to features.

We live in an "ER" world. Everyone is trying to be thinner, richer, smarter, happier, healthier and safer. Some people want to look younger longer; others hope to achieve professional success faster so they can buy a larger home sooner. This insatiable hunger for improvement has resulted in best-selling books with upbeat titles (*Becoming a Better You: Seven Keys to Improving Your Life Every Day*), popular television networks (HGTV and the Food Network) and hundreds of how-to articles in magazines and newspapers across the country. The instructions can be as lightweight as how to build a better burger, included in a special BBQ issue of *bon appétit*,[1] or as serious as how to instill ethics in teenagers for *Living With Teenagers*.[2] Forget the old advice that writers should write about what they know. How-to articles enable curious writers to research and write about what they would *like* to know.

It's a fact: How-to articles sell magazines. Imagine that you're walking through an airport en route to catch a flight. You pause briefly at a news-stand to pick out a couple of magazines to pass the time between naps. How do you choose among this month's issues of *People, Vanity Fair* or

Elle? What causes you to reach for *Fitness* rather than *Self?* Your flight is boarding; you only have a few seconds to make your decision, so you can't dawdle over the tables of contents. If you're like most magazine buyers, you make your selection based on two factors.

- First, the face featured on the cover tells you that a profile article is inside the issue. (See Chapter 14, Profiles.) If the person—usually an A-list celebrity—interests you, chances are you'll buy the magazine to learn more about the personality behind the photo.
- Second, the cover lines highlight the most provocative contents. We discussed these four- to six-word blurbs in Chapter 3, but now it's time to consider the psychology behind them. One editor we know describes cover lines as little "marquees"—usually arranged on either or both sides of the celebrity's cover photograph—that showcase key articles inside. Editors write cover lines carefully because they know the impact that the blurbs have on single-copy sales.

Among the most successful cover lines are those that promote how-to articles. Many newsstand browsers will buy a publication because a how-to article, touted on the magazine's cover, has succeeded in its mission to grab the attention of shoppers.

LOOKING FOR ANSWERS

How-to articles fall into the general category of "service articles" because they promise to be of benefit or service to readers. Some service articles impart information in standard paragraph form; others take a more instructional approach and walk readers through detailed steps arranged in a 1–2–3 or bulleted format. The unspoken message of a how-to article is: "If you buy this magazine, read this article and follow this advice you'll be better, smarter, happier, thinner, richer" or some other desirable characteristic. How-to articles are mainstays of home remodeling and decorating magazines—think *This Old House* or *Martha Stewart Living*—but they're equally appropriate for publications that focus on fitness, business, women, travel, gardening, sports or investments. Editors like them because they invite readers to get involved and experiment with the advice that the authors share.

Some magazines use bullets to cluster entire packages of advice, which they tout under single headings on their covers. The assumption seems to be that if one bulleted story doesn't grab your attention, perhaps the next one will. As an example, a summer issue of *Prevention* promised to give readers:

Easy New Ways to:

- live longer
- conquer pain naturally
- boost heart health
- fight cancer
- get your energy back[3]

Kiplinger's Personal Finance magazine took a similar approach when the editors assembled a timely package that was circulated during the height of an economic slowdown. The heading suggested that readers could:

Beat the High Cost of:

- gas!
- food!
- credit!
- & more![4]

In both of these examples, the "how-to" element is understood even though the exact words aren't articulated. Each of the bulleted topics could be expressed in more predictable language: "How to live longer;" "How to conquer pain naturally;" "How to get your energy back;" and "How to beat the high cost of gas."

KEYS TO SUCCESSFUL SERVICE FEATURES

The most effective service articles share three important characteristics. Their topics are specific and timely; the author shapes the information to meet the needs of a tightly defined audience; the advice is fresh and comes from credible sources.

The more specific and timely the how-to article is, the more irresistible it is to the reader. An article that promises to tell golfers "How to Shave Five Strokes off Your Game This Winter" is more powerful than merely "How to Play Better Golf." An article that outlines "Three Steps to Beating the Holiday Blues" is more engaging than "How to Overcome Depression." Whatever the words, the underlying promise is that this article is going to give readers information that they can use in their lives *right now* to reap quick, positive results.

Because how-to articles address readers' current concerns, the writer must tune into the issues that are on the minds of the target audience. A cover line in *Marie Claire* magazine touched a nerve at a time when many companies were downsizing and distributing pink slips to employees: "How to Survive a Layoff—and Spot One Coming." The topic was especially pertinent for the publication's readers, whose median age is 33 and 76 percent of whom are working women.[5]

Shaping an article to fit the audience often involves doing research on the topic, followed by additional research on the anticipated readership. When novelist Shirley Jump was launching her career as a freelance journalist, she looked for how-to topics that she could sell and resell to a variety of publications. As an example, she would research a broad subject such as "How to Buy Health Insurance for Your Employees" and then tweak it for different audiences. "Every industry has to buy health insurance," she explains. Her core research on health insurance would remain the same, but one article might advise small business owners on buying health insurance, a second article might offer tips on buying insurance for a large, blue-collar workforce.[6]

Another way to shape an article to fit its readers is by writing in a style and tone that is conversational for the audience. Aware that the *Marie Claire* article on surviving a layoff would be read by young, professional females, author Lea Goldman chose this lead: "Here's a stark news flash: The pink slip is back, big time. Call it the latest grim reminder of these hard times, alongside gas prices inching to $4 a gallon and higher prices on everything from Cheerios to chicken wings."[7]

The final key characteristic of effective service articles—fresh advice from credible sources—is the one that students frequently ignore. Beginning writers too often cast themselves as the "experts" who are sharing information with readers. A writer may have a genuine interest in and some knowledge about a topic, but that doesn't qualify him as a quotable expert. In addition to facts gathered during interviews, the service journalist also uncovers statistics and other data from recent studies, surveys and reports. As an example, the article about "How to Survive a Layoff" contained current unemployment numbers and the names of well-known companies that had cut jobs in recent months.

FOUR STEPS TO THE HOW-TO ARTICLE

Popular how-to articles often are very specific, relatively short—1,200 to 1,500 words—and usually contain four parts, the last of which is optional. Here's the formula that many writers follow:

- introduction
- transition
- steps/tips
- wrap-up (optional)

Because the goal of a how-to article is to instruct or educate readers, the author wants to get to the points as quickly as possible. The introduction is sometimes the only place that the writer can exhibit creativity; even so, the opening paragraph should be short and tightly written. The "job" of the introduction is to set up the rest of the article. Let's look at two examples of effective introductions.

Ask a question

For a January issue of *CompuServe Magazine,* a how-to article about tension and stress began this way: "Prediction: This year—if it's anything like last— more than 65 percent of all visits to family doctors will be for stress-related problems. What are some quick techniques for relieving pressure on and off the job? Allan Stevens, manager of the Health and Fitness Forum, suggests four easy stressbusters that can reduce tension and boost energy."[8]

The topic of stress is an old one, but the author makes the article timely by opening with a New Year's prediction (remember, this is a January issue) and a surprising statistic (again, fresh research is a key to all how-to articles). Since the article was packaged as a sidebar to a major story with a title that suggested that readers should "Make Wellness Your First New

Year's Resolution," it could occupy only one page in the magazine. The limited space required the writer to move from the introduction to the four steps/tips very quickly. She used a question ("What are some quick techniques for relieving pressure on and off the job?") to set up the heart of the sidebar article. Each of the four steps was given a boldface subheading and then explained in a paragraph or two.

Create a scene

A scenario is another good way to introduce a how-to article. An introduction that describes a brief moment that readers can relate to is particularly effective if they've been in a similar situation. Example: Say you are writing an article titled "How to Make a Speech . . . and Survive!" Chances are, readers who have suffered wobbly knees and near-panic attacks when standing in front of an audience will want to learn how to ease their nervousness. The writer establishes additional common ground with readers with this introduction:

> Your heart was pounding as you took a final gulp of ice water and blotted your mouth with the napkin. Breathe deeply, you told yourself. Inhale . . . one, two, three . . . exhale . . . one, two, three. Why had you ever accepted the invitation to speak at the mother-daughter banquet?
>
> The waiter cleared the last dish from the head table, and the emcee began her introduction. There was no turning back. You were on.[9]

Having grabbed the reader's attention with the scenario, the writer next creates a transition sentence or paragraph and introduces the expert. This person might assure readers that they can survive the ordeal of making a speech if they will follow five (or whatever number you choose) easy steps. These steps, often packaged in a bullet format, offer specific strategies to help readers through their next public-speaking obligation. The bullets, containing words of advice from one or more experts whom you've interviewed, might look like this:

- **Slow down:** Sometimes nervousness causes you to speak too fast. Prof. John Smith suggests that when you rehearse your speech you should keep an eye on the clock. "Try to talk at a rate of about 120 words per minute," he recommends.

- **Dress code:** Strive for a look that is slightly more formal than your audience, says fashion coordinator Mary Brown. A navy blue suit and crisp white shirt will help you feel like the cool professional that you are. As an added benefit, the jacket will provide a dark background that will hide the inevitable clip-on microphone.

The most credible experts are those who have impressive titles, important positions and a wealth of experience. Strive for variety. In the bulleted pieces of advice above, the sources have a blend of professional training and field experience. Note, too, each piece of advice is supported by a quote or by an illustration.

And in closing . . .

The final element of a how-to article is the optional conclusion. If you have a strong wrap-up comment from one of your expert sources, this is where to use it. Otherwise, you can merely end the article with the last step or tip. Remember: It was the advice rather than your clever introduction or closing paragraph that attracted the reader to your article in the first place.

DELIVER THE GOODS

A how-to article must deliver what it promises. If a title and cover line promise an article that will explain how to relieve pressure on the job or how to survive a public-speaking ordeal, the article inside should offer new information from reliable experts. You damage your credibility by luring readers into an article with a provocative title and then rehashing information that is common knowledge or easy to find on the Internet. This was the case several years ago when a women's magazine offered this cover line on a December issue: "How to Look Like You've Lost 10 Pounds Overnight." Readers who bought the magazine were dismayed by the article's tired suggestions: Wear something black and remember to stand up straight.

A good service article should cause readers to clip and save the steps and tips. These steps should be so creative that readers cut them out, tack them on bulletin boards, tuck them under magnets on their refrigerator doors and stuff them into their wallets and purses.

TANGIBLE VS. INTANGIBLE HOW-TO ARTICLES

Most how-to articles fall into either the tangible or the intangible category. The tangible variety offers steps that, if followed, will lead to the creation of an object or an event. The results are visible. Three examples of this type of service articles are:

- "How to Plan a Garden Wedding Under $500"
- "How to Launch a Home-Based Business"
- "How to Create a Low-Maintenance Garden"

Keys to writing a successful tangible how-to article are to keep the directions simple and illustrate the directions with examples and anecdotes. Too many steps can overwhelm and confuse readers. One way to avoid a complex topic is to narrow the focus. Example: "How to Plan a Garden Wedding Under $500." This variation of a broader article—"How to Plan the Perfect Wedding"—limits the focus by season (summer), location (garden) and budget ($500).

Intangible how-to articles often are described as "self-help" articles and reap results that may not be visible. Instead, they may involve personal changes. Three examples of this popular category are:

- "How to Be More Content in Your Job"
- "How to Control Your Jealousy"
- "How to Cope with Failure"

The types of expert sources will vary widely, depending on which type of how-to article you write. For the tangible service article you will want to talk with persons with first-hand experience and a great deal of expertise in the topic—a wedding planner, a small-business owner, a landscape architect who has created dozens of low-maintenance gardens. Remember, your best friend isn't a quotable expert on weddings just because she planned her own ceremony. She may make a good anecdote or an example, but she does not have the credentials necessary to serve as your expert source.

For an intangible how-to article you typically will interview a person with impressive academic degrees or formal training in the topic—a counselor or a psychologist. Otherwise, the article will have what we call the "authority problem." This means that the author writes in his or her own voice, doesn't give examples and fails to quote experts or authorities about the subject of the article. The reader may distrust the information and react by thinking, "Who says so?" As an example, we recall a writer who once wrote about how to use proper nutrition and vitamins in solving common medical problems. Since she had no training in medicine or nutrition, we questioned her authority in giving advice on the issue.

HOW-TO ARTICLES AS SIDEBARS

Editors often want article packages. These packages generally include a main story plus related sidebars, graphics and other illustrations. Taken together, a package can be more visually attractive than a single article because it involves several elements that break up a text-heavy page. The package also benefits readers because it offers variety and choice. A reader can read any or all of the elements on the page. How-to articles often make good sidebar accompaniments to long articles. Here are some examples:

Main Article	**How-to Sidebar**
Five Off-Season Honeymoon Cruises	How to Pack for a Week at Sea
Road Rage Heats Up	How to Keep Your Cool
Training Tips for Your First Marathon	How to Choose the Right Shoes

When packaged as a sidebar, a how-to article should not exceed one-fourth of the length of the main story. It shouldn't repeat any information or quote the same sources as the article that it accompanies. It complements the main story and is placed in close proximity to the major feature. Many readers choose to read sidebars before they decide whether to read the longer story. Because of their short length, sidebars seem less intimidating and require less of a commitment on the part of readers.

WHERE TO LOOK FOR HOW-TO IDEAS

Because the how-to article is in demand at most magazines and newspapers, writers interested in earning bylines and building portfolios should master the format. Where are the best ideas for how-to articles? A writer's personal experience is the most obvious place to begin the search for topics. For example, we know an animal activist who created a series of how-to articles aimed at pet owners, pitched the articles to the features editor of her community's daily newspaper and was rewarded with a weekly column. Even with her extensive knowledge of animals, this writer probably couldn't sustain a column for several months (or years) if she depended only on her personal experience. She supplements her knowledge by frequently interviewing veterinarians, trainers and other experts who provide a stream of fresh insights and information.

Sometimes it's fun to brainstorm with friends about problems they would like someone to solve or questions they would like someone to answer. *More Magazine* came up with a list of 18 "things you should know by now" for their target readers (female, age 40+). The result was a package of short how-to articles that told readers how to: bluff at poker, make an entrance, get a passport at the last minute, overcome writer's block, put out a fire, make a sales call, etc. Each standalone article contained a nugget of valuable advice from an expert. A television actress offered tips on how a woman can make a dramatic entrance to a room; a successful novelist provided ideas on beating writer's block; a Georgia firefighter suggested ways to put out a fire.[10]

Another way to discover viable how-to topics is to think in terms of crossroads. People typically face many crossroads in their lives—decision points where they must choose to follow one course of action or another. They look for help in making the right decisions at these crossroads, and help can come in the form of how-to articles. Here are several examples:

Crossroad	How-to Article
Graduation	How to Master the Job Interview
Serious relationship	How to Know if You're Compatible for Life
Buying a home	How to Avoid Hidden Closing Costs
Retirement	How to Know When to Go
Family illness	How to Choose the Right Nursing Home

Because today's magazines are so specialized, you can tune into a publication's demographics and surmise the decisions—minor and major—that its readers are likely to face. For instance, *Child* magazine is obviously aimed at families with young children. In its promotional letter to prospective subscribers, it promises articles that will show parents how to choose kids' books, pick the best preschool, solve sleep problems and decorate a nursery. On the other end of the age spectrum, *More Magazine* appeals to prospective subscribers in its letter by promising articles that will help readers learn how to "unscramble your nest egg," how to rejuvenate vitality with natural products and how to survive an adult child who moves back home.

An obvious place to look for how-to article ideas is within the back issues of the publications that you plan to approach. Many magazines have perennial how-to topics, and they are always looking for fresh angles and new sources. For example, *Prevention* magazine runs some variation of a "how to lose weight" article in almost every issue. *Runner's World* frequently revisits the topic of how to choose running shoes. *Consumer Reports* tells readers several times a year how to purchase some kind of computer hardware.

Another place to look for strong how-to article ideas is in broadcast and print media that typically report new research and surprising statistics. A retirement bulletin, for example, revealed that in the next 18 years, an American will turn 50 every 18 seconds and that more than 22 million Americans are in their 50s. The smart writer takes those bits of information and asks: What kinds of help will these people need to cope with all the changes they will face in the upcoming years? What crossroads will they encounter? What how-to articles will they be interested in reading? The answers should keep writers supplied with enough ideas to explore for a long, long time.

PULLING IT ALL TOGETHER

The following article was among the winners in the 2008 annual writing competition sponsored by the Association for Education in Journalism & Mass Communication. Author Josh Patterson, a student at The University of Kansas, used a conversational tone to share advice with fellow students about giving bicycles a spring tune-up. Although the article is less than 700 words in length, the author conducted four interviews with knowledgeable sources. He also established his own credentials in the second paragraph.

DUSTING OFF THE GEARS[11]

A tune-up and some springtime TLC will keep your hip ride rolling smoothly all year long.

By Josh Patterson

It's been a long winter. If you feel weary of the endless days of rain, sleet and snow, rest assured that your bicycle suffers with you. Whether you neglected your trusty steed by leaving it locked outside your dorm or actually braved the ice and salt-covered streets, your bike will last longer if you give it a little care each spring.

Years of working in bicycle shops have taught me the value of preventive maintenance. Spending a little time and money to keep your bike rolling and shifting smoothly keeps your bike from becoming a money pit. Andrew Slater, Overland Park junior, is one of those intrepid souls who brave the elements to commute to class each day. To cut down on maintenance, he wipes down his bicycle's drivetrain with warm water after each ride and lubes his chain once a week.

Jordan Ferrand-Sapsis, a bicycle mechanic at Sunflower Outdoor and Bike, adjusts a customer's mountain bike on Feb. 24. Jordan says her interest in bike repair started when she was using a bicycle for transportation and decided it would be a worthwhile investment because she didn't own a car.

If you store your bike outside, at the very least you'll need to lube the chain and probably pump up the tires. Additionally, when exposed to harsh winter weather, many parts of your bike will rust. It's very common to have to replace chains on bicycles at the beginning of each season because of rust. Rusty chains squeak and can develop stiff links that, if left unchecked, will ruin the rest of your bike's drivetrain—forcing you to spend significantly more money. A replacement chain will set you back $10–20. Expect to pay another $8–10 in labor fees to have the chain installed.

Many times, people bring their bikes to repair shops after they've been stored all winter and the first thing they'll say is, "My tires are flat, I need new tires." Ninety percent of the time the tires are fine. Unlike a car, bicycles rely on tubes within the tires. Your bicycle's inner tubes have lost air, but the tires themselves are fine—the distinction matters when you talk to your bike mechanic. Keep in mind the inner tubes are made of rubber, which is porous. Over the course of several months it is natural for the tubes in your tires to lose air pressure. Nick Gardener, mechanic at Cycle Works, 2121 Kasold, notes that bicycle tubes lose an average of 5 psi a week naturally, whether they sit or are being ridden. I always told customers, if they were unsure if their flats were caused by a puncture or if they'd just been sitting too long, to start by airing the tubes up. If they hold air overnight they're fine. If not, then your inner tubes must be replaced.

The ability to make your bicycle stop on your terms is good. Without brakes, your bike is less a method of transport and enjoyment than it is a vehicle with kamikaze tendencies. Winter riding tends to wear down your bike's brake pads. "Road grit and grime gets onto your rim and really sands the pads down," says Gardener. So, to prevent a possible "Oh, shit!" scenario, please, have your brakes checked as well.

Adam Hess, service manager at Sunflower Outdoor & Bike Shop, sees a lot of weather-beaten bicycles this time of year. Most of the bikes he's been servicing need new chains and some kind of lube and tune-up. If your bike has been fighting the elements all winter, Adam recommends getting a brake service tune-up. It costs $30 and includes servicing your bike's brakes, adjusting the gears, and lubing the cables and drivetrain.

There are three bike shops in Lawrence, and they all provide free estimates. Customers can expect to be without their bikes for two to three days. Or, if you use your bike for daily transport, make an appointment and pick your bike up the same day you drop it off.

ENDNOTES

[1] Tony Rosenfeld, "Blueprint for a Perfect Burger," *bon appétit*, July 2008, 89.

[2] Dave Rahn, "Putting Integrity to the Test," *Living With Teenagers*, Nov. 2007, 8.

[3] *Prevention*, Aug. 2008, cover.

[4] *Kiplinger's Personal Finance*, Aug. 2008, cover.

[5] *Marie Claire*, July 2008, cover.

[6] Presentation by Shirley Jump, July 26, 2008.

[7] Lea Goldman, "Surviving A Layoff," *Marie Claire*, July 2008, 94–97.

8   Holly G. Miller, "Tense? Me, Tense?" *CompuServe Magazine*, Jan. 1991, 16.

9   Dennis E. Hensley and Holly G. Miller, *Write on Target* (Boston: The Writer, Inc., 1995), 71.

10 Rebecca Adler et al., "18 Things You Should Know by Now," *More Magazine*, Oct. 2007, 137–148.

11 Josh Patterson, "Dusting Off the Gears," *Jayplay*, Feb. 28, 2008. Used by permission.

17

CONNECTING CONTENT TO
THE CALENDAR

Your takeaway . . .

Although magazine writers create articles weeks—even months—
in advance of publication, the stories need to seem timely when
they appear in print. One way a writer can add relevance to a
topic is by linking it to the calendar. This chapter shows you how
to plan ahead to produce stories that relate to a season, a holiday,
an anniversary or a special observance. The key is writing and
submitting articles six months in advance of that holiday or anniversary because Christmas comes in July for many magazine
editors.

The assignment seemed routine: Write a one-page personality profile article
(650 words) about Robin Roberts, former college basketball standout,
ESPN sportscaster and current co-anchor of ABC's "Good Morning
America" (GMA) show. What made the story interesting and timely were
three calendar-related facts. The article was slated for a magazine's October
issue because October is Breast Cancer Awareness Month; the issue would
hit the newsstands close to the one-year anniversary of Roberts' public
announcement of her breast cancer diagnosis; the interview coincided with
the release of Roberts' new book that dealt with her cancer experience.
These factors gave the writer a clear focus for the story and assured her that
the article would occupy a prominent place in the magazine and on the
magazine's Web site. Knowing the story's angle also helped the writer come
up with open-ended questions to ask during her interview with Roberts.
As examples:

• As you mark the one-year anniversary since your cancer diagnosis, how
  are you different? What did the experience teach you?

- In your new book you talk about your family's strong religious beliefs. What role did your faith play in your treatment and recovery?
- You will be making many public appearances linked to the release of your book. What message will you carry to your audiences? What do you hope people will take away from your experience?[1]

FAST FORWARD FOUR MONTHS

Timing is everything in magazine journalism, and an article linked to Breast Cancer Awareness Month (October) needs to land on an editor's desk in early spring (May). With lead times that vary from four to six months, writers and editors generally work at least a season or two ahead of the calendar. This means they're planning back-to-school issues in March, considering Christmas fiction submissions in July and looking for spring gardening features in November. Since monthly and quarterly magazines can't compete with the Internet, television, radio, daily newspapers and weekly magazines in reporting breaking news, the staffs at these publications must be creative if they are to ensure relevance in the material they offer readers.

Some calendar-related features are perennial favorites, and readers look forward to them year after year. *Sports Illustrated*'s famed swimsuit edition has become a pre-summer tradition since its launch in 1964; *Vanity Fair* does a popular "green" issue each year that focuses on the environment; and *Yankee* produces its special New England travel issue each May-June.

Beyond these well-known themes, calendar-related material includes articles that are linked to events and activities (June weddings, October tailgate parties), stories that mark anniversaries (9/11 terrorist attacks, Martin Luther King Jr.'s death) and features that call attention to special observances (Father's Day, Mother's Day, Labor Day). The smart writer looks to the calendar for timely article topics and submits them to publications at precisely the right moment.

To tune into the creative ways that editors tie content to the calendar, simply compare several magazines published in the same month or two. Note the seasonal articles promoted on the covers and listed in the tables of contents. For example, a June issue of *Food & Wine* offered an "Ultimate Summer Wine Guide" and "Buying a Grill: What You Need to Know."[2] In

July, *Family Fun* suggested "10 Ways to Enjoy a Summer Day,"[3] and *Ebony* listed "24 Things to Do in the Sun."[4]

Calendar-linked articles can deal with serious and lightweight topics. A spring issue of *Scholastic Instructor*, a magazine geared to teachers, suggested "Poolside Picks: Top Professional Titles"[5] for subscribers who wanted to catch up on educational reading during their summer vacations. Because the first issue of any year is a logical time to help people make their annual resolutions, *Smart Money* once urged readers to "Set Your Course Now for the Year Ahead."[6] April is an appropriate month to publish articles related to finances because readers are feeling the pinch as they prepare their income tax returns. Thus, "Get the Paycheck You Deserve" drew attention to an April issue of *Self.*[7] *Smithsonian*, known for its serious journalism, had fun when it marked the 30th anniversary of Elvis Presley's death by running an article about Elvis impersonators or "tribute artists" as they call themselves.[8]

CREATING A SEASONAL LINK

Occasionally a writer manipulates an article to make it seem seasonal. A visit to a southern spa once resulted in a feature story for a November issue of *The Saturday Evening Post*. It began with the question: "Time for a winter tune up? Florida's newest spa will strip you of stress, wrap you in luxury and send you home fit for the holidays." Had the writer offered the same article for publication in a May issue of the magazine, she might have changed the introduction to: "Time to shape up for swimsuit weather? Florida's newest spa will strip you of stress, wrap you in luxury and send you home fit for long afternoons at the beach."[9]

A creative writer with a good topic can tweak a feature story to make it seem appropriate for any season. An article about home security—"How to Burglar-Proof Your Home"—might point out that intruders often take note of houses left vacant during the summer vacation season. A different spin on this same topic might remind readers that winter weather keeps neighbors inside where they're oblivious to the sights and sounds of nearby break-ins. Since the topic is an evergreen—of perennial interest to readers—it takes on an element of importance with the insertion of a few sentences that link it to the season.

Some months lend themselves to easy content-calendar connections. December is the most obvious because of the holidays. Every year readers can expect to see cover lines such as *Redbook*'s "51 Great Gifts Under $40" and "New Holiday Traditions You'll Love."[10] Other months, like February and March, seem to challenge writers and prompt them to stretch to come up with timely ideas. Two competing magazines—*Parents* and *Parenting*—once featured similar cover lines for their February issues. The title of one article was "Be My Valentine: Sweet Ways to Make Your Kids Feel Special";[11] the title of the competition's article was "I Love You: Little Ways to Make Your Child Feel Special."[12] Apparently the editors were on the same wavelength.

When brainstorming topics with a calendar connection, writers need to keep a magazine's demographics in mind. As an example, the majority of *Hallmark Magazine* readers are female, married and age 35+. Those subscribers probably liked a February issue that had red roses on the cover and cover lines that promoted three seasonal stories: "One-of-a-Kind Valentines," "Romantic Dinners" and "12 Real-Life Stories of How We Met."[13]

FORGET "THE FIRST THANKSGIVING"

If the calendar is a good place to begin hunting for timely article ideas, it's only a starting point. You have to look beyond the obvious and avoid predictable topics that sound like retreads from your sixth-grade spiral notebook of essays. No editor is interested in your take on "The First Thanksgiving," your musings about "What Christmas Means to Me" or your recollections of "How I Spent My Summer Vacation." One of our writing colleagues used to warn her students against "I-strain," her label for the dangers of writing from a first-person point of view.

An easy way to move beyond predictable article ideas is to brainstorm with a calendar in front of you. For January, move past the general topic of New Year's resolutions and think about specific changes that you've heard people say that they want to make in their lives. January gives them the feeling of a fresh start, a clean slate, a new beginning. Perhaps this is the year they hope to get out of debt, go back to school, lose weight, start exercising, kick a bad habit or strengthen a key relationship. Each resolution can lead to a how-to feature (see Chapter 16). For example, readers who resolve to get out of debt and be more fiscally responsible this year might want to read an informative article titled "How to Cut Your Credit Card Debt in Half." Its timing seems right on target in January.

For a June publication, a student writer might ask a handful of college professors, college administrators and prominent alumni to offer parting words of wisdom to the senior class that is about to graduate. The writer might follow up with this question: "What do you know now that you wish you had known when you walked across the stage and picked up your diploma so many years ago?" (Beware: Some interviewees, when asked such open-ended questions, can't resist delivering lofty sermons.)

CONNECTING THE DOTS

Two of the best Web sites for ideas related to the calendar are www.butler-webs.com/holidays and www.history.com. Plan to spend a good deal of time exploring both resources, and be prepared to let your imagination run rampant. The first Web site (butlerwebs.com/holidays) allows you to choose a month and then scroll down day by day to learn of holidays, special observances, anniversaries, and the births and deaths of prominent people.

For example, among its many designations, May is Better Sleep Month. Combine this bit of trivia with recent research that found that too many Americans aren't getting the recommended seven-to-eight hours of sleep a night. Add the fact that most colleges and universities schedule their final exams during May, and you come up with an ironic conclusion: Many students become sleep-deprived zombies during Better Sleep Month. Could this be the beginning of a feature story? Start your background research by visiting the Web sites of the National Sleep Foundation (www.sleepfoundation.org) and the American Sleep Association (www.sleepassociation.org). Next, conduct interviews with faculty and students to elicit their advice and anecdotes about prepping for finals—the right and the wrong way. Create a sidebar that lists the value of caffeine, energy bars and other products that inhibit sleep. The result is an informative and timely article.

The second Web site (history.com) makes it easy for you to connect the past with the present and come up with some colorful story ideas. For example, you can type in an area of interest such as "women's rights" and learn that one of the founders of the women's rights movement (Elizabeth Cady Stanton) was likely the first bride to omit the word "obey" from her marriage vows. Use that as a springboard to a feature article about contemporary couples who are writing their own vows and tailoring their wedding ceremonies to express their personalities and beliefs. Make the point that this trend is nothing new; in fact, it dates back to Elizabeth Cady, who promised 170 years ago to love, honor but not necessarily *obey* her husband. Interview two or three couples as well as a sampling of clergy who officiate at these unique ceremonies. Offer it for publication in a June issue of a magazine.

The key to a successful anniversary article is making the topic relate to the present. Whereas writers should weave enough history into a feature story to educate readers on the event's significance, they should avoid merely retelling what historians have already documented in textbooks. Among the most interesting calendar-related stories are those that bring to the forefront anniversaries that are unknown to most people. Let's look at several diverse examples.

Historic event

In 1869, attorney Arabella Babb became the first woman to gain admittance to the bar.

Anniversary article idea: Almost 150 years later, what kind of progress have women made in the legal profession? How many women make up the student bodies of law schools today? Are they as successful as men when they establish their practices? It's important to note that Arabella Babb would not be the focus of this article; she would merely be a way of getting to the issue.

Historic event

Sometime between 1832 and 1839 a man named Robert Anderson invented the first electric carriage that ran on rechargeable batteries.

Anniversary article idea: Here we are, so many years later, and we still don't have a viable electric car. In light of the rising cost of fuel, why are 21st-century Americans so reluctant to give up the traditional gas guzzler? What alternative means of transportation are in the developmental stages?

Historic event

The luxury steamship Titanic, on its maiden voyage in April 1912, sank after hitting an iceberg. More than 1,500 persons died.

Anniversary article idea: In spite of numerous books, films and documentaries that have told and retold the story of the ill-fated ship, people are still fascinated by it almost 100 years later. As the centennial approaches, what kinds of commemorations are planned? What Titanic memorabilia are available on eBay? What are people willing to pay for keepsakes? With all of the tragedies that have claimed many more lives, why does the Titanic story endure?

Historic event: In 1927 the first federal prison for women opened its doors (and cells). More like a fashionable boarding school than a jail, the facility taught its inmates to can vegetables and fruit and offered them singing lessons.

Anniversary article idea: In 2012, on the 85th anniversary of the prison's opening, a timely article might compare prison life for women, then and now. The story is pertinent to the increased number of women currently serving sentences for everything from white-collar crimes to murder.

NEW LIFE FOR OLD TOPICS

Even a tired topic gains new life when it is tied to an observance or an anniversary. Many writers have probed the serious issue of teen pregnancy, but Mother's Day provides an appropriate time to revisit the topic. The resulting article—call it "Moms Too Soon" or "Premature Moms"—might update readers on current teen-pregnancy statistics and on new efforts to discourage the trend of kids having kids. The Mother's Day connection also might prompt an article about professional women who delay motherhood until they've successfully launched their careers. Again, the topic isn't new, but the calendar connection makes it seem worthy of another look.

The idea of one generation passing its wisdom on to the next may be tired, but if the advice is offered in conjunction with Father's Day, it still can work. Consider interviewing three or four successful people from different walks of life who credit their adult success to their fathers' influence when they were children. Include lots of anecdotes as you tell their individual stories in a round-up article. Or talk with a handful of well-known people and ask them to recall the best advice their fathers ever gave them. *AARP* magazine did this for a May-June issue and called it "Tops of the Pops." The secondary title explained: "Some of our favorite people recall the lessons they learned from their dads."[14]

Major historic anniversaries often serve as the foundations of major magazine articles. When the United States observed the 60th commemoration of D-Day, the Allied forces' invasion of Europe during World War II, the story made the cover of *Time*. Much more than merely reminding readers of the date and recapping the event, *Time* made the statement, "D-Day: Why It Matters 60 Years Later."[15] A second story featured the recollections of 10 veterans who witnessed the Normandy landings.

The anniversaries of landmark Supreme Court cases give writers good reasons to revisit hot topics. Brown vs. the Board of Education of Topeka, Kan., which led to public-school desegregation, was decided in May 1954. Fast forward 50 years and many magazines took a look at education in America and questioned if schools are offering equal opportunity to all students. Another important case, Roe vs. Wade, legalized abortion in the United States. The court handed down its decision in 1973, and writers have revisited the controversial issue on subsequent anniversaries.

BIRTHDAY ISSUES REAP REWARDS

Sometimes editors create anniversary issues that directly or indirectly celebrate the publications that they edit. These often generate extra advertising revenue and attract record newsstand sales. *Rolling Stone* produced three special issues in 2007 that celebrated the magazine's 40th anniversary. In 2008, *Esquire* began a year-long commemoration of its 75-year history. While most anniversary issues mark the birth of a magazine, at least one served to memorialize the end of a publication. This was the case in April 2008 when *CCM* produced its final print edition on the 30th anniversary of its founding. It survives as an online magazine (www.ccmmagazine.com).

Typically magazines use five-year markers to call readers' attention to anniversaries. A 10th, 15th, 20th, 25th anniversary is more appropriate than a 17th, 23rd or 51st anniversary. Of course, some calendar-related events are so extraordinary that magazines begin the celebration well in advance. This was the case when the millennium approached. Starting in April 1998, *Time* issued a series of editions that cited the most influential people of the past 100 years. The project, according to managing editor Walter Isaacson, was "more popular than we dared dream."[16] For its last magazine of the century, *Time* announced its choice as "Person of the Century"—Albert Einstein.[17]

To show how a writer can pursue an unusual angle on a story, let's look at a millennium-related feature that was published in *Indianapolis Monthly* as part of what the magazine touted on its cover as its "Special Millennium Issue" (Dec. 1999). Among a range of articles linked to the calendar was "Living History," which had a clever gimmick at its core. The editor assigned a writer to locate and interview three Indianapolis residents who shared one common characteristic: All three had lived in three centuries. How is that possible? These senior citizens were born late in the 1800s, had lived through the 1900s, and when they woke up on Jan. 1, 2000, they entered their third century. The resulting article is a round-up feature because it solicits comments from different people on a central topic. The article is also a series of mini-profiles as well as a calendar-related story.

As you read "Living History," ask yourself these questions:

- What difficulties might the writer have encountered in interviewing these people?
- What kind of research, besides the three interviews, adds depth to the story?
- How do the subheadings help the writer make transitions from one interview to the next?
- How does the ending bring the story full circle to the beginning?

LIVING HISTORY[18]

While some people read about the past in textbooks, others saw it with their own eyes.

Their partying days are over. An exchange of kisses at midnight is unlikely, and compiling a list of resolutions seems presumptuous. On Jan. 1, at midnight, an exclusive group of Hoosiers will move quietly into the next century: their third. Born in the 1800s, they've lived through the 1900s and soon will wake up to the year 2000. Not that the Millennium means much to people who have defied the actuary tables by decades, watched the passing of 19 presidents from Cleveland to Clinton, and experienced the coming and going of a hundred New Year's Eves.

From retirement homes, continuing care centers and assisted living communities around the city, they remember the past in amazing detail and aren't shy about sharing their views on politics, sex and scandal. Just mention Bill Clinton's name, and expect the unexpected. "What he did wasn't right," concedes Frata Sarig, 105, who served as executive secretary to Reginald Sullivan, a Democrat mayor of Indianapolis in the early 1940s. Then, as an afterthought, she adds, "But he sure is good-looking."

They're at their best when recalling vivid moments that aren't connected to any major historical event. They don't remember much about Prohibition, D-Day or women's suffrage, but they can describe the interior of their first Chevy and recall their family's first telephone and the ring—"one short, three longs," says Frata—that distinguished their calls from those of their neighbors. "Of course, everybody listened in on the party line."

The war hero

"I remember the day I got my card from the draft office and figured, 'What the hell, I might as well enlist,'" recalls Gustave Streeter, reminiscing from a huge green lounge chair—an unlit cigar between his fingers and an erasable tablet and marker within arm's reach. His hearing and eyesight are failing, and visitors who want to tap into his vast memory bank have to print their questions on the tablet in oversized black letters. It's worth the effort. He's a bona fide war hero, and proof of his bravery is pinned to his shirt under his Perry Como cardigan. It's a handsome green and white medal, the Croix de Guerre, awarded by the French government in 1999 to commemorate his service during World War I. He was a gunner, took part in seven campaigns in France and Germany, was hobbled by shrapnel in both legs, treated himself from his first aid kit and kept going. "I was a pharmacist," he explains. "I knew if I reported my injuries they'd send me to a hospital. I wanted to stay and fight."

Streeter stayed, and in one bloody exchange was responsible for saving the lives of several U.S. Marines. He later wrote about his war experiences in a collection of reminiscences published by the Little

Sisters of the Poor and aimed at the next generation. "I can't remember many [fellow soldiers'] names," he wrote, "but frequently during these twilight years of my life, I can see them pass in review, their heads high, their bodies erect and their expressions noble."

He lives at St. Augustine Home now, his room decorated with pictures from the Great War and mementos from his most recent birthday, his 103rd. There are framed greetings from Bill, Hillary and the senior Bushes, a stack of cards and a helium-filled balloon with the message, "Aged to Perfection." Trading his independence for institutional life was difficult a couple of years ago, especially since current house rules prevent him from enjoying two long-standing pleasures of his past: a cigar in the afternoon and a Rob Roy before dinner. Shortly after he moved into the Catholic retirement center, Streeter confided to one of the nuns that he sure missed the ritual of an evening cocktail. "That night I came back to my room and sitting right here by the bed was a gold-rimmed, stemmed glass with a Rob Roy in it," he says with some surprise. "I don't know where it came from, and it only happened once."

A miracle.

The doctor's wife

"You'll think I'm a little goofy," confides Beaty Segar, 100, "but every night when I go to bed, I sing the same three songs: 'Hello, Dolly,' 'Singin' in the Rain' and 'Tea for Two.' Of course I usually go to sleep before I get to the third one."

Music has been a part of her life since her early years in Chicago, when she and her sister sang for the troops who were home on leave from World War I. She moved to Indiana in 1922, the bride of Dr. Louis Segar, the state's first full-time pediatrician, and together they were active in community theater and "went to the symphony from the day it opened." Dr. Segar, an IU graduate, had interned at Boston's Children's Hospital, where he traded rotations with other young doctors, taking on extra pediatric assignments so he could get additional experience. "He came back to Indianapolis, opened an office and sat there day after day," says Beaty. "Nobody came in. At one point he told his father he was going to quit medicine. Then, finally, he got a call to consult on a case of scarlet fever." He was good, word got around, and his long, successful career was launched.

As newlyweds, the Segars lived on North Alabama Street, and each afternoon Beaty would walk to her husband's downtown office so she could accompany him on his house calls. "We rode all over the state," she says. If a call came late at night, Beaty would slip a robe over her nightgown and travel with him. "He was a 24-hour-a-day doctor, and he carried his black satchel with him everywhere."

Sometimes he prescribed a dose of common sense rather than a shot of medication. "One child refused to talk," recalls Beaty. "His parents knew he could speak, but they couldn't convince him to do it. Finally, my husband put the boy in the hospital with instructions to leave him alone and not to feed him. After one day the kid said to the nurse, 'Damn it, I'm hungry!'" He was cured.

She's been a widow for 35 years now, and describes her health as good "from the neck up." When problems with her eyesight threatened to curb her insatiable appetite for reading she discovered books on tape. She just finished a biography of FDR and has moved on to an in-depth look at Truman. "I'm probably better educated now than I have been in a hundred years," she says. Reading about the Depression has put into perspective the lean years when her husband's patients often couldn't pay for the medical services he delivered. No one withheld treatment, and no one filed a lawsuit. Beaty remembers the butcher settling a bill with a pound of ground chuck, which she promptly stretched into a meatloaf. She recalls the Shapiro family, of delicatessen fame, helping out by sending over dinner. "They gave us enough food for a week."

If she misses anything about days gone by, it's the sense of friendliness that permeated the neighborhoods. "We grew up without fences," she says. "Kids played in each other's backyards. Our doors were open, and so were our refrigerators. Today things seem more divided. My daughter, who lives out of state, just told me about being in a grocery story and talking to a little boy. His mother rushed up, grabbed the child and said, 'I told you not to talk to strangers!' Things like that hurt."

The career girl

Frata Sarig drove her little Chevy until she had a fender bender at age 98. No one was hurt, but she reluctantly hung up her keys because "I felt from then on, no matter what the trouble was, the insurance people would say it was my fault." Now, at age 105, she still recalls the wonderful sense of independence when, years ago, she drove solo from one coast to the other. "I would stop for gas, and people would ask me where I was going. I always fibbed about it because I didn't want anyone to know I was alone and traveling so far. I didn't want them to follow me."

Sarig had already had two careers when she and her husband moved to Indiana more than 65 years ago. She had taught in a one-room schoolhouse in Iowa and had worked in a Kansas City biological laboratory. Once settled in Indianapolis, she joined city government and eventually served on the mayor's staff as executive secretary. Later she sold real estate, retiring at age 75. "A home back then cost anywhere from $12,000 to $35,000," Sarig says. She sold her share of them, "made quite a bit" and invested well. Good thing, she notes, because "I never expected to live this long."

As progressive as she was in her professional life, so was she ahead of her time when it came to her health. She never drank alcohol or used tobacco—"my grandmother, dear soul, smoked a clay pipe"—and she underwent hormone replacement therapy before it was fashionable. Sarig stopped taking hormones at age 70, and later, when a niece asked her why, she answered, "I guess I took the Bible literally. I didn't think I would live beyond three score and 10 years." That was 35 years ago.

Cheers

All three centenarians agree that tomorrow isn't quite as mysterious when you've already seen 100 years of yesterdays. Beaty Segar's love for words once prompted her to consider writing a book about the people she's known, but the project seemed daunting, and she settled for poems instead. She recites from memory the lines she composed to mark her 100th birthday in July. Its closing words say: "I have cherished every year. You see me standing here. Believe it or not, it's really me, and I have lived a century."

She took poetic license with the line "you see me standing here." These days she travels by wheelchair, although that hasn't slowed her pace. "I don't think anybody ever lives too long," she says, "not if they have something to offer." Segar dismisses the foibles of age as inevitable, and refuses to dwell on them. "Everybody has aches and pains," she says. Failing eyesight? "I know my lunch is in front of me, but if I put in my fork I'm not sure what I'll come up with." Hearing loss? "Yesterday I was talking with a woman and I said, 'It's a beautiful day.' She answered, 'I'm so glad you like it. I haven't worn it for a while.'"

Like birthdays, ringing in another year—even another century—"doesn't mean much at this stage of life," admits Sarig. For persons who have seen a hundred years, any celebration is likely to be quiet and private. A chorus of "Hello, Dolly" would be nice, followed by a memory of tapping the accelerator of a little Chevy, and toasting the journey with something cold. Make it a Rob Roy.

ENDNOTES

[1] Interview with Holly G. Miller, June 25, 2008.
[2] *Food & Wine*, June 2008, cover.
[3] *Family Fun*, July–Aug. 2008, cover.
[4] *Ebony*, July 2008, cover.
[5] *Scholastic Instructor*, May/June 2004, cover.
[6] *Smart Money*, Jan. 2004, cover.
[7] *Self*, April 2007, cover.
[8] "Elvis Lives," *Smithsonian*, Aug. 2007, 64.
[9] Holly G. Miller, "Southern Comforts," *The Saturday Evening Post*, Nov./Dec. 2001, 62–63.
[10] *Redbook*, Dec. 2007, cover.
[11] *Parents*, Feb. 2004, cover.
[12] *Parenting*, Feb. 2004, cover.
[13] *Hallmark Magazine*, Feb.–March 2008, cover.
[14] Al Roker and Friends, "Tops of the Pops," *AARP*, May–June 2005, 29–30.
[15] *Time*, May 31, 2004, cover.
[16] Walter Isaacson, "Why Picking These Titans Was Fun," *Time*, Dec. 7, 1998, 6.
[17] *Time*, Dec. 31, 1999, cover.
[18] Holly G. Miller, "Living History," *Indianapolis Monthly*, Dec. 1999, 134–137, 212.

TRENDS, ISSUES AND CONTROVERSIES

Your takeaway . . .

Trend, issue and controversy stories inform the public about matters that affect their health, finances, safety and general welfare. Every field of special interest covered by magazines has trends, issues and controversies—hobbies, health, entertainment, sports, science, politics or religion. You will learn how to analyze trends and issues and recognize the groups that get hurt or benefit from them. You will also learn tips on finding ideas, developing creative angles and reporting these stories in the most interesting way.

Many parents try to do the right thing by using safety seats, but actually put their small children in greater danger. According to the *Reader's Digest* story, "Kids at Risk: The Alarming Truth About Safety Seats," more than 30,000 injuries and 200 deaths occur every year to small children while riding in child safety seats. Safety experts have concluded that more than 90 percent of these seats are not properly installed by parents. This widely reprinted article had a significant influence on new safety legislation passed by several states.[1]

Stories such as "Kids at Risk" perform an important public service by alerting the public to risks and dangers they may not know about. Sometimes they prompt new legislation to protect public health and safety. Trend, issue and controversy stories can also be called "news features" or "current-event features." They investigate beyond "what happens" and analyze "why" and "how" events happen and how they affect readers. They differ from news stories because they don't report on a single news event, but result from a complex web of events. They may start with an isolated incident—such as the death of a child using a safety seat who is involved in an auto accident. Then the writer links a series of similar events—"connects the dots" if you will—to answer the question "Why?"

Trend, issue and controversy stories don't have clear-cut boundaries between them, and some stories may contain elements of all three. These definitions and examples, however, will help you understand the distinctions.

Trend

A phenomenon that is increasing or decreasing in frequency. Trends always have a quantifiable dimension and can occur in society, pop culture or any field of endeavor.

Examples:

"The Record Industry's Slow Fade" (CD and album sales declined from 785 million to 588 million between 2000 and 2007)—*Rolling Stone*[2]

"Warming Trends" (coat manufacturers are responding to global warming with slim styles that use high-tech materials)—*SmartMoney*[3]

Issue

A phenomenon or development that poses a risk or danger to the public or some segment of the population. Since some issues may benefit some population segments and hurt others, the solutions are debatable.

Examples:

"Perverted Justice" (convicted sex offenders in Miami are forced to live under bridges because local ordinances prohibit them from living anywhere else)—*Details*[4]

"Strong Medicine: What's Ailing the FDA?" (insiders say the Food and Drug Administration is underfunded, dangerously understaffed and fractured by internal tension)—*Reader's Digest*[5]

Controversy

A prolonged, intense debate about a public issue without an immediate or easy solution. The difference between "issue" and controversy is one of the degree or intensity of the public disagreement.

Examples:

"Santa Impersonators Face Internal Schism" (The Amalgamated Santas, one of the nation's largest Santa groups, is dealing with a schism in its ranks)—*The Wall Street Journal*[6]

"Death in Georgia" (a multiple-murder case results in controversy over Georgia's death-penalty law)—*The New Yorker*[7]

These stories help readers understand their world by explaining what, why and how things happen and how they affect readers. They report on many fields of human interest and endeavor and get published in many different types of magazines. They are not limited to politics or public affairs.

COMMON CHARACTERISTICS

These common characteristics will help you research and write these stories:

- Their purpose is to inform and educate readers about a trend, issue or controversy and how it may affect them.
- Every field of special interest covered by magazines has trends, issues and controversies—hobbies, health, entertainment, sports, science, politics or religion.
- Trends often benefit one group or sector of the population while hurting others. Both sides must be covered fairly.
- Your reporting must cover the viewpoints and experiences from many sources. These stories are more challenging to report than others because they can't focus on a single person nor rely on a single interview.

- Trends, issues and controversies can become quickly outdated. You must continually look for fresh angles and approaches to these topics.

Here are some tips on recognizing and writing each type of story.

Trends

A trend is a social or economic phenomenon with quantifiable dimensions such as growing, declining, increasing or decreasing. Some trends may be dangerous or controversial while others are positive or light-hearted. In his article, "What's Up, Doc? The Prestige of Honorary Degrees Falls to Record Lows," Joseph Epstein poked fun at the decreasing prestige of honorary doctorates because so many universities have offered them to non-qualified celebrities and donors.[8]

In "Why U.S. Workers Are Losing the Tug of War Over Toilet Paper," *The Wall Street Journal* reports on the "controlled delivery" trend in company and public restrooms. They save on paper costs by making dispensers tricky to use. It quotes a building-services manager who defends the practice, and includes statistics related to the most popular complaints about public restrooms.[9]

Trends with harmful consequences turn into controversies as people debate solutions to the problems they bring. For example, in February 2003, *Jane* reported on "Women Who Rape: A Scary Trend You Don't Hear About: Female Sex Offenders." This story reported on the increasing number of female sex offenders. In "Why Some Brothers Only Date Whites and 'Others,'" *Ebony* quoted experts who attributed the rise in interracial dating and marriage partly to the cross-racial, hip-hop culture.[10]

"Those trend stories can start with the anecdote or the big picture. Trend stories can come from statistics and can come from having a friend who is having some problem," says Ted Spiker, a journalism professor and former senior editor at *Men's Health*. Spiker says anecdotes bring a story to life, but the statistics add credibility. "If you don't have a number there, you haven't proven to me there's a trend," he says.[11]

However, writer-editor Gail Belsky says that trend stories originate in everyday life before they show up in statistics. "When I was the executive editor of *Working Mother*," she says, "the census had just come out that showed for the first time in 24 years that the number of women who returned to work after having a baby went down."

Yet she says she already knew about it. A couple of years earlier, a young colleague told her at lunch that she did not have a single friend who had gone back to work after having a baby.

> To me, that speaks volumes. That is the trend, far more than waiting for the census bureau to spit out a number. You see that kind of anecdotal information once you start looking around and seeing what's going on. You see it once, you think 'hmmm.' You see it twice and you know there must be a third one. You know if you do a little walking and talking, you're going to come up with more.[12]

Belsky says that another trend she has noticed in the New York City area where she lives is an increase in knitting. She has observed it among young women on subways. Shortly after that interview, when we asked students in a magazine-writing class whether any of them knitted, about three of 15 students raised their hands. One of them held up a sweater she had knitted.

Issues

CQ Researcher, as explained in Chapter 4, offers a great source for ideas and background for articles on current events issues. It provides a balanced overview of issues the media and public are discussing, such as human rights in China, the accuracy of the Internet, cyberbullying, the gender pay gap and the future of airlines.

For example, a recent edition focused on "Race and Politics: Will Skin Color Influence the Presidential Election?" It identified three major issues in the 2008 presidential race:

- Has Republican Party identification with white Southerners cost it support in other regions?
- Can the Democrats attract white, working-class votes outside the South?
- Is race a major factor in the 2008 presidential election?

Another edition of *CQ Researcher* focused on "The Global Food Crisis: What's Causing the Rising Prices?" You can create a local angle on one of these national issues. You could write a story on how it's affecting donations to local food pantries and whether they have seen increased requests for assistance. Additionally, you can take a national issue and develop an interesting angle for the niche audience who reads a special-interest magazine. For example, you could write an article for a denominational magazine explaining how church-operated food pantries are affected by increased food prices.

Controversies

Some trends and issues turn into controversies because people disagree intensely about their causes, solutions or both. Sometimes the opposing groups are clearly defined, such as labor and management, faculty and administration or Republicans and Democrats. At other times, supporters and opponents come from less clearly defined coalitions. For example, rising fuel costs motivated public support for ethanol, which in turn made more farmers start growing corn. But as demand for corn rose, food prices rose, shortages resulted and a controversy developed over whether tax-subsidized ethanol production was the cause and whether it did any good to alleviate high gasoline prices. Some newspapers and magazines ran "pro" and "con" articles about whether ethanol was causing rising food prices and shortages.

Newspaper feature editors want balanced stories with comprehensive, equal coverage of opposing points of view. Magazine editors may permit writers to argue a point of view depending on the magazine's tradition. In the two examples that follow, *National Review* is one of the most conservative commentary magazines while *The Nation* is among the most liberal. Each wrote the story from its own point of view favoring one side or another.

National Review: "PETA vs. KFC: A Dirty War Against the Colonel." This story criticizes People for the Ethical Treatment of Animals (PETA) because of tactics it used in a campaign charging that Kentucky Fried Chicken (KFC) treated chickens inhumanely.[13]

The Nation: "Fields of Poison: While Farm Workers Are Sickened by Pesticides, Industry Writes the Rules." This story examines numerous health dangers faced by farm workers who use pesticides, charging that the farm industry pressured the government against adopting protective regulations.[14]

Controversies and trends begin behind the scenes before they turn into news stories or statistics. You can get a real "scoop" if you're the first to report them. These stories often begin with a hunch based on personal observations and conversations. Following that hunch into interviews and research can give you the scoop. For curiosity-filled writers, it's the most exciting and interesting type of story to write.

CHOOSING THE BEST ANGLE

Every trend and controversy offers a dozen angles to pursue. You can look at the people who are for it, the people who are against it and the people who just don't care. If it's a trend, you can look at the people it hurts or the people it helps. Some people remain unaffected, but have definite reactions to the trend. To help in choosing the best angle, start by analyzing it from these three perspectives: central development, benefits to some, harm to others.

Central development

Something begins to happen. For example, American electronics companies begin exporting jobs and factories to countries with cheaper labor.

Benefits for some

As the development advances, it affects people, places or institutions in specific ways. Consumers get cheaper televisions, DVD players, cell phones and other gadgets. Developing countries get new jobs and a higher standard of living.

Harm to others

As the effects take place, impacted groups react to this development. Labor groups may pressure Congress for import restrictions. Some communities lose factories and jobs and look for ways to rebuild their economies.

Each of these three phases of development, however, involves different directions for the writer. For each one you can look at *magnitude* (how much, how many, how often); *location* (which states or regions are most affected); *diversity* (which groups of people are affected); or *intensity* (to what degree or extent they're affected).[15]

These four perspectives on three central developments give you at least a dozen angles from which to pursue the story:

- **Central development:**
  Magnitude (how many?)
  Location (where?)
  Diversity (to whom?)
  Intensity (to what extent?)

- **Benefits for some:**
  Magnitude (how many?)
  Location (where?)
  Diversity (to whom?)
  Intensity (to what extent?)

- **Harm to others:**
  Magnitude (how many?)
  Location (where?)
  Diversity (to whom?)
  Intensity (to what extent?)

In summary, every issue or trend has at least a dozen ways you can go with it. The direction you take will depend on several factors:

- the nature of the audience for whom you are writing
- what other authors have written about the topic
- which questions remain unanswered
- which experts and affected persons you have access to
- any other primary-source information you can uncover

If you can find new sources of information and answer unresolved questions, then you're on your way toward a great story.

DOING THE REPORTING

Feature stories on trends and conflicts can't depend on a single source. Hal Karp, a contributing editor to *Reader's Digest* and *Parents* magazine, says, "What people don't understand—feature writing is even more about reporting than hard news reporting because you have so much more depth. [Feature articles] take a lot of time and require a lot of sources." Karp wrote the *Reader's Digest* "Kids at Risk" story mentioned at the beginning of this chapter. These trend and conflict stories require reporting from four different sources.

1 **People who are the players.** The players in the events are principal sources—the people involved at street-level in the nitty-gritty of the action. These are the mothers who lost a child in an auto accident or the police officer who filed the accident report.
2 **People who are experts.** The experts earn a living from finding, fixing or dispensing information. They may be doctors, lawyers, researchers, academics or auto mechanics.
3 **Facts** come from both interviews and background research. The facts add background, context and depth. They can let you know where, when, why or how these types of events occur.
4 **Numbers** convey the magnitude, enormity or frequency of any phenomenon. Numbers are especially important in trend stories. They add credibility to your main points and demonstrate that you did your homework.

A solid story may require dozens of hours in the library followed by dozens of interviews. They depend on background research for context and interviews for color. Too much secondary research without interviews will make them dull. Likewise, interviews alone with too little background research will make them irrelevant or outdated.

Hal Karp says the first step is to read everything published on your topic. "The most important thing I can do is locate what's already out there. I have to do as much research as possible, which is incredibly time consuming. I ask myself, 'Who's looked at this topic?' and 'What science is behind it?' I will really dig into the research and find all the primary materials."

Karp says that good features require a combination of anecdotes and hard factual evidence:

> You have to have both. Anecdotes bring it to life and make readers see themselves in the topic. You can read statistics all day long about how many kids die in car crashes, but you may not think about it much until you read about a mother who lost her kid in a crash. It's really important to have both.

He says advocacy groups are a good source. Any type of social problem or issue probably has an association or advocacy group representing it. "A lot of the time those people are going to be my best finders," says Karp. "They're interested in getting the word out because that's their job. They want to help journalists." You can find thousands of these groups in the three-volume *Encyclopedia of Associations* or the Internet Public Library's Association Directory (www.ipl.org/div/aon/) mentioned in Chapter 4.

WHEN TO QUOTE

Stories can contain too few or too many quotes. Stories with too few quotes run the risk of boring readers or overwhelming them with too many facts. Stories with too many quotes can make them work harder to interpret what's being said. Most readers prefer a healthy balance of interpretive reporting by the writer with colorful and insightful quotes from sources.

Hal Karp says, "I use quotes kind of like exclamation marks as the final point—the point that really drives it home. I also use quotes to balance an article. People like reading articles that contain some quotes and some paraphrases. Sometimes you quote because you just need to break it up."

In general, paraphrase facts and numbers in your own words. Use direct quotes from the actors, experts or observers in these three cases. First, use a quote when you have an expert source and the quote adds weight and credibility that it wouldn't hold if it came in the writer's own words. Second, use a quote when the quote is colorful and adds a touch of humor or irony to the issue you're examining. Third, use a quote when it expresses a key point in a particularly trenchant or concise way.

Finally, good pacing depends on the logical movement of ideas throughout the article. You can improve the pace of these stories by ensuring that each paragraph or section thematically progresses from one to the next in a logical fashion. Sentences and paragraphs should follow one another in logical sequence. And each paragraph must contain a significant idea about your main theme. Each paragraph must contain a unique idea that in some manner develops the theme.

You've probably heard the saying, "It's better to light a candle than curse the darkness." This phrase originated with former presidential candidate Adlai Stevenson when he praised Eleanor Roosevelt during an address to the United Nations General Assembly in 1962.[16] "She would rather light candles than curse the darkness, and her glow has warmed the world," he said. Think of writing trend, issue and controversy stories as "lighting a candle in the darkness." You perform a public service for readers and make a crazy world easier for them to understand.

ENDNOTES

[1] Hal Karp, "Kids at Risk: The Alarming Truth About Safety Seats," *Reader's Digest*," March 1999.

[2] "The Record Industry's Slow Fade," *Rolling Stone*, June 6, 2007. Accessed at Rollingstone.com, July 21, 2008.

[3] "Warming Trends," *SmartMoney*, Jan. 2008, 103.

[4] Ian Daily, "Perverted Justice," *Details*, July 7, 2008. Accessed at Details.com, July 18, 2008.

[5] Alexis Jetter, "Strong Medicine: What's Ailing the FDA?" *Reader's Digest*, Aug. 2008. Accessed at www.rd.com, July 18, 2008.

[6] Jim Carlton, "Santa Impersonators Face Internal Schism," *The Wall Street Journal*, July 10, 2007, A1.

[7] Jeffrey Toobin, "Death in Georgia," *The New Yorker*, Feb. 4, 2008. Accessed at www.newyorker.com, July 18, 2008.

[8] Joseph Epstein, "What's Up, Doc? The Prestige of Honorary Degrees Falls to Record Lows," *National Review*, May 26, 2008, 10.

[9] Jared Sandberg, "Why U.S. Workers Are Losing the Tug of War Over Toilet Paper," *The Wall Street Journal*, Sept. 10, 2003, B1.

[10] Zondra Hughes, "Why Some Brothers Only Date Whites and 'Others,'" Ebony, Jan. 2003, 70–72.

[11] Interview with David E. Sumner, Toronto, Ontario, Aug. 5, 2004.

[12] Telephone interview with David E. Sumner, Nov. 15, 2003.

[13] Jay Nordlinger, "PETA vs. KFC: A Dirty War Against the Colonel," *National Review*, Dec. 22, 2003, 27–29.

[14] Rebecca Claren, "Fields of Poison: While Farm Workers Are Sickened by Pesticides, Industry Writes the Rules," *The Nation*, Dec. 29, 2003, 23–25.

[15] Credit to William Blundell in *The Art and Craft of Feature Writing* (New York: Penguin Books, 1986) as the original source of these concepts.

[16] *The Phrase Finder*. Accessed at www.phrasefinder.co.uk, July 21, 2008.

WRITING TO INSPIRE
AND MOTIVATE

Your takeaway . . .

Faith-related articles are in high demand at secular and religious magazines. Think about it: Wars are fought over religious differences, politicians are grilled about their spirituality and many of today's hot-button issues center on matters of faith. This chapter introduces you to the world of inspirational/religious periodicals— many of which are available by subscription only—and shows you how successful contributors have mastered the art of "writing in degrees," depending on the targeted publication and its audience.

Most feature writers begin their careers as generalists. Equipped with basic journalism skills, they're able to take on a variety of assignments and turn out a range of articles worthy of publication. At least one of these freelancers, a friend of ours, describes himself as a "hired pen." His pitch to editors goes like this: "Tell me what you need and when you need it. I'll deliver the package on time and on target." He likes the challenge of tackling different topics for different audiences. Other writers prefer to move from generalist to specialist as soon as possible. They narrow their interests, refine their skills and develop writing niches. They become travel writers, education reporters, sports journalists, political columnists or celebrity interviewers. Some, who are motivated by readers' growing interest in religious issues or by their personal convictions, write faith-related articles for secular publications or for the hundreds of inspirational and "crossover" periodicals that are published today.

Proof that religious topics are welcomed throughout the industry comes from the annual Amy Foundation writing competition. For several years, this Michigan-based organization has awarded $34,000 annually in prize money to journalists who place Christian-themed articles in nonreligious publications. The contest attracts about 700 submissions each year, and past winners have included articles that appeared in such widely circulated publications as *The Boston Globe, The Philadelphia Inquirer, The Dallas Morning News* and *Time Magazine.* (For contest rules and sample articles, check www.amyfound.org.)

In this chapter we concentrate not on writing about religion for the secular media; instead, we focus on the opportunities and challenges of writing for the hundreds of publications that consider themselves part of the religious press. In that marketplace, the rules vary because many of the magazines and their respective writers and readers have deeply rooted points of view.

THE BUSINESS OF PUBLISHING

Writer-editor Terry Whalin cringes when he remembers a manuscript that an author once sent him via e-mail with this note attached: "God told me to write this. You need to publish it." Without intending to alienate Whalin, the writer had committed two serious mistakes. First, he had assumed that Whalin had time to open the file containing the unsolicited article, format its many pages, print them and read them. Second, by crediting God with the submission, he had irritated the seasoned editor. His not-so-subtle message was: How could Whalin possibly risk rejecting a submission sent from heaven by way of the Internet?

"Because they see their writing as a ministry, many inspirational writers don't understand that they have to exhibit the same level of professionalism as secular writers," explains Whalin, a former associate editor at *Decision,* the author of 60 inspirational books, creator of the *Right Writing News* electronic newsletter and an active literary agent. "Religious publications have higher standards than they used to have, and the challenge for every writer is to study a magazine, understand its purpose and figure out what its editors want."[1]

In *Right Writing News*, Whalin emphasizes that religious publishing is a business and "at the end of the day, editors have to make a profit if they are to stay in business." Although not all inspirational publications are commercial enterprises—many are sponsored by church denominations and other faith-based organizations—their editors expect the same excellent writing as editors whose publications compete on the newsstand. Their goal is to turn out first-class products that please subscribers and, in some cases, attract advertising dollars.

It isn't easy. Many fine inspirational magazines—*Moody, Aspire, Clarity, Virtue* and *Eternity* among them—have ceased publication for reasons usually related to red ink on the bottom line. Others, such as *CCM Magazine* that covered the Christian music scene for almost 30 years, have dropped their print versions and now offer only electronic editions. Even those print publications that are financially secure generally have smaller circulations and sell fewer advertising pages than their secular counterparts.

Still, the inspirational magazine industry is growing, as is the sub-category labeled "crossover" publications. Editors here are open to inspirational topics if the articles are well written, not "preachy" in tone and don't offend readers of different faiths. Jim Watkins, author of *Communicate to Change Lives* and a magazine editor and contributor, defines a crossover writer as one who carries the cross over to secular readers. Crossover material typically deals with spiritual issues but is written with a light hand and is aimed at readers regardless of their beliefs. Examples might include:

- profiles of Olympic athletes who use their high visibility to speak out about their faith
- how-to articles that help readers who struggle with spiritual issues such as "How to Forgive and Move On," "How to Raise Mission-Minded Kids" and "How to Plan an Inter-Faith Wedding Ceremony"
- essays that explore life-changing personal experiences, such as "My Battle With Clinical Depression"

At a time when Judeo-Christian values are a popular topic for politicians of all persuasions, they're certainly fair game for the media. The key to an article's success is the writer's ability to adjust the intensity of the spiritual content to suit the comfort level of readers.

width:1057px; height:1637px;

SIDEBAR 1

Networking Opportunities

Rubbing shoulders with established religion writers and editors is a great way for students to earn assignments, compete for writing awards and gain recognition. At least five trade organizations fund scholarship programs, sponsor job boards, offer contests, host annual conventions and create professional-development opportunities.

- Associated Church Press (www.theacp.org) is the oldest religious press association in North America and encompasses some 200 publications, Web sites and news services. ACP offers student memberships.
- Catholic Press Association (www.catholicpress.org) is an organization of almost 200 publications in the United States and Canada. A section of its Web site lists the names and e-mail addresses of freelance writers along with the writers' areas of specialization.
- Evangelical Press Association (www.epassoc.org) is the world's largest professional organization for the evangelical periodical publishing industry. Its membership represents 320 publications with a combined circulation of 22 million readers. Its annual competition honors winners in 38 categories.
- The American Jewish Press Association (www.ajpa.org) represents almost 250 newspapers, magazines, journalists and affiliated organizations. Its Web site includes the editorial calendars of Jewish publications.
- Religion Newswriters Association (www.rna.org) advances the professional standards of religion reporting in the secular press. Student members are welcome.

LEARNING TO WRITE IN DEGREES

If you've ever prepared a bath for a young child, you understand the importance of getting the water temperature just right. Typically one hand adjusts the faucets while the other hand makes sweeping motions under the tap.

You are at the controls, and constantly testing to make sure the water is not too hot for the child.

Inspirational writers go through a similar exercise. They, too, are at the controls and must take care not to deliver a message that is uncomfortably "hot" for their sensitive readers. They regulate the flow of the words and intensity of the message. If the story becomes too emotional, too dogmatic, too manipulative or too religious, their readers are likely to complain—loudly. The magazine that publishes such an article can expect angry letters complaining that the publication is preaching to them. "If I want a sermon I'll go to church!" is a familiar line.

Smart writers place magazines on an imaginary continuum. At one end of the continuum are publications that would never run an inspirational article regardless of how "cool" the message. On the other end of the continuum are magazines geared to the most devoutly religious readers. The challenge is to study the glut of magazines between the two extremes and discern their likely positions on the continuum. Some publications might consider stories that are morally uplifting (tepid); others might include material that falls into the "lite-inspiration" category (lukewarm); still others might be willing to publish downright spiritual articles (hot). A skilled writer can take the same topic and write it differently depending on the magazine's place on the continuum.

For example, we know a writer who once interviewed a TV anchorwoman in the Midwest and sold one version of the profile article to an inspirational women's magazine and another version to a secular city magazine. In the article aimed at religious readers, the writer traced the anchorwoman's "faith journey" and explained how she had had a "spiritual reawakening" and now was including brief inspirational stories as part of the evening newscast. The version published by the city magazine took a less emotional approach and explained the anchorwoman's efforts to balance bad news with good news and occasionally "mention God in a sound bite." The city magazine also chose to include comments from critics who objected to what they perceived as overly "sunny material." Although the subject of both articles was identical (the anchorwoman's picture ended up on the cover of both publications), the language and tone were different. The profile in the inspirational magazine was much like the "portrait" article that we described in Chapter 14. Its content was 100 percent positive. The city magazine's profile resembled the warts-and-all "photograph" article explained in Chapter 14.

AVOIDING THE SEVEN DEADLY WRITING SINS

Whether your goal is to sell articles to inspirational or crossover publications, you need to beware of certain minefields in the marketplace. In keeping with this chapter's topic, we call them the seven deadly sins of prospective inspirational writers. Here's how you can avoid them.

Recognize and reject tired topics

When it comes to looking for appropriate article ideas, too many inspirational writers can't think beyond complex and worn-out topics. These include abortion, prayer in public schools, gay marriage, the death penalty, sexual abstinence for singles and dozens of other subjects that deserve a rest. Yes, these issues are important, and that's precisely why they have been the subjects of endless speeches, sermons, editorials, articles and books. Our best advice: Don't add to the overload. If you must write about a tired topic, focus on a small piece of it. Jim Watkins recommends summarizing your message in three words. Then, as you review your research, eliminate everything that doesn't relate directly to the three words.

Know your audience

To their credit, many inspirational writers can quote the Bible by chapter and verse. But they make a mistake if they assume that their readers are equally knowledgeable. Too often these writers include in their articles shorthand references to scripture that mean nothing to persons who didn't grow up in the church. Especially if you are trying to reach a crossover audience, you cannot alienate readers with words like, "As we know from the story of Mary and Martha . . ." What story? Mary who? Martha who? Are we talking about Martha Stewart?

Watch your language

Some inspirational publications put restrictions on some words. Paul W. Smith, a senior editor for Gospel Publishing House, explains that "words such as 'golly' are viewed as euphemisms for the word 'God'" and are not appropriate for the publications he oversees. Ginger Kolbaba, editor of *Today's Christian Woman*, urges writers to strip their texts of jargon. She lists her pet peeves as words and phrases such as: abundant life, getting into the Word, prayer warrior, eternal reward, God's chosen lamb, living victoriously and traveling mercies. Such language confuses readers who aren't fluent in "evangelical-ese."

Style is another concern. Some publications are specific about how they handle references to the deity. For example, after the first mention of God, should a writer capitalize "He" and "Him"? And how about words like heaven, scripture and gospel?

Balance your arguments

The writer who explores just one side of an issue without acknowledging that another side exists is being unfair. Many articles that qualify as "inspirational" take a distinct point of view. They advocate or support certain behaviors and beliefs. That's acceptable, but it doesn't mean that an inspirational writer should preach to readers, manipulate information to support an argument or fail to mention the other sides of an issue. Accuracy, balance and objectivity are equally important whether you are writing to inform, to inspire, to motivate or to accomplish all three goals.

Tap sources with clout

The persons you choose to interview for an article depend on the readers you're trying to reach. We know a writer who earned a byline in a Christian magazine for an article about how to communicate with teenagers. Her expert source was a doctor who had written several books aimed at Christian parents and who was a frequent guest on Christian talk radio. The doctor's name was familiar to people who consumed Christian media, and his advice had clout within that audience. Interestingly, he was virtually unknown in the secular world. This meant that if the writer wanted to rewrite the same article for a secular or crossover publication, she would need to find an expert whose credentials would impress secular readers. The Christian world and the secular world are often worlds apart.

Keep in touch with reality

Along the same lines, inspirational writers who want to reach a wide audience need to know the world they want to change. This means becoming familiar with pop culture, keeping up with trends, consuming newspapers and best-selling books, knowing which films people are flocking to see and which TV shows draw the largest audiences. Writers who don't approve of what's happening in society and therefore retreat from it often have difficulty connecting with contemporary readers. They can't use examples with mass appeal; they can't drop names that everyone recognizes.

Write well

The skills that translate into success for a secular writer serve the inspirational writer equally well. Just because a writer professes to support the beliefs of a certain publication doesn't mean the writer's bad articles automatically will be published. Among the most serious "sins" of a writer is to churn out boring manuscripts. Ginger Kolbaba of *Today's Christian Woman* suggests that a writer should ask a friend to read an article before it is submitted to an editor and mark any place where the reader's mind starts to wander. The chances are good that the manuscript needs to undergo an additional draft that will delete the dull parts.

SIDEBAR 2

Sample Query Letter

Like all pitch letters, the query that is aimed at the religious press needs to stress an article's timeliness and should reflect the tone of the finished feature. As an example, writer Cathy Shouse prepared this letter for Relevant *magazine, a bimonthly publication that describes its readers as "culturally savvy 20-somethings."*

Dear Ms. _____:

Jon McLaughlin, 24, sings on the soundtrack of "Enchanted," the Disney movie, has been on Jay Leno, and was written up in *USA Today*. His co-written song "Beautiful Disaster" is a social commentary on teen girls and their images. A Christian who's finding success in the general market, he's a great representative of popular culture and might be worthy of a profile.

I'm a journalist with credits in *Family Fun* magazine and *The Saturday Evening Post* and am a contributor to *Focus on the Family* parenting newsletters. I interviewed Jon for an hour and developed a 1,500-word piece, although that could be trimmed and shaped to the *Relevant* style. I have some photos of his performance at a mall and also have publicity photos.

My Web site has dozens of published clips, and I'm attaching three recent ones here. Because most of the reporting is complete, I could have this story to you by December 1.

Sincerely,
Cathy Shouse[2]

WALKING THE FINE LINE

America has always been called a melting pot because of the ethnic, cultural and religious diversity of its citizens. Although most Americans identify themselves as Christians, other faiths are represented and growing. For this reason, some magazines try hard to be inspirational without being overtly Christian. This presents challenges for writers who have to walk a fine line. They want to appeal to readers' spiritual side but not their religious side. They want to write in a way that is meaningful to all, offensive to none. At the same time they don't want to water down their inspirational message to the point that their articles are bland.

The article that we include in this chapter, "The Least of These," was written by Holly G. Miller and published in a magazine geared to women of all faiths. In fact, the phrase on the magazine's cover explains that the publication is for "the thinking, believing woman." As you review the article, ask yourself these questions:

- Recalling the continuum of magazines, from overtly secular to overtly religious, how "hot" is the inspirational content of this message? Where does it belong on the continuum?

- Whereas the article mentions God several times, is it aimed at a particular faith or denomination? Would it be equally acceptable to Christian, Jewish and Muslim readers?
- What does the author hope the readers of this article will do with the information it contains?
- If the author wanted to recycle this article for a secular magazine, how would she need to change it?
- How does the author turn this local story into a national story?

THE LEAST OF THESE[3]

By Holly G. Miller

Versions of this story, written by other authors, have been published in numerous secular magazines and newspapers. This version appeared in Clarity, *June-July 2000.*

Debi Faris had one eye on dinner and the other on the 5 o'clock news the night she heard the story that changed her life. Someone had abandoned a baby several miles from her hometown of Yucaipa, Calif., and the televised account of the tragedy left her immobile, too horrified to walk across the kitchen floor to silence the report's graphic details. She could do nothing but stand there and absorb the painful description of a newborn boy who had been stuffed into a duffel bag and tossed from the window of a car speeding down a freeway. The story ended with the assurance that police were looking for the parents, and viewers should stay tuned. Not that Debi had a choice. "I couldn't move," she says. "I kept thinking, 'How can this be? How have we become a society that throws away its children as if they are nothing?'"

Four days later, the story still haunted her. Somehow she had to find out what happens to a child's body that no one claims. Is the baby given a name? Does he have some kind of funeral? Does anyone say a prayer over his grave? She thought about contacting the police, the Los Angeles County coroner, somebody, but she didn't know what to say or how to explain her growing obsession with the little boy. "I didn't know why this particular child was touching me so deeply," she says. "I didn't know why I couldn't get on with my life. Finally, I asked God what he wanted me to do, and I felt him saying, 'Debi, pick up the phone and make the call for me.'"

An act of love

The information she gathered did little to relieve her anguish. The investigator in the coroner's office was kind, but the procedure that she described seemed routine and uncaring. The bodies of abandoned babies—and the county tallied as many as 15 a year—were assigned numbers, were eventually cremated, and the ashes were stored until enough had accumulated to justify the opening of a common grave. Debi thought about the newborn, the duffel bag, the speeding car and the freeway. "I just can't have that for this child," she said.

With the blessing of her husband, Mark, and their three children, she asked that the authorities release the baby to her for burial. She secured permission, and in her conversations with Gilda—the coroner's investigator who was fast becoming her friend—she learned of another unidentified newborn awaiting cremation. Could she care for him too? she asked Gilda.

While she waited for the answer, her search for two burial places took her to Desert Lawn Cemetery in Calimesa, where an attendant pointed out an available plot in one area and another in a different section. "Somehow I knew we would be caring for more babies than these two," says Debi, "and I wanted a special place where they could all be together." She asked if there was a larger open area, and soon settled on what has become "a cemetery within a cemetery"—a peaceful portion of Desert Lawn that she calls the Garden of Angels. Her premonition proved right; more babies were in her future.

"Gilda called me one morning and said that the two little boys were ready for release and that I could come pick them up. Then she hesitated and told me that they also had the body of a little girl, about age 2, who had washed up on the beach in Malibu some time ago. She said, 'We know she belongs to somebody. She's been on this earth close to two years; who wouldn't miss her?'"

The coroner had been given the order to cremate the child's body. Gilda asked, "Debi, would you be willing to take care of her too?" Overwhelmed, Debi told Gilda she needed time to think, but she never doubted her response.

"I knew when I hung up the phone that we would be taking three caskets to the cemetery, but first I needed time alone with God. I remember praying, 'I don't think I can do this, God. I don't think I have the courage.' I stayed quiet for a while until I sensed that what we were doing was right. It was an act of love, and at that moment I made a commitment to offer it to any child who needed it."

A gift from God

Of the 41 babies she has helped bury since that August in 1996, Debi has given names to five of them herself. (She has enlisted help from others to name the other babies.) The gesture is symbolic rather than official since the law prevents a stranger from naming a baby. The first three, Mathew, Nathan and Dora, were easy to bestow. Each name means "a gift from God," and she believes all children are just that. Then there was 5-year-old Jeremiah, "seeker of truth"—whom the coroner had labeled "John Doe" during the months his body was stored at the morgue while police officers struggled to piece together clues to his identity, his death and the whereabouts of his parents. Most recently Debi named an abandoned newborn for the maintenance worker who found him among the refuse piled high in the bed of his trash truck. Tiny "Joel" had been alive when his mother discarded him, but had bled to death because she did not clamp his umbilical cord before putting him into a beachside Dumpster.

As a way of offering healing to the police officers who investigate the deaths of abandoned children, Debi invites them to name the babies and participate in the services that honor the children. "They're the ones who have to remove the babies from the trash cans, the Dumpsters and the roadways," she says. "I thought it might help for them to be part of something loving that was planned for these children." The police often accept her offer, arriving at the cemetery in full dress uniform and carrying stuffed animals to tuck into the small caskets. "Sometimes they even bring their pastors with them, or they buy the blankets to wrap around the children, or they read poems and release doves as part of the services," says Debi.

The bigger picture

Word of Debi's ministry has spread, and volunteers have rallied to help with details that range from making pillows to tuck under the babies' heads to tending the flowers that decorate the Garden of Angels. She has recruited a group of pastors to conduct the services, and her dad makes the white crosses that serve as markers. Local students plan fundraisers to help with expenses, and Debi's 14-year-old daughter, Jessica, sometimes accompanies her mom to the morgue to accept the small bundles that are wrapped in plastic. "At first I was leery because I wanted to protect Jessica from seeing such things, but she's very mature and has asked to go," says Debi. "Preparing the babies [for burial] is the hardest thing I do. I think it's an honor to put my arms around these children, love them and pray for them."

Until recently she handled all of the arrangements from a spare room in her home. Thanks to an anonymous gift she has moved this year to an office in the center of Yucaipa, where she spends more and more time overseeing efforts to lobby government in favor of a "safe abandonment" law. She hopes California soon will follow the lead of Texas in giving reluctant parents—who are often panicked teenage girls—an alternative to the reckless acts that end in death for their newborns. Under a safe abandonment law (which several other states are also in the process of developing), a mother could bring her unwanted baby to a safe place, such as a hospital emergency room or a police station, with the assurance that she won't be prosecuted. The legislation is controversial because opponents believe it allows parents to duck their responsibility and casually dispose of a child whose arrival is inconvenient.

Even more controversial is the notion of baby banks, where a mother can "deposit" her newborn into an incubator-like receptacle equipped with sensors that summon caregivers on call. The idea isn't new—Hamburg, Germany, currently is phasing in a pilot program. A group of churches is working to bring the idea, which they've dubbed "Safe Arms," to Southern California.

The silence within

By lobbying for legislation and investigating programs like Safe Arms, Debi hopes to reduce—better yet, eliminate—the need for her Garden of Angels cemetery. Until then, she tends the garden and honors its babies by telling their stories to service clubs, church groups and middle-school students. "It will always be our mission to try and keep children from coming to the Garden of Angels," she tells her audiences. "Until then, by sharing the stories of the children who rest there, we have become their voices."

People who hear the stories often are moved to come to the garden and see for themselves. First-time visitors usually compliment Debi on the lakeside setting with its well-tended flower beds and the tidy white markers decorated with pink and blue hearts, all bearing names. Sounds from the nearby freeway serve as a daily reminder of a baby's death four years ago that caused her to pause and listen to God. "When I see people rushing to get from Point A to Point B, I remember how important it is not to miss what is between one place and another," she says. "I think about the importance of stopping and listening to the urgings of our hearts."

ENDNOTES

[1]   Interview with Holly G. Miller, July 16, 2004.
[2]   Used by permission.
[3]   Holly G. Miller, "The Least of These," *Clarity*, June-July 2000, 48–51.

WRITING FOR PROFESSIONALS AND PRACTITIONERS

Your takeaway . . .

Thousands of magazines, newsletters and Web sites comprise the trade or "business-to-business media," which serve readers in specific careers and industries. An even larger number of magazines serve members of nonprofit associations, organizations, denominations, religious groups and alumni from colleges and universities. This chapter introduces you to their readers and offers tips on finding a publishable idea and choosing a target magazine. It also offers tips on writing annual reports for companies and organizations, a lucrative market for freelance writers. Finally, it concludes with explaining career opportunities and advantages of working for trade and sponsored publications.

When most people think "magazine" they think of the typical consumer titles they see every day in grocery or department-store display racks. These consumer magazines include the women's, men's, health and fitness, automotive, outdoor, celebrity, travel, hobby and leisure sectors and more. A consumer magazine is any magazine accessible to the general public through subscription or single copy sales. Yet consumer-magazine titles comprise only a third of more than 19,000 magazines published in the United States.

Trade magazines and those published by various organizations and nonprofit associations comprise the vast majority of the other 13,000 magazines. Opportunities for careers and freelance articles sales exceed those at consumer magazines.

A business-to-business (B-to-B) or trade magazine offers news and features to help people in specific professions and occupations become more successful at their jobs. Organization magazines—sometimes called sponsored publications—are published by professional associations, fraternal and hobby associations, churches and religious organizations, and colleges and universities for their alumni. Although loosely called the "nonprofit sector," organization magazines can also include magazines published by large companies for customers and employees.

In general, both sectors publish the same types of articles as consumer magazines: profiles, dramatic stories, trends and issues, how-to, calendar-related, etc. Their articles employ the same principles and techniques of writing that we've taught throughout this book. Freelance writers use the same techniques of publishing articles by studying the markets and writing query letters.

The major difference between consumer, trade and organization magazines is the specialized nature of their audiences. Just as each consumer magazine aims its content at a well-researched niche, readers of trade and organizational magazines comprise even more specialized niche audiences. When you approach these markets with ideas, it's even more essential to know your readers.

ORGANIZATION AND ASSOCIATION MAGAZINES

AARP Magazine, the nation's highest-circulation magazine, with more than 20 million subscribers, is an association magazine, not a consumer magazine. The American Association of Retired Persons sends the magazine free to all of its dues-paying members. One of the nation's oldest and most prestigious magazines, *National Geographic*, is technically an association magazine. Originally created in 1888 as a side benefit to members of the National Geographic Association, the magazine is a perk for readers who don't "subscribe" but "join" the association.

Organization magazines are published by companies for their employees or customers, universities for their alumni, denominations or religious organizations for their members, and professional and hobby associations for their members. It's difficult to estimate the number of magazines in this group, but 7,000 is a reasonable estimate. Organization magazines differ from consumer magazines because neither are they sold in stores nor can the general public subscribe. They are published by their sponsoring organizations and generally sent free as a membership benefit. That's why they are sometimes called "public relations magazines" or sponsored publications.

These magazines create an essential link between sponsoring organizations and their members. The only contact many members ever have with the association or organization to which they belong is the magazine they receive in the mail. Universities rely upon their alumni magazines to maintain the goodwill, loyalty and financial support they receive from their graduates. Magazines published by civic groups, such as Kiwanis or Rotary, serve as vital communication links between the local clubs and the international organizations.

The quality and scope of feature stories in these magazines is not in any way "second rate" or inferior to that of consumer magazines. Their editorial content does not simply contain news about the business of the organizations, but first-rate features that keep their readers informed about current events, issues and trends.

Here are some examples of organization and association magazines that accept articles from freelance writers who are not necessarily required to have a membership in the sponsoring organizations:[1]

- *Kiwanis* magazine seeks "articles about social and civic betterment, children, science, education, religion, family, health and recreation; emphasis on intelligent analysis and thorough research of contemporary issues."
- *American Legion*, which has more than a million subscribers, solicits articles focusing on "the American flag, national security, foreign affairs, social issues, health, education, ethics and the arts" that appeal to its audience of military veterans.
- *Reform Judaism* wants "exposé, general interest, historical, inspirational, interviews and profiles, opinion, personal experience and travel articles."
- *Concordia University Magazine*, which is 60 percent freelance written, seeks "general interest, historical/nostalgic, humor, interview/profile, opinion and personal experience" articles.
- *US Airways Magazine* looks for "smart, pithy writing that addresses travel, food, lifestyle and pop culture" relevant to its passengers and most common destinations.

The best Web gateway to association magazines is the Society of National Association Publications (www.snaponline.org) or the National Council of Nonprofit Associations. The Internet Public Library (www.ipl.org)

maintains the best online directory of associations and organizations. Learn more about publishing in religious magazines through the four groups representing thousands of these publications: Associated Church Press, Catholic Press Association, Evangelical Church Press and the Jewish Press Association. Each of these groups has Web sites that are listed in Chapter 19 or easily located with any search engine.

Two dozen professional writers associations (see Sidebar 1) serve writers specializing in areas ranging from dogs and cats to science and the military. Their Web sites can give you links to more magazines and publishing opportunities and tips on getting published.

Specialized Writers Associations

All of these associations have Web sites you can find easily with any search engine. Use them to learn more about writing for specialized magazines in these areas. Many of them have online job listings and opportunities for freelance assignments.

American Agricultural Editors' Association
American Business Media
American Medical Writers Association
American Society of Business Publication Editors
Association of Health Care Journalists
Catholic Press Association
Cat Writers' Association Inc.
Dog Writers Association of America
Evangelical Press Association
Fraternity Communications Association
Garden Writers Association
International Federation of Agricultural Journalists
International Food, Wine & Travel Association
Jewish Press Association
Military Reporters and Editors
National Association of Science Writers
National Council of Nonprofit Associations
National Education Writers Association
Outdoor Writers Association of America
Religion Newswriters Association
Society for Technical Communication

SIDEBAR 1

Society of American Business Editors and Writers
Society of American Travel Writers
Society of Environmental Journalists
Society of National Association Publications
Society of Professional Obituary Writers

The advantage of writing for organization and association magazines is the more frequent opportunities they offer for writing on topics of special interest to a writer. Their editors may be more accessible by telephone or e-mail and quicker to respond to queries. Circulations are less than those at consumer magazines and range from a few thousand to millions. The pay for freelance writers is usually less than consumer magazines and often varies in the $500 to $1,000 range for feature articles. In most cases, you don't have to belong to the sponsoring organizations to write for these magazines, but you do need to understand their readers and agree with the goals of the sponsoring organization.

Kathryn Keuneke, a 2002 college graduate, is editor of *Million Dollar Round Table*, a Chicago-based magazine serving a national association of certified financial advisers. She started as an editorial assistant five years ago and quickly worked her way up to editor.

> I answered an ad for a job at an association. Though I had a double major in journalism and economics, I knew nothing about the industry I was entering. It didn't matter. As the content experts, our members provided us with the information. We just had to help them present the information to each other in a polished way. Working for an association provides me with opportunities I wouldn't likely have at a consumer publication. From my first day, I was writing, editing and assisting the editor in moving the magazine through the publishing process. After five years, I became the editor of the magazine, and I have complete control over the focus and content of our 52-page bimonthly publication. You get a real education in subjects that can be very interesting and helpful in your own life.[2]

BUSINESS-TO-BUSINESS MAGAZINES

You've probably never heard of these titles: *Pizza Today, Party and Paper Retailer, Playground Magazine, American Window Cleaner, Balloons and*

Parties, Onion World, Portable Restroom Operator or *Wines and Vines*. All of these publications are listed in *Writer's Market* and solicit articles from freelance writers. Sometimes called trade magazines, their main purpose is to provide news and features to professionals in specific jobs, careers or industries. Some offer paid subscriptions, while others are supported entirely by advertising and sent free to key executives and decision-makers in various industries. Advertisers of products for specific industries and occupations are so eager to reach these key decision-makers that they're willing to pay the entire cost of publishing the magazine.

For example, *Onion World* covers the world of onion production and marketing and targets readers who are growers and shippers. *Balloons and Parties* magazine is published for professional party decorators and gift delivery businesses.

"Writers who have discovered trade journals have found a market that offers the chance to publish regularly in subject areas they find interesting, editors who are typically more accessible than their commercial counter-parts and pay rates that rival those of big-name magazines," says *Writer's Market*.[3]

For example, Allured Publishing Corporation is an 80-year-old Chicago-area company specializing in magazines, Web sites and trade shows serving the cosmetics, personal care and fragrance industries. Its magazine titles include *Cosmetics & Toiletries, Global Cosmetics Industry, Skin Inc., Journal of Essential Oil Research* and *Perfumer & Flavorist*.

Writer's guidelines for *Pet Product News International* state: "We're looking for straightforward articles on the proper care of dogs, cats, birds, fish and exotics as information the retailers can pass on to new pet owners." The editor advises prospective writers, "be more than a pet lover. Talk to pet store owners and see what they need to know to be better business people in general, who have to deal with everything from balancing the books . . . to animal rights activists."[4]

Campus Activities is sent free to entertainment buyers on every college campus in the United States. It features stories on performing artists, speakers and programs at individual schools and buys 40 articles a year from freelance writers. *Playground Magazine* describes itself as "a trade journal that offers up-to-date industry news and features that promote play and the playground industry." It covers playgrounds, play-related issues, equipment and industry trends while targeting a readership of recreation and parks managers, school administrators and child-care facility owners.[5]

Guidelines for *Woman Engineer* explain that it wants, "Articles dealing with career guidance and job opportunities for women engineers and manuscripts showing how to land an engineering position and advance professionally." *Mountain Resort Magazine* covers the ski and snowboard resort industry for people who work at resorts, but not necessarily the high-level managers: "Shoot ideas by e-mail and please include any relevant on-hill experience. Be young; be funny. Tell us a story you heard in a locker room rather than drone on about what's happening in a board room," its guidelines say.

While most consumer magazines have Web sites that replicate their print content, B-to-B companies are more likely to update their content daily or weekly. Whitney Sielaff, publisher and editorial director for *National Jeweler*, says that his magazine was historically known as a news magazine in the jewelry business. "The Internet forced us to change it to a news-analysis magazine. We had to back that up with a hard news site that provides constantly updated news to our readers." The extension into various forms of content delivery means, "We are not just writers for a magazine; we are content providers," says Sielaff.[6]

The most mistaken notion about trade magazines is that you have to be an expert or practitioner in the field to write for one of its magazines. Almost all trade journal editors and publishers say they have had better success hiring journalists and training them in the specialty than they have had hiring experts and training them in journalism. Experts more likely write with technical jargon that even readers of a particular specialized magazine might not understand.

Whitney Sielaff says when he hires writers or editors for *National Jeweler*, he looks primarily for a journalism degree and news-writing experience. "I want someone who knows how to turn around copy and meet deadlines. I want someone who can copy edit, who knows AP style and knows how to use a dictionary. I want people who are curious, interested and willing to learn," he says.

"Surprisingly, I knew little about healthcare coming into my first, part-time position at *Modern Healthcare*," said Nicole Voges, copy editor and Webmaster at *Modern Healthcare*, a magazine aimed at hospital and healthcare administrators. "I took a copy editing test and there were some words related to the industry where I had to pick the correct spelling, and the copy I edited was actual copy from the magazine, but otherwise, it's all been on-the-job learning."[7]

All you really need to write for a trade magazine is an interest in the field and access to some of its practitioners. While highly technical magazines may require some expertise of their writers, others deal with everyday products and services sold in almost any town. Does one of your relatives own a successful carpet-cleaning business? Then send a query to *Cleaning Business*, which looks for "interviews with top professionals on how they manage their business." Do you know about a great Mexican restaurant in your town? Then look up *El Restaurante Mexicano* in *Writer's Market*. Editor-owner Kathleen Furore, who is based in the Chicago area, says she looks for stories about "unique Mexican restaurants and about business issues that affect Mexican restaurant owners." She adds, "No specific knowledge of food or restaurants is needed; the key qualification is to be a good reporter who knows how to slant a story toward the Mexican restaurant operator."[8]

HOW TO FIND A MAGAZINE

The best online source for information is American Business Media's Web site: www.americanbusinessmedia.com. Founded in 1906, American Business Media represents 350 companies that produce 6,000 print and online titles and 1,000 trade shows each year. You can click on the "membership directory" link to browse through an alphabetical listing of these 350 companies, links to their Web sites and names and addresses of the magazines that they publish. Or you can search for specific magazines by category or geography.

The best print source is the venerable *Writer's Market*, which contains listings for more than 1,500 trade publications in 60 categories. For the same price (about $30), you can purchase a year's access to writersmarket. com, which contains guidelines with frequently updated information on these same 1,500 publications. We explained more of these resources in Chapter 6.

Another way is to ask people who work in that field what magazines they read. Chances are you have favorite restaurants, retail stores or service providers who are especially good at what they do. Maybe you have noticed something unique or outstanding at their places of business. Strike up a conversation with the manager, and it probably won't take long to learn what accounts for the difference. Ask about the manager's favorite trade magazines, and you may be ready to send a query letter to one of its editors.

CAREER OPPORTUNITIES AND ADVANTAGES

The major reason the B-to-B media offer good career choices is that they publish twice as many magazines as the consumer press. Experts estimate the number of consumer magazines around 6,000 while trade, associations and nonprofit organizations number around 13,000. While most consumer magazines are published in New York City, business press publishers are scattered around the country in cities such as Atlanta, Cleveland, Chicago, Denver, Detroit, Houston, Kansas City, Seattle and Washington, D.C. New York City may be a wonderful place to build a magazine career, but many people simply don't want to live there.

Carol T. Fletcher, a magazine journalism professor at Hofstra University on Long Island, says that jobs are more plentiful at trade magazines than consumer magazines:

> The jobs are there and often the publishers and editors come here recruiting our students. Our students are reluctant to take the jobs because they're not as sexy as consumer magazine jobs. But when they do, they always report having great experiences and really enjoying it. The magazines pay well, get them up and running right and give them important assignments. They get lots of experience writing, reporting and editing.[9]

The B-to-B magazines can also offer a stepping stone to consumer magazine jobs. "I also came out of school during a recession. I started out at *The American Lawyer* magazine. It wasn't my passion to write about law, but I learned a lot and worked incredibly hard," says Kristin Granero, editor of *Seventeen*.[10]

"The advantages to working at a B-to-B over working at a consumer magazine are numerous," said Nicole Voges. "Compensation is the first thing that comes to mind—because I've found that B-to-Bs are almost always more willing to pay more for good people than consumer magazines are—because consumer magazines have people tripping over themselves to take jobs, lowering the salary range for most entry-level positions. Trade magazines are more lucrative because there is less competition."

She said another advantage is that staffs are smaller. "So the opportunity to help with projects outside the scope of your position might be more plentiful than at a large consumer magazine where your only job is as a fact-checker or copy editor."[11]

If you're looking for a job, the best place to do a geographic search is the *Gale Directory of Publications*, which most large libraries carry. This four-volume annual directory contains an alphabetical state and city listing of all radio and television stations, magazines and newspapers published in every U.S. city.

Whitney Sielaff of *National Jeweler* has spent his 15-year career in the business-to-business media. He sees three advantages to a B-to-B career over a consumer-magazine career: more opportunities to write, more influence on your audience and more interaction with an educated professional audience.

First, he says, "If you really want to write, you can get that done easier in this field. The Web offers some good opportunities as well." Second, "You're catering to a higher level of educated audience. Most of those you're writing for are heads of companies or business owners and smart entrepreneurs. If you're writing for a newspaper, chances are you're out there talking to people on the street." And third, he says, "You can really have an effect. You are helping people improve in what they do on a daily basis. You can become an integral part of their work."[12]

GHOST STORIES: ANOTHER CHANCE TO WRITE FOR PAY

Organizational downsizing has created many opportunities for feature writers who want to gain experience and earn money but who don't care about public recognition for their work. Corporations and nonprofit agencies often hire freelancers to research and write annual reports that they distribute to their stockholders (if they are publicly traded companies), customers, patrons, employees, members, donors and other key audiences. The good news is that the pay is generous and the work is steady. The writer who delivers a top-quality product usually can depend on the same assignment year after year. The bad news is that organizations often don't publish the names of the freelancers they hire. An outside contributor must be satisfied with ghostwriter status. He or she receives a check but no byline.

In recent years the business of producing annual reports has changed radically. Many publicly traded companies, required by law to issue annual reports to their investors, have trimmed the size of their books. The feature stories and the colorful (but costly) photographs are luxuries of the past. Companies continue to print and distribute the financial information that the government mandates, but the photos and feature stories are reserved for the online versions of their reports. Not only does this save hundreds of thousands of dollars in production and postage costs, it also allows companies to update their Web pages frequently with new material and integrate audio and video clips. Feature assignments are still available, although the stories tend to be shorter.

If opportunities to write annual reports have decreased in the corporate world, they have increased in the nonprofit community. Organizations have to tell their stories in compelling terms if they want to attract donors, members, patrons and clients. Especially during difficult economic times, human-interest stories that put a "face" on a product or service can pique interest and generate support. Organizations that need support—museums, community foundations, symphonies, hospitals, libraries, ministries, etc.— produce annual reports as a way to connect with and be accountable to their audiences.

For example, a nonprofit community foundation uses its annual report to encourage donations from the community to continue its work. A recent annual report included feature stories and photos about three groups that received grants the previous year. They included a group offering aid to military veterans struggling with homelessness and substance abuse, a women's shelter providing a home to domestic-abuse victims, and a men's shelter providing food and housing for homeless men.

The words "annual report" may sound intimidating. Writers often plead ignorance when it comes to economics. They think they could never tackle an organization's annual report because they aren't fluent in the mysterious jargon that explains assets, liabilities, profits and losses. They think they surely would need a degree in business to have a hand in producing a publication that contains endless pages of numbers, pie charts and bar graphs.

Think again. Accountants provide the financial information, which is carefully scrutinized by attorneys. Feature writers do what they do best: conduct interviews and create memorable "people" stories. Similar to a high-school or college yearbook, an annual report chronicles the events, successes and failures of the previous 12 months. Editors typically choose a theme and then create feature material to support it. Often outside writers bring a fresh perspective to an organization's stories. The result isn't objective journalism but advocacy journalism. An annual report doesn't constantly pat its sponsoring organization on the back, but it does maintain a positive point of view.

ENDNOTES

[1]   Robert Lee Brewer (ed.), *Writer's Market 2009* (Cincinnati, Ohio: F&W Publishing, 2008).

[2]   E-mail to David E. Sumner, Aug. 28, 2008.

[3]   Robert Lee Brewer, *Writer's Market 2009*, 765.

[4]   Writer's guidelines quoted in this chapter were published in Robert Lee Brewer, *Writer's Market 2009*.

[5]   Robert Lee Brewer, *Writer's Market 2009*, 889.

[6]   Telephone interview with David E. Sumner, Aug. 2, 2004.

[7]   Telephone interview with David E. Sumner, March 31, 2008.

[8]   Robert Lee Brewer, *Writer's Market 2009*, 860.

[9]   Telephone interview with David E. Sumner, Aug. 20, 2008.

[10] Kristin Granero, "Chat with an EIC: *Seventeen*'s EIC, Ann Shoket." Accessed at www.ed2010.com, Aug. 20, 2008.

[11] Telephone interview with David E. Sumner, March 31, 2008.

[12] Telephone interview with David E. Sumner, Aug. 2, 2004.

WRITING FOR ONLINE PUBLICATIONS

Your takeaway...

Great writing is great writing regardless of the medium. Yet writing for online publications and Web sites poses unique challenges. You will learn five ways that writing for online publications differs from writing for print publications. You will also learn several specific ways to find the best places to publish your online work. The chapter concludes with 10 practical tips for success such as using links, keywords, subheadings, bulleted lists and emphasizing useful information.

The Internet market for writers will continue to grow as more people use the Internet and wireless access expands. It's easier to get an article accepted on a Web site or Internet-only publication than in print. While the pay is less, many editors purchase first electronic rights, which allows you to continue to look for print publishers for the same material.

The success of all Web sites depends on one thing—their ability to make users return on a regular basis. The only way to do that is offer original content and update it often. Consequently, writing for the Internet requires top-notch research skills. Online readers are highly literate and probably know what's been in recent newspapers and magazines. So when they come online, they expect fresh information.

According to Jacquelyn Wilson, an associate features producer for CNN.com:

> There also has to be a reason for you to write the story in the first place. It has to have a news peg. Perhaps this is even more prevalent in online writing because of its immediacy. Why would a reader go to your story on

a topic when they can dig up archives from the 1990s about the same topic?[1]

ADVANTAGES OF WRITING FOR ONLINE PUBLICATIONS

Writing for online publications has three advantages over traditional print magazines and newspapers. First, you can reach many more readers than in print publications, which are limited to subscribers and single-copy purchasers. Online users can read your work any time of day or night in any part of the world.

Thomas Didato, in an article for *The Writer* magazine, says:

> I have received dozens, if not a hundred e-mails from people who read my work in online magazines. I have received one [from someone] who read my work in a print magazine. I know that my online work is read, while my print work in some pretty good literary magazines is sitting in a dusty box in a closet . . . somewhere.[2]

Second, new writers can more easily get published because thousands of online magazines and Webzines have a continuous demand for fresh new material. Online editors are more accessible by e-mail and are always looking for new material. You will probably get a much quicker response to your e-mail query or submission.

Third, your online articles have an unlimited shelf life if the publication stores them in a public archive. Most subscribers tend to toss their print magazines after a month or two. Stories published on the Web remain accessible for an unlimited time and will continue to find new readers.

The disadvantage of online publishing is less pay and prestige than publishing in a "name brand" consumer magazine. Book author Dee Power did an informal survey of writers who wrote for online publications. She found that payment averaged around $20 for 500-word articles, $50 for 1,000 word articles and $150 for 2,500 word articles.[3] While that's considerably less than most consumer magazines, the main goal for a new writer should be getting published anywhere. Once you get some publication credits, you can leverage your success and start working your way up the pay scale.

WHERE TO GET PUBLISHED

The Internet provides thousands of sites that offer paying markets for freelance writers. They include print magazines that publish additional content on their Web sites, Internet-only magazines or Webzines, specialized-content sites such as travel, health or hobbies, and trade and professional association sites. While we can't possibly review all the Webzines or other places to get published, we can point you in the right direction and give you a few leads.

First, the Yahoo magazine directory links to more than 3,500 online magazines in 60 special-interest categories (http://dir.yahoo.com/News_and_Media/Magazines/).

Once you find a magazine that interests you, look for a link for its writer's guidelines, guidelines for contributors or a similar term.

Second, the annual directory *Writer's Market* has both print and online editions. While a Writersmarket.com subscription isn't free, it will give you constantly updated writer's guidelines and leads to key paying markets.

Third, the monthly magazines *Writer's Digest* and *The Writer* both publish regular "markets" departments offering leads to print and online magazines seeking articles. These departments, however, are not published in their online editions. Most university and public libraries will probably carry subscriptions. In addition, *Writer's Digest* offers its annual listing of "101 Best Web Sites for Writers" in each June issue.

Fourth, use your favorite search engines with keywords that will lead you to online magazines that publish writer's guidelines. Use one of the terms listed below followed by the type of magazine or content that interests you. For example,

"writer's guidelines" + gardening
"submission guidelines" + political magazines
"submissions policy" + health and fitness
"author guidelines" + religion
"contributor guidelines" + pet magazines
"guidelines for contributors" + music
"write for us" + news stories

These search terms were all tested and yielded several possible publications suited for those particular types of articles. However, if your first try doesn't yield useful results, try exchanging the terms such as submissions policy or contributor guidelines followed by the type of magazine you want to write for.

SIDEBAR 1

Web Sites that Pay for Articles or Share Revenue With Writers

www.articlewarehouse.com
www.associatedcontent.com
www.authorconnection.com
www.constant-content.com
www.lifetips.com

Web Sites With Leads to Freelance Writing Assignments (Print and Online)

www.freelancewritinggigs.com
www.allfreelancewriting.com
www.freelancewriting.com
www.journalismjobs.com
www.mediabistro.com

WHY INTERNET WRITING IS DIFFERENT

Knowing the differences between print and online writing will help you succeed when you research and write articles for online publication. Amy L. Webb, editor of an online magazine, told *Writer's Digest*: "The Web requires many more elements. Digital storytelling means that a piece may have 500 words in print, a two-minute audio clip, 37 links, photos and a searchable database. Writers hoping to break into Web publications must think of themselves as 'information brokers' rather than reporters—they need to be capable of collecting information for multiple platforms."[4]

That doesn't mean you have to be able to provide all of that "multimedia" information when you prepare an article, but you will help your chances of publication by including at least some photos and links to additional information. A print magazine will not want to publish a 1,500 word article without any art or photos and an online magazine will even less likely consider it.

The Internet has probably decreased the attention span of most users, and the average person will less likely read a 2,500-word article on a computer screen than the same one in print. Screen text is more difficult to read for five reasons:

- First, screen text requires more concentration from the reader because the text has less resolution. Laser printer text has 600 dots per inch and a full-color magazine photo may have 2,400 dots per inch. Computer screens, however, only have between 72 and 96 dots per inch.
- Second, screen text reading is slower. One study found that most people read screen text 25 percent slower than print text. They will likely spend less time in reading an Internet article than a book or magazine. And they often comprehend and recall less.
- Third, screen text lacks the context of print material. You can't view as much screen content as you can on a magazine or newspaper page. Therefore, online text lacks the visual cues of magazines (sidebars, subtitles, captions, photos, etc.) that shed light on the text's meaning. When you pick up a magazine, you usually look first at its cover and contents page. When you turn to an article, you glance at the photos and other graphical material. Internet users, however, can jump straight to an article from an outside link without ever seeing the home page or other contextual material.
- Fourth, screen text lacks the permanence of print material. It's "here" right now but gone in a click—sometimes an accidental click. When you read a magazine article, you can flip back to the previous page to refresh your memory. Internet text requires more time and effort to move back, forth and around. Readers get more easily distracted and may not return after clicking a link to another site.
- Fifth, reading screen text feels like work for many people—not fun— because it's part of their job. These people turn to the Internet for work-related reasons, not for entertainment.

These obstacles make writing for the Internet more difficult than it appears. You can't write in the same style you do for print publications. Magazines and newspapers can't "dump" their print material onto a Web site and expect users to read and enjoy it in the same way. Any print magazine article more likely gets read by subscribers than the same article on a Web site where thousands of surfers click in and click out daily.

TEN TIPS FOR INTERNET WRITING

"When you're writing for the Internet, you have to understand that the average reader will skim your piece," said Jacquelyn Wilson.

> I once saw a comic strip that said reading a newspaper online is like trying to meditate in a casino. There are too many bells and whistles (ads, links, audio, video). A reader will immediately jump to anything on the page that looks more interesting than what they're reading. They're distracted, bouncing their attention all over the place. So *every* part of your story has to have some kind of golden nugget in it.[5]

These principles of Internet writing are based on the premise that busy readers zoom in and out of Web sites quickly. One editor says, "Online writing needs to be snappy and exciting because it's harder to read on computer screens, and I think much harder to retain the information. . . . Use provocative leads, short paragraphs and lots of subheads to break up the text and make it easier on the eyes."[6] Therefore, we offer these practical suggestions to make electronic writing more compelling and keep your readers' eyes on the screen.

1. Begin with the Most Important Information

Internet articles are more likely read when the most important information comes first. Writers, therefore, may have to use the traditional "inverted pyramid" structure of newspaper writing. Print magazine readers more likely remain with a writer's logical presentation of evidence through to the conclusion of a 2,500-word article. But Internet readers will more likely decide whether to read an article based on skimming the first paragraph.

Not only should the most important idea introduce an article, Internet writers should begin every paragraph with its main point. "Research on reading printed text shows that people generally understand and remember paragraphs best when the paragraphs start out with the main point. When people skim through text on a page, they are most likely to read the first sentence of every paragraph," say Jonathan and Lisa Price in *Hot Text: Web Writing That Works*.[7]

2. Think Links

The right links add credibility to your material by linking to sites with examples and substantiating evidence. They can include tutorials or "how-to" Web sites, case studies and examples, reports or background information. You can place links in a separate sidebar or within the text itself. When you include links within your text, attach them to keywords at the end of the sentence or paragraph. Links are two-edged swords, however. Too many can distract readers and tempt them to leave the page.

3. Emphasize Keywords

Look for keywords in your content that can be used to link to other sites with similar content. As suggested above, include these keywords at the end of sentences and paragraphs if possible. Internet search engines rank results according to how often key phrases are linked with other sites with similar content. Or they may be ranked according to how often keywords appear in a document. You can also emphasize keywords by linking to other Web sites with similar content as the keywords.

4. Create Subheadings

Internet writers structure and organize their material into chunks of easily highlighted information. Subheadings that preview the content ahead are a great convenience for readers. Remember that Internet readers often will browse through the subheadings of an article before deciding to read it. "Subheads are also extremely important because no matter how boring print is on a page, print online can make your eyes go blurry. You have to have points of interest (like tourist traps) along the way to break up the cornfields," says Jacquelyn Wilson of CNN.com.

5. Use Bulleted and Numbered Lists

Internet readers look for quick bites and chunks of information. Bulleted and numbered lists provide several advantages.

- They quickly capture the reader's scanning eye.
- They highlight important information.
- They summarize main points.
- They provide contrast and emphasis.

Lists do another favor for the reader. In essence, the writer edits the material for the reader and says, "If you've only got a minute, here are the most important things you need to know."

6.   Emphasize Useful Information

Users more likely come to the Internet seeking specific information rather than entertainment or amusement. It's just not as much fun to read a page-turning novel on the screen as on a couch. Therefore, you'll find a higher predominance of service journalism content on the Internet than in print. Consumers want to know where to go on vacation, what kind of tires to put on their cars, medicine to use or where the good restaurants are.

7.   Use Fewer Words

Writing short and simple is a time-tested principle of print journalism, but the Internet requires you to economize even more for its impatient readers. You don't have to avoid profound ideas or complex information. It simply means you have to work harder to present profound ideas and complex information in a shorter space. For example, suppose an editor assigns the same story to two writers about how a local hospital staff makes bioethical decisions involving life and death. Suppose that story involves 20 facts. Writer "A" comes back with a 1,000-word story, while Writer "B" returns with a 2,000-word story. Therefore, Writer "A" has used "50 words per fact" while writer "B" used "100 words per fact." Like a hybrid car with higher gas mileage, writer "A" is a more efficient writer.

8.   Short Sentences and Paragraphs

Use simple declarative sentences with a subject, verb and direct object. Think of the period as your best friend. Use it frequently to avoid compound and complex sentences. In general, limit paragraphs to three to five sentences.

9. Use Everyday, Concrete Language

Imagine that every reader has a split-second to comprehend every word you use. If it doesn't register in the brain in that split second, then it's lost. Consequently, choose nouns that describe everyday objects and events and verbs that display specific actions.

10. Make It Punchy and Personal

You have more freedom to put voice and style in Internet writing. Make it quick and punchy with a little "attitude." Let the reader feel emotion and detect the voice behind your writing.

Jacquelyn Wilson says:

> My best piece of advice is to have fun with it. While newspapers are trying to mix it up a bit, the Internet really is the place to do that. Online you are freer to use the unconventional to catch someone's attention. You can link to audio and video that will support your point. You can be a little sensational and still keep good journalism at the heart of your story.

Writing for Internet magazines requires more of the writer's personal involvement. Some of its best writing steams with emotion and attitude, which get readers' attention.

KNOW YOUR ELECTRONIC RIGHTS

Electronic rights have become a battlefield between writers and publishers. In the 2001 decision, "Tasini v. *New York Times*," the U.S. Supreme Court ruled that newspapers and magazines had to obtain the writer's permission before selling their freelance contributions to electronic databases such as Lexis Nexis. The court also ruled that "first rights" meant first rights for one medium only (such as print or Internet), but not both unless specifically agreed upon.

While that sounds like good news for writers, its consequence means that more magazines demand "all rights" from freelance writers so they can publish the articles in any medium. We know of one writer who sold an article and then saw it posted on the magazine's Web site. She went back to the editor and demanded more payment. Unfortunately, she had sold all rights without realizing it. So if you plan to sell to an online-only magazine, make sure you're specific about selling "electronic rights" or "first electronic rights," so that you have the freedom to seek a print publisher.

Once an article is on a Web site, regardless of whether the writer sold specific "electronic rights," the author might have difficulty selling it elsewhere. That's because many print publishers regard anything published on the Internet—including personal Web sites—as previously published material.

Handheld computers now allow wireless access to the Internet—even in automobiles—where a hi-fi network exists. Hundreds of restaurants and coffee shops offer wireless access to their customers. Despite growing pains, the electronic market is expanding and will continue to grow as more people use the Internet and wireless access expands. Jacquelyn Wilson from CNN.com offers this concluding advice: "Don't be so afraid of writing online that you forget you're still writing. You're still a journalist. It's still a story. There has to be a beginning, middle and end. There has to be solid interviews, good quotes and interesting anecdotes."

LOST SOMETHING? CHECK THE VIRTUAL LOST AND FOUND

By Jacquelyn Wilson
June 30, 2008
www.cnn.com/2008/LIVING/06/30/lost.found/

(**CNN**)—Michael and Sharon thought the photos from their wedding were lost forever. Then a friend called the newlyweds and told them their photos were online.

The friend recognized Sharon in her beautiful white dress, holding a bouquet of yellow flowers, on a blog titled "Found Cameras and Orphan Photos." Within a week, Sharon had claimed the photos on the blog and had the photo CD back in her hands.

Matt Preprost's blog is full of successful reunions like this one.

A coach recognizes lost—or "orphan"—photos belonging to some of her high school cheerleaders; a Japanese exchange student gets back photos from her first American family Thanksgiving.

For anyone who's ever left a camera in a hotel, lost a hat in the wind, or dropped a glove on the street, Web sites like "Found Cameras and Orphan Photos" are a sign of hope.

While most people spend their time on the Internet searching for information, others are online looking for something a bit more tangible. And now several Web sites are making it easier than ever to retrieve your lost stuff.

Preprost's blog posts photos that people have found, either physical photos or those on cameras and memory cards. People can email Preprost three photos from the set, along with information about where and when they were found. Preprost then posts the three online and hopes that someone spots themselves in the photos and claims them.

The blog's inspiration came from a secret posted on PostSecret.com that read "I found your camera at Lollapalooza this summer. I finally got the pictures developed and would love to give them to you." Preprost contacted the secret poster Frank Warren and decided to start a blog based on the lost camera concept.

Now nearly 100 photo sets have been posted to the blog, and 9 or 10 of them have been claimed. The 10 percent success rate encourages Preprost to keep up his work. "These cameras contain memories that their owners thought were gone for good. To give them hope and inspiration that one day a total stranger will do a good thing to help them out is a very positive thing," Preprost said.

That connection with a total stranger is part of the reason Davy Rothbart runs FOUND magazine and FOUNDmagazine.com.

"We all have a curiosity about the people we share the world with," Rothbart said. "The fact is, when you find a note blowing down the street, it's a fragment of a story. It's up to you to fill in the blanks. There's something exciting about that."

FOUNDmagazine.com takes submissions of everything from random notes to diaries to photos to postcards. A lot of the submissions are random pieces of paper that are funny, but no one would really want back. But other finds are spotted online or in the magazine and claimed by their rightful owners.

A 20-year-old letter-writing correspondence between a student studying abroad in Japan and her boyfriend at Brown University was recognized in the magazine's third issue. A container of the boyfriend's stuff had been found in a basement at the university.

"We had an entire box of the letters," Rothbart said. "She asked if she could have them back. There was a passport and everything, and it was returned to her."

Some of the stuff claimed to be lost online may seem trivial—a recipe for raspberry Danish, for instance—but even that could be a treasure passed down from generation to generation. *America's Test Kitchen* has a forum where people can ask for recipes they've lost. And Uncle Phaedrus, consulting detective and finder of lost recipes, will personally search the Internet and other resources to find food favorites from your past.

Other lost items like jewelry, clothing and pets can be found at The Found Bin. This Web site allows you to search under multiple categories or by location. The results use Google Maps to show you exactly where the item was found, making it easier to determine if it was yours.

Even lost cars can find their way home. Keith Ingersoll, from The Lost Car Registry, helps owners who regret selling their beloved vehicles find them again. Many of the site's visitors own or are buying cars and want car history information. But a few are searching for a specific car, sometimes one that belonged to a relative who recently passed away.

And for those with a slight foot fetish, Humphrey Dunn runs a photo gallery of lost shoes. He wanders beaches, streets and even cemeteries with a camera in hand. Some are obviously forgotten, the lone flip flop on the beach. But others are so obscurely placed Dunn wonders how they could ever have been abandoned.

One of his favorites is that of a four-inch heel sitting atop a large boulder on a very rocky beach. "I guess the owner discovered that they should have worn something else that day," Dunn said with a laugh.

Fortunately, he can't remember ever losing a pair of his own shoes. "But if I did, I'd hope someone would post a picture of them on the Web so I could track them down. Although, I am pretty happy that the owners of the ones I found in the cemetery didn't come back in person to claim theirs."

ENDNOTES

[1]   E-mail to David E. Sumner, July 22, 2008.
[2]   Thomas Didato, "Now Is the Time to Write Online," *The Writer*, February 2008, 30–33.

3   Dee Power, "Begin Writing for Internet Markets," *The Writer*, July 2008, 46.
4   Debbie Ridpath Ohi, "Cast a Wider Net," *Writer's Digest*, Jan./Feb. 2007, 50.
5   E-mail to David E. Sumner, July 22, 2008.
6   Quoted in Anthony and Paul Tedesco, *Online Markets for Writers* (New York: Henry Holt, 2000), 43, 48.
7   Jonathan and Lisa Price, *Hot Text: Web Writing That Works* (Indianapolis: New Riders, 2002), 199.

PART V

POSTSCRIPT

Magazine journalism is a competitive business. Writers vie for slots on a publication's masthead just as their articles compete for inclusion in its table of contents. Some of the same strategies that help a job applicant secure an entry-level position also catapult a manuscript out of the field and into print.

22

LAST CHANCE: THE FINAL DRAFT

Your takeaway . . .

Too often a feature article is one draft short of an "A" if you are submitting it to a professor for a grade; or it's one draft short of acceptance if you are submitting it to an editor for publication. This chapter shows you how to step back and review your copy as a professional evaluator does. Our 20-point checklist serves as an assessment tool to help you identify and fix common writing errors.

As a feature writer, you want to create *quiet* manuscripts that are free of communication noise. That doesn't refer to sound, but to any distraction that tugs a reader's attention away from the article's content. If the noise is loud enough (think fire alarm), the reader may concentrate on the distraction rather than on the message. Writing problems such as a lack of focus, weak quotations, poor word choice, grammatical errors and run-on sentences qualify as communication noise. They can cause a professor to lose patience and a student to lose points. Likewise, they prompt editors to reach for their ready stack of rejection slips.

Before you submit your article for a grade or for publication, evaluate it against this checklist. Many of the criteria on the list are familiar because we've discussed them earlier in this book. We offer them here as a final reminder.

1 **Required word count.** Editors and professors are precise in the number of words they expect in the article packages they assign. *Writer's Market*[1] gives the range of 1,000 to 6,000 words for articles, but that is too broad. Check the writer's guidelines of a publication to learn the recommended length. If an editor specifies 1,500 words, you can

slice that number in a variety of ways—a main article of 1,000 words, two sidebars of 225 words each, and an info box of 50 words. Length is a good indicator of the depth an editor or professor expects.

2 **Tightly focused idea.** Topics that are too broad can sprout legs and take off in multiple directions. If you make the mistake of pursuing all the directions, you may end up running around in circles and going no place. Summarize the central point of your article in one clear sentence. Include that sentence within the first three or four paragraphs of your story. Result: A nutgraf, which points the reader to what's ahead and provides a convenient stopping point if the content fails to interest the reader.

3 **Strong lead.** Ask yourself these questions: "Does my lead grab reader interest? Does it establish the right tone? Does it establish my chosen voice? Does it serve as a legitimate gateway to the topic?" A lead paragraph that is too long (more than four sentences) can intimidate readers. A lead can be shocking, sensational, funny or dead serious— but never boring.

4 **Anecdotes.** Have you included enough stories and examples that illustrate the main points? Do they add color and human interest? Re-read the little stories that you've sprinkled throughout your article. Make sure you haven't used two anecdotes to illustrate one point. To qualify as an anecdote, a story needs to describe a situation and reach a conclusion. Pare your anecdotes down to their bones.

5 **Smooth transitions.** Look at the way you move from one point to another. Read your text out loud and listen for clumsy or abrupt transitions. If your editor or professor allows you to use boldface subheads within the text, place them judiciously throughout your copy to move the story forward. Coherence means that the parts of a story—facts, quotes, anecdotes, etc.—fit together in a way that flows and makes sense to the reader.

6 **Quotations.** Do enough interviews so that you can include a lively quotation from a credible source in at least every third or fourth paragraph. Direct and indirect quotations represent people, and people add depth and color to an article. An article without quotations tends to preach or drone. As you skim your manuscript, look for (and eliminate) all bland and "cheerleader" remarks.

7 **Defendable sources.** Everyone who is quoted in an article should bring insight to the topic. Don't add boring or meaningless words just to have a quote. Think of your sources as "voices" and strive for variety

and credibility. Can you defend the presence of every source that populates your article?

8 **Originality.** Will every paragraph make the reader think, "Wow, I didn't know that!" or "I never heard that before"? Or have you simply recycled old news that anyone can find by "Googling" the Internet? We often read articles by students that elaborate on common sense and what most people can easily find online. Examine each sentence and paragraph to determine if they add fresh, original information to your main theme.

9 **Add some sidebars.** Editors love sidebars. Readers love sidebars. When readers scan pages, sidebars catch attention and pull them into the article. A sidebar may include a table or list, but you can also excerpt text and narrative and put them into a sidebar. Sidebars enhance the graphical appeal of a page with contrast and emphasis and also summarize complex information concisely. They bring to the page what graphic designers call "points of entry." Look for any set of paragraphs that can be read alone as self-contained information.

10 **Library and online research.** Have you added enough depth? By doing substantial, in-depth background research you can add interest and gain readers. By setting a local story in a national context you broaden its appeal and marketability.

11 **Strive for unity.** Weave the article around one central idea or main theme. As you edit the first draft, clarify your main purpose and include only ideas and concepts that fulfill that purpose. Sticking to your topic gives unity. A single purpose helps you collect and organize information economically. Unity means that a story focuses on one topic only. It gives the reader the sense that it was written for one purpose using one voice, tense and tone.

12 **Consistent viewpoint.** Viewpoint is a choice, but once established, it needs to be consistent. Make sure you've selected the right viewpoint and have maintained it. First-person viewpoint (I) is the obvious choice for a personal essay; second-person (you) creates intimacy with readers; third-person viewpoint (he or she) works well when you want to be objective. The key is to avoid switching from one viewpoint to another.

13 **Consistent tone.** Think about the kind of audience you are writing for and make sure that the tone you have selected is appropriate. You might choose to sound conversational, formal, sassy, academic, witty . . . and the list goes on. Again, the key is consistency. Knowing what

tone is appropriate for your article will guide you in the use of slang, sentence fragments, contractions, etc.

14 **Consistent style.** If you are writing for the feature pages of a newspaper, you will probably follow the *Associated Press Stylebook*. If you are writing for a literary magazine, you need to brush up on *The Chicago Manual of Style*. Many large publications develop their own style sheets and expect writers to adhere to the rules. Once again, the best advice is to be consistent. Don't abbreviate a word in one paragraph (Sept.) and spell it out in the next (September).

15 **Clever title and cover line.** Although editors reserve the right to change the title of an article, the writer always wants to offer a suggestion. Take a cue from the pages of the publication. Some magazines like puns, other like labels, a few combine the two. (*The New Yorker* once ran an article about infants who suffer from colic and called it "Crybabies.")[2] Your challenge is to provide a title that looks as if it fits perfectly into the publication that will receive it.

16 **Few adjectives and adverbs.** Pay particular attention to adverbs that you have tacked onto attributions (she said *softly*; he said *loudly*). Can you substitute one word for two (*whispered, bellowed*)? Adjectives and adverbs should never be used to inflate the word count of an article.

17 **Action verbs.** Watch for "is," "are," "was" or "were" verbs and see if you can figure out a way to replace them with a strong, action verb. Look for sentences beginning with the dead constructions "there is" or "there are" and rewrite them to begin with a noun and action verb. You'll find that it's easy to rid your copy of "dead expressions."

18 **Satisfying ending.** Reread your article and make sure you've answered all the questions that you've raised. End with a strong final quote or the wrap-up to the anecdote that you used as your lead. Don't summarize what you've already written in the body of the article.

19 **Obvious purpose.** Ask yourself, "What was I trying to accomplish with this feature?" Among your possible answers are: to educate, activate, motivate, commemorate, explain, demystify, inform, influence, inspire, honor, entertain, warn, persuade, argue. Now ask yourself, "Did I accomplish my purpose?"

20 **Proofread carefully.** Don't rely on your computer's spelling and grammar check to get it right. It will not catch spelling errors like using "complement" for "compliment" or "principal" for "principle." A computer can never replace a careful set of eyes with an old-fashioned dictionary by your side.

Prepare to Delete

Cleanse your copy of redundancies, qualifiers and clichés that editors dislike. These wordy expressions creep into our spoken language, but they have no place in our written text.

A majority of (most)	For the purpose of (for)
At this point in time (now)	Free gift (gift)
Brand new (new)	Gather together (gather)
Due to the fact that (because)	In order to (to)
Easter Sunday (Easter)	Make a conclusion (conclude)
End result (result)	Mental attitude (attitude)
Exact opposites (opposites)	Past history (history)
Filled to capacity (filled)	Write a summary (summarize)

Qualifiers: *If you can delete a word without losing meaning, the word is unnecessary. Get rid of it.*

Completely demolished	Slightly disappointed
Little confused	Somewhat surprised
Rather important	Totally ruined
Readily available	Very obvious

Clichés: *Avoid them like the plague.*

At the end of the day	Right on target
Fact of the matter	Step up to the plate
Get a life	The name of the game
Out of the box	You go, girl!
Put it on the back burner	24/7

SIDEBAR 1

ENDNOTES

1   Robert Lee Brewer, "Editor FAQs," in *2008 Writer's Market* (Cincinnati, Ohio: Writer's Digest Books, 2008), 77.
2   Jerome Groopman, "Crybabies," *The New Yorker*, Sept. 17, 2007, 46.

23

HOW TO FIND A MAGAZINE JOB

By David E. Sumner

Your takeaway . . .

This chapter explains four steps to help you prepare for a magazine career and three steps to follow when you begin your job search. Strategies include creating good work habits, getting media experience and building the portfolio, doing two or more internships and creating a writing specialty. Steps to follow later include setting a specific goal and pursuing it relentlessly, writing an original cover letter with each application, and making telephone calls and visits to prospective employers.

As coordinator of the magazine program at one of the nation's 10 largest journalism schools, I have spent the past 20 years teaching magazine courses and helping students find jobs in the industry. I've given dozens of lectures about how to write a résumé, improve a portfolio and search for editorial positions. Former students are working for dozens of magazines—print and online—from New York to California. Of course, others have had to settle for jobs in real estate, office work and even retail stores, at least on a short-term basis.

Consequently, I have observed the work habits and study skills of students who have succeeded in magazine publishing and those who haven't. The students who succeed as magazine writers and editors don't simply have good luck or follow a better job-search strategy. They have developed important skills, work habits and attitudes in college that have carried over into their careers. This chapter, therefore, has two parts. The first explains what to do now to prepare for a magazine career. The second part advises what steps to take after you start your job search.

STARTING NOW

Create good work habits

The first step is to develop good work and study habits that will carry over into your professional career. Mediocre students may take comfort in the fact that numerous studies show little correlation between grade-point average and later career success, which is true in journalism as well. But most of my students who succeeded as magazine editors and writers earned all A's or mostly A's in their journalism courses, if not in other courses.

If you develop good work and study habits, many professors will go out of their way to help you find a job. I've gone the extra mile many times to help deserving students find a magazine job. What impresses professors so that they will give you a glowing recommendation and make telephone calls to help you find a job? Here are some suggestions:

- Never be late to class.
- Never miss the deadline or fail to turn in an assignment, no matter how minor.
- Never miss class except for illness or personal emergency.
- Be sociable and polite with fellow students and the professor; this includes disagreeing in a civil and rational manner.
- Do more work than expected or required on all of your assignments.
- Display a teachable attitude and don't act like you know it all.

While doing these things may seem like sucking up or brown-nosing, they are the same work habits that guarantee success in the workplace.

When asked about common mistakes she sees among interns and recent graduates, Ann Shoket, editor of *Seventeen*, says, "Gossiping and showing up late. When you're first coming out of school, it's so hard to understand the business world. Make sure you're modeling your behavior after the executive level instead of the other interns or entry-level staffers. Stay focused on the next level up."[1]

Lauren Gelman, a senior editor at Parents.com, advises students to turn in assignments early:

Turning in assignments early (or at least, not late) is a good habit to get into now. Especially now as magazines are expanding their brands online with blogs and other daily forms of content, there's something so valuable about editors and writers you can trust to meet their deadlines—and that frees you up to pitch or ask for other or more challenging projects or assignments.[2]

Kathryn Keuneke, editor of *Million Dollar Round Table*—a magazine for financial advisers—says the "teachable attitude" is important in the workplace:

> Go into your first magazine job without the attitude that you already know everything. It's hard not to feel that way after you've gone through all those specialized classes . . . but you still have a lot to learn. An editor will be a lot more eager to share information with you and involve you in things if you are appreciative of the learning opportunities.

She adds, "I have trained both types of people here, and you're more likely to be trusted with more responsibility if you're not afraid to admit you're not perfect and have areas you need to improve."[3]

"Learn that a job is all about criticism," says Adam Bornstein, assistant editor at *Men's Health*. "A lot of people who don't make it here can't take the criticism. The editor is there to make you better and not criticize you personally. If you go in with the right attitude, expect to be criticized, and accept it with the right attitude," says Bornstein.[4]

Doing more than expected can also make the difference between a great and a mediocre story, says Lauren Gelman:

> Whether it's a feature-writing assignment for a magazine-writing class or a 750-word article for the school newspaper, always show you're willing to get in the trenches and cover all your bases. You may only need two sources for an adequate story, but maybe it's the third or fourth interview that'll give you the amazing pull-quote or totally change your lead.

Ted Spiker, a magazine journalism professor at the University of Florida, says the "hustle factor" distinguishes his most successful magazine students from others. "The big factor that ties them all together is that they've got the ability to hustle when they report. A lot of students can write well and have good ideas, but the difference is their willingness to take the extra step to make the story succeed. Magazine editors look for the hustle factor. Are you going to settle for three sources or are you going to go for 30 until you have all the information you need?"[5]

Get experience and build the portfolio

Student media experience is essential—not optional. I encourage our magazine majors to work at least a year on the student magazine and a year on the student newspaper. Working on the magazine gives them feature writing, editing and design experience. Working on the daily student newspaper gives them experience meeting daily deadlines and reporting and writing stories quickly. Since our student newspaper is published daily (except on weekends) and the student magazine is published three times a year, they get more clips and build their portfolios more quickly with newspaper writing.

Every year I conduct exit interviews with graduating seniors from the magazine journalism major. To graduate, they must have a portfolio that contains writing samples from the student magazine, newspaper and internship experiences. Every year a few students bring a portfolio without any published clips—only a few articles written for their journalism classes. Without exception, no graduate without published clips ever found a newspaper or magazine job. These are the students who must settle for jobs in real estate, office work or retail sales. Students without at least five to 10 published clips usually don't find media-related jobs.

"This probably sounds trite, but it's really about experience, experience, experience," says Lauren Gelman at Parents.com. Nichole Screws, fashion market editor at *Esquire*, says, "The best advice I can give is write, write, write. Get clips through the school paper, magazine and local online magazine. Students are lucky these days because they have a whole new medium—online—to get work published. Use it. Clips and experience are the holy grail of magazine entry," she says.[6]

Complete two or more internships

Most journalism students complete an internship, but two or more internships make you stand out from the crowd. You don't have to do two summer internships. Fall and spring internships are less competitive and easier to find. Do a fall or spring semester internship, even if it means moving elsewhere and not taking any classes. Graduates with two internship experiences get the best jobs and get them more quickly than those with only one.

"Two of my earliest internships were at a local newspaper and a small trade magazine, where I got tons of clips, interviewing experience and great fodder to use for future interviews," says Lauren Gelman at Parents.com. "As you get closer to junior/senior year, if you want to work at a major publication in New York City, then you should go for an internship at one of the big publishers—Hearst, Condé Nast, Meredith, etc. The contacts you can make at an internship there can be very helpful when you're job-hunting for real."

"Some of my best magazine students have done four or five internships by the time they graduate," says Larry Stains, director of the magazine journalism program at Temple University. Some of his former students are now working at *People, Entertainment Weekly, Harper's Bazaar* and other well-known consumer magazines in New York City.

"The most successful students have a good balance of internships," says Ted Spiker at the University of Florida. "They have some local magazine experience and they have interned at a big one to see how the inside of a big magazine works. They've also worked on the local newspaper and obtained daily reporting experience."

An unseen advantage of internships is the networking opportunities they provide. "The skill I wish they would teach more in journalism school is the art of networking. Being able to make and maintain relationships in the magazine industry is key to breaking in and staying. Whom you know is a huge advantage," says Nichole Screws. "Once a relationship is started . . . maintain it by staying in touch. Write an occasional note, remind them about you. If they show interest in your career, update them on internships and job changes," she advises.

Create a specialization

Although not usually required, a specialty in a field of interest can give you an edge in finding a job. A writer with a specialty in a particular field can always write general-interest articles. But a general-interest writer may not always have the ability to write specialized articles.

Adam Bornstein, an assistant editor at *Men's Health* and University of Florida graduate, says that his specialty in health and fitness writing helped him land this job. "I advise finding a niche and becoming a more specialized writer. For me it was health and fitness. What separated me from other applicants was that I had different types of certifications and research experience in this field that made me more marketable. They were a combination of my personal and professional interests," he says.

SEARCHING FOR A JOB

Decide what you want and pursue it aggressively

When you start the job search, which should be in your junior year, the first thing to do is decide exactly what you want to do and where you want to do it. *What Color Is Your Parachute: A Practical Manual for Job Hunters and Career Changes* by Richard Bolles is the world's best-selling job-hunting book.[7] Originally published in 1970, it has sold 8 million copies in 12 languages, averaging 20,000 copies per month in sales.

Deciding what you want and pursuing it aggressively is the central tenet of Bolles' advice, which he based on extensive research of successful job hunters. The most successful job hunters have a clear goal that they relentlessly pursue until reaching it. I've given many lectures to students on finding jobs based on Bolles' five best and five worst ways to find a job (see Sidebar 1).

Best and Worst Ways to Find a Job

In *What Color Is Your Parachute: A Practical Manual for Job Hunters and Career Changes*, Richard Bolles offers "Five Best Ways to Find a Job" and "Five Worst Ways to Find a Job." His tips are based on documented research and echo advice given by recent graduates and professors quoted in this chapter.

Five best ways to find a job

- asking for job leads from family, friends, professors or anyone you know (33 percent success rate)
- knocking on doors of any company that interests you, whether you know it has a vacancy or not (47 percent success rate)
- using the Yellow Pages® to find companies that interest you in cities where you want to work (69 percent success rate)

SIDEBAR 1

- with a group of friends, using the Yellow Pages® to find companies that interest you (84 percent success rate)
- the creative approach: decide exactly what your skills are, where you want to work and what you want to do and pursue your goal relentlessly in any way possible (86 percent success rate)

Five worst ways to find a job

- using the Internet (10 percent success rate)
- mailing out résumés at random to employers (7 percent success rate)
- answering ads in trade and professional journals (7 percent success rate)
- answering local newspaper ads (5 to 24 percent success rate)
- going to employment agencies and search firms (5 to 24 percent success rate)

Journalism professors and recent graduates interviewed for this chapter consistently echo Bolles' advice. "My most successful students have a persistent and unshakeable goal and desire to get to where they want to get to. They have a single-minded determination and never give up," says Larry Stains at Temple University in Philadelphia. Determination is more important than talent, he says. "They may not be the best writer; they may have less talent. But the key factor in their success is determination."

"The biggest mistake some of my students make is not having a focus to their job search," says Prof. David Abrahamson at Northwestern University's Medill School of Journalism.

> They don't really know where they want to work. What they have to do is to cast a very wide net, look closely at a lot of magazines, and then, most importantly, establish their own priorities. Make up an A list, a B list and a C list of publications, based on their own enthusiasms or interests. It's okay if they end up with a total of 20 or 30 or even 50 magazines, as long as they can put them in a rank-order that reflects their own preferences. Then they should concentrate on making contacts and getting interviews at those magazines.[8]

Lauren Gelman, a former student of Abrahamson's at the Medill School of Journalism, says, "Target 10 or 12 publications that you really want to work for and you're passionate about. And your passion will come through in your letter and your communication. You will also impress the editors if you show you've been a reader of the magazine before you go on the job interview."

"Figure out what your priorities are. Is it to work at a specific genre of publication (women's magazine, fashion book, newsweekly), to work in a certain city, like New York, to edit a certain kind of content, like health or politics? Then, leave no stone unturned," says Gelman.

Finally, strike a balance between having a focused goal and being flexible when an opportunity presents itself. Although you should have an ideal job as your goal, most people don't find their ideal job until after working years in less-than-perfect jobs.

"Don't let the perfect job be the enemy of the good job," says David Abrahamson. "Students should have enough flexibility to recognize when a good opportunity presents itself, even if it isn't exactly what they originally had in mind."

Write an original cover letter that proves you know the magazine

The cover letter offers a great chance to display your creativity and writing ability. Your letter should display knowledge of each magazine you apply to and explain how your talents can serve its interests. Talk about how your skills can help this magazine or publishing company. Don't send the same boiler-plate cover letter to every company you apply to. Don't talk about why you want the job or what it will mean for your career. Don't paraphrase your résumé in a cover letter.

"Never send a generic cover letter that begins with 'to whom it may concern,'" says Nichole Screws from *Esquire*. "A cover letter is your first chance to impress the editors with your passion for working where they work. Be specific, cite examples, anecdotes and show creativity. Prove that you read the magazine, at least a few issues, and start with something that will keep them reading past hello," she says.

Lauren Gelman says, "When you're mass applying to multiple jobs a day, remember to be careful and give due diligence to each application. Research the publication thoroughly and have a very clear understanding of what it's about, who the reader is, what makes it unique and why you want to work there."

"The cover letter offers a perfect opportunity to show you can capture the tone of the magazine. If you do a lot of homework on the company, you can show that in the cover letter. You have the chance to produce the kind of writing they are looking for," says Adam Bornstein.

Make telephone calls and visits

In *What Color Is Your Parachute* Richard Bolles estimates that up to 80 percent of all job vacancies are not advertised in newspapers, magazines or on the Internet. All companies would prefer to fill vacancies without having to go through the time and expense of advertising for at least three reasons. Advertising their vacancies can bring hundreds of applications, and they don't want to spend time sifting through and replying to each one. If they can get a few strong applicants through word-of-mouth referrals and unsolicited applications, then there's no need to advertise. Second, résumés and cover letters don't reveal invisible qualities like honesty, reliability and initiative and can cover up character deficiencies like substance abuse or a criminal record. If an employer can get enough qualified applicants through word-of-mouth referrals and unsolicited applications, again, why advertise? Third, public advertising of jobs puts employers at risk of lawsuits if rejected applicants feel they've been discriminated against for any number of reasons.

Therefore, even if you don't feel adept at networking, a phone call or e-mail to the right editor at the right time can put your foot in the door before everyone else's.

Lauren Gelman says informational interviews can make a big impression:

> People love to help students and are usually willing to spend some time on a desk-side informational interview. Make a list of all the publications or companies you'd love to work for and e-mail a couple of editors introducing yourself and asking for an informational interview. You'll learn a little bit about their job, what the publication looks for in pitches from writers or potential staffers, and you'll have a contact to follow up with down the road. Even if it doesn't pan out to anything right away, you'll still have made a face-to-face contact and have gotten your name out there, putting yourself in a more valuable position should something open up later.

"Everyone is going to have a cover letter, résumé and clips," says Adam Bornstein. "The biggest thing you can do to get noticed is your willingness to show up or place a phone call. You can only see so much about my personality on a piece of paper, but personal contact can make a huge difference."

After he applied for his job at *Men's Health*, he says, "They gave me an opportunity for a phone interview or coming up in person. It was a no-brainer; I made the trip. By the time I had my layover on the way home, I already had a voice mail offering me the job. If you impress the right people, it will open doors for you."

Best Places to Look for Magazine Jobs and Internships

www.ed2010.com (managed by young New York magazine editors)

www.mediabistro.com (the best source for consumer magazine jobs and internships)

www.asbpe.org (American Society of Business Publication Editors)

www.snaponline.org (Society of National Association Publications)

www.careerhq.org (jobs at nonprofit associations)

http://careers.associationforum.org (jobs at Chicago-area professional associations)

See also the list of specialized writers associations in Chapter 20.

SIDEBAR 2

IS A MASTER'S DEGREE USEFUL?

Many students ask whether a master's degree in journalism will help them find that first job. If all other qualifications are equal, a master's degree could give you the nod over another applicant. But a master's is not that helpful in getting a job if you have earned an undergraduate degree in journalism and obtained some good experience in student media and internships. Most master's degree programs offer few, if any, advanced skills courses like "advanced magazine writing" or "advanced investigative reporting." Master's degree courses focus on topics like research methodology, research statistics, media history, media theory or law.

Some students in some situations, however, could benefit from a master's degree and gain a definite edge in the job market. First, master's programs are an excellent option for career-changers or students who have an undergraduate degree in another major. Sometimes we get students with an accounting degree or social-work degree who spent a few years at a job they didn't like. So they returned to college to earn a master's degree aiming to start a second career in journalism. If you enter a master's program with no undergraduate courses in journalism, most universities will require you to take up to 15 hours in skills courses like reporting, feature writing or news writing. Time spent while earning the master's degree will also allow you to get experience with an internship and work on a student newspaper or magazine.

Second, a master's degree in journalism from a prestigious university can give you an edge in getting a job even if you have an undergraduate degree in journalism. Probably the most prestigious graduate programs are at Columbia University, Northwestern University, Syracuse University, University of Missouri and the University of California at Berkeley. These programs also offer a professional emphasis with skills courses and admit students with undergraduate degrees in many majors. Most of the traditional Ivy League schools like Yale or Dartmouth do not offer journalism majors at undergraduate or graduate levels.

Third, a master's degree in a specialized field of interest could give you a competitive edge in becoming a writer in that field. If you're interested in religion journalism, consider a master of divinity or master of arts in religion. If you're interested in business reporting, consider a master's in business administration. An M.B.A. can also give you an edge in moving up the ranks as an editor or publisher.

Fourth, a master's degree is essential if you entertain any thought of teaching journalism. You cannot get a tenure-track position at an accredited university without a master's degree. At the best-known schools, a Ph.D. is necessary. Most journalism faculty members today have spent five to 20 years as professional journalists before deciding to enter the academic world. Many journalists tire of the daily grind of deadlines and return to graduate school to pursue a second career as a professor of journalism. It's always easier to get graduate degrees when you're young and single instead of later in life. If you have any thought of becoming a professor, get the master's degree now.

WHAT ABOUT NEW YORK?

The majority of well-known consumer magazines are published in New York City. If you want to work for one of them, then you should find a way to get there.

The advantage of working in New York is the ability to network and move easily from job to job as you progress up the career ladder. Large companies like Time-Warner, Hearst and Condé Nast publish more than 200 magazines (total) and prefer to promote from within their own ranks. National associations like the Magazine Publishers of America, American Society of Magazine Editors and American Business Media are located here and offer educational and networking opportunities to meet people from outside your own employer. Smaller groups like Ed2010 offer social, educational and networking opportunities for young editors and writers who are just beginning their magazine careers. Several local universities offer a chance to get a master's degree and other specialized courses while you work.

The disadvantage is the cost of living. The most expensive section of the city is Manhattan, where apartment rents start at $2,000 a month and more. Most young people starting their careers in New York use local networking opportunities to share costs with roommates. Those who work in Manhattan, the downtown section, often commute from the less expensive boroughs of Brooklyn, Queens, Staten Island, the Bronx, Queens or New Jersey, Connecticut and other parts of Long Island. But you don't need a car to live in New York and can also expect higher salaries than elsewhere. Public transportation is relatively inexpensive and extends into all the boroughs and nearby Long Island, New Jersey and Connecticut.

"I always suggest to journalism students to try New York," says Nichole Screws, *Esquire*'s fashion markets editor.

> If they have the support and are able to swing it, this is where the industry thrives and there is nothing like the exposure of the national stage. In saying that, if you come and nothing is sticking, you will know when it is your time

to bow out. But if you leave with years or even a summer's experience, you can go anywhere and leave a mark. Being here is simply an invaluable publishing education.

In conclusion, if you want to become a magazine writer or editor, then don't settle for a career choice that merely offers a paycheck. We urge you to read and write every day. Fill your mind with great ideas while you follow your dream. When you begin applying for jobs, you may get dozens of "no" answers, but remember it only takes one "yes." The oldest, simplest advice is still the best: Never give up.

ENDNOTES

[1]   Kristin Granero, "Chat with an EIC: *Seventeen*'s EIC, Ann Shoket." Accessed at www.ed2010.com, Aug. 20, 2008.
[2]   E-mail to David E. Sumner, Aug. 15, 2008.
[3]   E-mail to David E. Sumner, March 30, 2008.
[4]   Telephone interview with David E. Sumner, Aug. 12, 2008.
[5]   Telephone interview with David E. Sumner, Aug. 13, 2008.
[6]   E-mail to David E. Sumner, Aug. 18, 2008.
[7]   Richard Bolles, *What Color Is Your Parachute: A Practical Manual for Job Hunters and Career Changes* (Berkeley, CA: Ten Speed Press, 2004).
[8]   Interview with David E. Sumner, Chicago, Aug. 6, 2008.

Appendix 1

SHOPTALK—A GLOSSARY OF MAGAZINE LINGO

Action: Changing from one place or situation to another by a person, entity or phenomenon. The description of change in feature articles makes them more appealing than those without any action.

Action verbs: Verbs that describe tangible action taken by people or things.

Active voice: A form of verb structure in which the subject of the sentence is the principal actor in the sentence. In passive voice, the subject is the recipient of the action.

Actor: Story sources directly involved with the event or issue that a story describes. Actors may be victims, perpetuators or participants in some other way.

All rights: The publisher can publish the article in its magazine, put it on its Web site, publish portions in another magazine it owns, or in a subsequent book with a collection of articles. The writer gives up any opportunity of selling or re-using the material.

American Society of Magazine Editors: The primary professional association in the United States for editors of major consumer magazines.

Analysis: The process of thinking through the topic you are writing about and breaking it down into smaller pieces for investigation. The results of research must also be analyzed to determine what to use and what to discard.

Anecdote: A true story used to illustrate the larger theme of a story. Anecdotes contain one or two central characters, some dialogue or quotations, and occur in a specific time and place.

Angle: The specific approach that you take toward covering a broad topic. Think of an angle like a small slice of a large topical "pie." Strong angles reveal fresh, original information.

Annual report: A publication produced every year by a company or non-profit organization explaining its significant accomplishments and financial activity for the previous year. These reports often contain some biographical information on key officers and board members.

Article package: Separate but related elements that cover a topic in a comprehensive way. In addition to the main story, these elements might include sidebars, data boxes, graphics and illustrations.

Attribution: Words that identify a speaker as the source of information. Most news articles use forms of the verb "said" (said Jones, says Smith). In a feature story the writer has the freedom to use other verbs of attribution (explained Jones, insisted Smith).

Author's bio: Two or three sentences about the author's background that appear at the conclusion of an article. Often called a "bionote."

Billboard paragraph: A paragraph usually placed immediately after the lead that tells in a nutshell what an article is about. Newspaper journalists call it the "nutgraf."

Breaking news: Newsworthy events that are unfolding right now. The reporter's challenge is to collect and verify the facts and relay them to readers quickly and without embellishment.

Business-to-business media: A term describing companies that produce magazines, tabloid newspapers, newsletters, Web sites and trade shows serving people who work in specific jobs, careers and professions. Their main purpose is to provide information that serves the professional needs of their readers.

Cheerleader quotations: Predictable and shallow observations that add little substance to an article. Example: "She is a very nice person"; "Everyone likes him."

Clips: Published samples of articles. Often writers include clips of their previous work when they approach editors with ideas for future articles.

Closing date: The deadline for submission of all materials, including advertisements, scheduled for a particular issue of a magazine.

Coherence: The unity of a story resulting from a logical organization of the facts, anecdotes and quotations that comprise it. The component parts fit together in a way that makes sense to the reader.

Common knowledge: Information that's available from several published sources and, therefore, not protected by copyright. Common knowledge falls into many categories such as art, geography, science, history, music, medicine and technology.

Complication: The central problem encountered by the central character in a story. The process of solving or overcoming the complication forms the plot for the story.

Conflict: Disagreement on issues or events by affected parties, such as labor and management, customers and owners, or faculty and administration.

Contributing editor: A title sometimes given to writers who frequently write for a publication but are not on the full-time staff. They earn a higher rate for their work and get first preference for story assignments.

Controlled circulation: Free subscriptions offered by trade publishers to targeted readers with key management or decision-making responsibilities in their companies or organizations.

Controversy: A prolonged, intense debate about a public issue without an immediate or easy solution.

Conventional wisdom: The most commonly held opinions and attitudes about various issues. Many creative and original articles call into question the conventional wisdom about the topics they address.

Convergence: The trend toward one company owning a variety of media outlets and having their writers and editors produce content for all, which may include newspapers, magazines, newsletters, Web sites and television and radio stations.

Cover line: Short catchy descriptions of articles that appear on a magazine's cover and try to catch the casual reader's attention.

Dead construction: A lifeless pronoun-verb combination at the beginning of a sentence such as "there is," "there are," "there was," "there will be," "it is," "it was," "it will be," etc.

Demographics: Vital statistics about readers such as age, education level, geographic location, employment, gender, political and religious leanings, number of children, hobbies and interests.

Departments: Sections of a magazine published on a recurring basis and covering the same general types of topics in every issue.

Description: Details about a person's appearance, clothing or surroundings that help reveal the person's character and personality.

Dialogue: The description of conversation between two people that occurs at a specific time and place. It differs from quotes that simply involve the reporting of later reflections and observations from one person.

Direct quotation: Exact words, spoken by an interviewee and placed within quotation marks and included in the body of an article. ("I grew up in the South during the turbulent 1960s," said Jones.)

Dramatic story: A true story that describes how a central character or characters encounter a complicating situation that they fight to overcome.

Editorial formula: The combination of types of articles used by a magazine on a regular basis. For example, some magazines may publish three news stories, two feature profiles and four standing columns in every issue.

Editorial packages: A feature article plus its sidebars, hotboxes, graphics and other related elements.

Evergreen topics: Article topics and ideas that publications revisit once a year or more and that readers are always interested in knowing about. For example, weight loss is an "evergreen" topic at many women's or fitness magazines.

Expert or voice of authority: An interviewee, who through virtue of job title, experience or education, is a credible source of information about a particular topic.

Exposition: Factual material in a story that explains needed background or context. Expository writing usually lacks people or action and should be limited.

Feature article: A term used mostly by newspaper journalists to describe stories that aren't "hard news." Magazine journalists use more specific categories such as profiles, how-to, travel, true-life narratives, inspirational, etc., all of which may be called "features."

Filler: An item that has little purpose other than to fill space on a page.

First reader: Often an intern or editorial assistant who opens unsolicited manuscripts and sorts them according to quality. If an article is publishable, the first reader directs it to the attention of an editor.

First serial rights (first rights): Rights sold to a publisher giving it the first opportunity to publish the article. After the article is published, writers retain the right to sell unlimited reprint rights to other publishers.

Gang query: A letter of inquiry written by a freelancer that proposes more than one story idea to an editor.

Hook, introduction, lead: The opening sentences or paragraphs of an article, designed to capture readers' attention and interest.

Indirect quotation: Words spoken by an interviewee but not placed within quotation marks. (Jones said that he grew up in the South during the turbulent 1960s.)

In-flight magazine: A sponsored publication published by an airline and available at no cost to passengers aboard one of the airline's flights.

Intangible how-to article: Self-help articles that often lead to internal changes rather than the creation of some object that you can see and touch. Example: "How to Feel More Content."

Intellectual property: Any work by a writer, musician, artist, sculptor or computer programmer capable of commercial use or distribution. Original creators hold legal rights to reproduction, distribution, public performance or public display of their work. They also have the right to sell part or all of their ownership.

Internet markets: Web sites that pay freelance writers to produce content. These sites may be sponsored by publications, companies, associations or nonprofit organizations.

Inverted pyramid: A way of organizing an article; the writer places the most important material first and then arranges subsequent information in descending order of importance.

Investigative reporting: Stories that report deceit, fraud or dishonesty on the part of corporate, government or public officials. After publication, they usually result in public controversy.

Issue: A phenomenon or development that poses a risk or danger to the public or some segment of the population. Since some issues may benefit some population segments and hurt others, the solutions are debatable.

Keywords: Words and phrases that emphasize the main theme of an article. Keywords should be used frequently enough to allow search engines to rank them highly in Web searches.

Kill fee: An amount of money that an editor pays a writer to cancel an assigned article. Typically a kill fee is at least 20 percent of the amount the magazine agreed to pay the author for a published article.

Lead time: The number of weeks or months required by a publication's staff to produce an issue.

Lexis Nexis: A popular subscription-only database offering full-text access to thousands of newspapers and magazines, press releases, corporate information, court decisions and government records.

Linking verbs: Forms of "to be" verbs such as "is," "are," "was," etc., that link a subject to a similar object.

List article: A brief article that contains practical information presented in a 1-2-3 format.

Listserv: An electronic special-interest newsletter subscribed to by people interested in that topic. Any subscriber can send e-mail questions or comments to all of the other subscribers.

Literary nonfiction: The term that eventually replaced "New Journalism" (see below). Both refer to the use of fiction techniques in nonfiction reporting.

Loaded words: Words that convey the writer's opinion toward a topic or a person.

Luggage paragraph: A catchall for information; the writer dumps an assortment of facts into one paragraph, often making it long and confusing.

Masthead: Often positioned near a magazine's table of contents, it lists editors and other staff members affiliated with a publication.

Narrative: A story with a chronological structure that proceeds from one event to the next.

National Magazine Awards: The most prestigious awards given in the magazine industry. The annual competition is sponsored by the American Society of Magazine Editors.

New Journalism: A writing genre that developed during the 1960s later called "literary nonfiction." Its distinguishing characteristic is the use of fiction techniques—especially narrative, dialogue, description, scene-by-scene reporting—in nonfiction reporting.

News feature: A broadly used term that includes articles about trends, conflicts, investigative reporting and other issues that are not "hard news."

Newsgroup: Online discussion group on topics of special interest that anyone can read and contribute to. They differ from listservs, which have subscription-only access. Newsgroups can be accessed using Google's "group" function.

News peg: A current or recent event related to the topic that you are writing about; a news peg gives timeliness to a feature article.

News values: Certain characteristics of news and feature stories that make them interesting. The most common news values are novelty, conflict, magnitude, impact, tension and humor.

Niche: The narrowly defined content and readership that characterizes most magazines. While most magazines serve a narrow niche within a national audience, most newspapers serve a wide niche of ages and interests in one city or region.

Nutgraf: See **Billboard paragraph** above.

One-time rights: One-time rights are sold to several different publications giving them the right to publish the article simultaneously. Syndicated columns appearing in many newspapers are usually sold with one-time rights.

Online markets: Paying markets for writers that include not only Internet markets, but e-mail newsletters, private intranets and CD publishers.

On speculation: These words, often included in a query letter, indicate a writer's willingness to submit an article without any guarantee that the editor will accept it for publication.

On the record: A comment intended for publication; an **off-the-record** comment is meant to help the writer understand something but is not meant for publication.

Open-ended question: A question that cannot be answered with "yes" or "no" and strives to elicit an interviewee's insights.

Organization magazine: A magazine published by an association, company, university, religious group or other organization for its members. Sometimes called a "sponsored magazine" or "sponsored publication," its goal is to publish news and features about the organization and promote its goals and views.

Parallel structure: The use of the same verb tense, phrase and clause structure in sentences and paragraphs.

Partial quotation: Part of a sentence, spoken by an interviewee and placed within quotation marks. (Jones said he grew up in the South "during the turbulent 1960s.")

Participant: Someone with first-hand experience in dealing with the subject you are writing about. Participants will be "experts" by virtue of their experience.

Passive voice: A form of verb structure in which the subject of the sentence is the recipient of the action from another object in the sentence.

Plot: The problem or complication in a story that the central character(s) must solve. A good plot also creates tension and helps keep the reader interested and involved.

Primary source: The originating source for specific news and information. Primary source material has not been published or interpreted through other writers.

Profile article: Feature that looks in depth at one person.

Pronoun agreement: The use of singular pronouns to refer back to singular nouns, and plural pronouns to refer back to plural nouns.

Public domain: Written material not protected by copyright that anyone may use. Copyrighted material expires 70 years after the death of the author in the U.S. Anything published by the U.S. government is (with some exceptions) in the public domain.

Query letter: A letter written to the editor of a magazine that proposes the details of a story idea and explains the writer's qualifications to write it.

Regional correspondent: A writer responsible for generating articles from a specific geographic part of the country. These contributors live in the region and usually work out of their homes.

Reprint rights: The formal term is "second serial rights," which give a publication the opportunity to reprint previously published material. Most publications purchase reprint rights if the original publication's readership doesn't overlap with their own.

Resolution: In a dramatic story, the outcome of the central character's effort to solve the complication, which may involve happy or sad endings.

Rhythm: Variety in the movement or pace of writing. Strong rhythm results from varied sentence and paragraph length with frequent use of action verbs and active voice.

Round-up article: An article containing several persons' points of view on a common topic, often packaged as separate mini-profiles. Example: "Why I Home School My Kids—Five Families Share Their Experiences."

Run-on sentence: Two complete sentences incorrectly separated by a comma and not a period or conjunction.

Scene-by-scene reporting: A description of the unfolding scenes of a narrative as it moves from one event to another.

Secondary source: A secondary source is a "second-hand" source that stands between the reader and the originating source. Articles appearing in newspapers, magazines or Web sites are usually secondary sources.

Service journalism: Articles written to directly help readers in their everyday lives. Service journalism articles may provide practical help in improving readers' health, recreation, finances or careers. "How-to" articles are a special type of service journalism that focuses on completing a specific, immediate task.

Shadowing: A research technique that has the writer accompanying a subject as the subject goes about his day. The writer observes the subject in a variety of circumstances.

Scholarly journals: Journals whose content deals with academic disciplines and sub-disciplines whose authors are typically college professors. Articles are based on original research and must be approved by a review panel of academic experts prior to acceptance.

Shelf life: The length of time that a topic or an issue of a publication remains pertinent.

Short: Interesting, informative and intentional nonfiction items of various lengths.

Sidebar: Lists or pieces of related information presented outside the main body of the article in a separate space.

Single-copy sales: The opposite of subscription sales, these refer to newsstand sales of a publication.

Snapshot: A tightly focused, brief look at a person.

Special collections: Non-circulating documents held by libraries that often serve as useful information for journalists and researchers. Public officials and celebrities often donate their correspondence and documents to libraries for their special collections.

Specificity: Related to tangible facts or events that can be seen, felt, heard, smelled or observed.

Spin doctors: Writers and public relations persons who manipulate information to support their points of view.

Split anecdote: A story that is cut in half and separated by paragraphs containing other information. Often the first half of the anecdote serves as an article's lead and the second half brings the article to a conclusion.

Spreadsheet: A computer program that allows users to enter data and text in rows and columns and perform numerous statistical calculations on the data. Spreadsheets can create charts, tables and graphs.

Standing column: A regular feature that is present in every issue of a publication. The name of the column doesn't change; it usually appears in the same place and is written by the same writer.

State-of-being verbs: Non-action verbs that describe a person's attitudes, thoughts or feelings.

Structure: The way that the parts of a story—such as facts, quotes and anecdotes—are put together in a way that is most clear, logical and easy to read for the reader.

Style: A broad term describing the combination of voice, viewpoint, rhythm and tone in an author's writing.

Style manual: A guide to proper use of writing falling outside of normal rules of grammar. Commonly used style manuals are the *AP Stylebook*, *Turabian Guide* and *Chicago Manual of Style*. Some magazines write their own style manuals.

Subsidiary rights: Used in book publishing, subsidiary rights include all other rights such as movie or television rights, foreign editions, book-club rights, audio-book editions or electronic rights.

Summary lead: An article's opening sentences that answer the essential questions about an event: who, what, where, when, why and how.

Support interview: A supporting source of information; a person who adds a different point of view to a story.

Synthesis: The process of thinking about the "small pieces" of information resulting from your research and figuring out the best way to summarize and present them to the reader in the final story structure.

Talking points: Key information that an interviewee is determined to work into an interview regardless of the questions asked.

Tangible how-to article: Leads to the creation of something that can be seen and touched.

Tear sheet: A page torn from a publication that contains a sample of your writing.

Teasers: Similar to a magazine's cover line, they appear above a newspaper's nameplate on page one to promote stories inside the day's edition.

Tension: The introduction of an unsolved problem at the beginning of a story that writers use as a way of attracting and sustaining readers' attention.

Tone: The writer's attitude displayed in an article, which may be humorous, satirical, light-hearted, heavy, sarcastic, whimsical, persuasive, argumentative, self-deprecating, disparaging or respectful.

Trade magazine: A magazine whose main purpose is to provide useful information to practitioners of the various professions and trades; also known as business-to-business publication.

Transition: Words that serve as a "bridge" or a segue to move an article from one point to the next.

Trend: A phenomenon that is increasing or decreasing in frequency. Trends always have a quantifiable dimension and can occur in politics, pop culture or any field of interest.

Unity: Keeping the focus on a single angle in an article while using a consistent viewpoint, verb tense, voice and tone.

Viewpoint: The role the author takes in writing an article. First-person makes frequent use of "I" viewpoint, while second-person uses the "you" viewpoint frequently. Third-person uses primarily "he," "she" or "it" viewpoints.

Voice: How writers reveal their personality and identity in their writing style.

Writer's block: A "condition," claimed by many writers, when words don't flow and sentences don't find their way quickly onto paper or computer screen.

Zines: Sometimes called "Ezines" or "Webzines," these special-interest publications are published only on the Internet.

Appendix 2

SUGGESTED IN-CLASS ACTIVITIES AND ASSIGNMENTS

CHAPTER 1: CAPTURING READER ATTENTION

In-class activities

Instructor: Ask students to bring a favorite magazine to class or find its Web site during class. Students: Write a 50-word summary of the article you find most interesting. Read the summaries in class and discuss the action, angle and anecdotes contained in your stories.

Instructor: Ask students to recall a humorous or dramatic experience they have had during the past five years. Discuss their stories from the perspective of "action, angle and anecdotes" explained in this chapter.

Assignments

Students: Circle the leads from any 10 newspaper and 10 magazine features. Compare the number of magazine articles beginning with an anecdote lead with the number of newspaper stories.

Students: Interview five random people, asking these two questions and recording the answers: "What characteristics of any article you read make it interesting to you?" and "What characteristics of any article you read make it boring?" Bring the results of your survey to class. In small groups, determine common characteristics of interesting and boring articles.

CHAPTER 2: THE HUNT FOR FRESH IDEAS

In-class activities

Instructor: Give students 45 minutes to do anything they want to find a story idea for the next assignment. Give them the option to visit the library, read bulletin boards, telephone book yellow pages, browse the bookstore or call a friend. At the end of the time limit, ask them to return to class and report their story ideas.

Instructor: Bring to class a variety of brochures, advertisements, academic journals, posters, etc., and distribute in class. Students: Working in pairs, come up with an idea for a timely magazine article based on the item you have received.

Assignments

Students: Use magportal.com or findarticles.com to locate and read 10 articles on a single topic you are interested in writing about. Summarize each article in one sentence and then create a one-sentence idea for an original angle not covered by any of these articles.

Students: Start an "idea brainstorm list" using a small pocket notebook. For one week, create 25 one-sentence ideas from reading, television and movies, talking to friends and surfing the Internet. Revise and edit the ideas before turning them in.

CHAPTER 3: STRONG ANGLES AND FOCUSED IDEAS

In-class activities

Instructor: Display on a screen two feature articles that cover the same topic from a different angle. Discuss these two angles in class. Students: Working in pairs, create two additional angles on this topic for different demographics—i.e. one for men and one for women or one for young adults and one for middle-aged adults, etc.

Instructor: Divide students into groups of three or four. Assign each group a broad topic commonly covered in newspapers and magazines. Students: Create 10 one-sentence story ideas that bring a more tightly focused angle on that broad topic.

Assignments

Students: Pick a hot topic currently in the news. Do an online search and make a list of 10 articles with different angles on that same topic. Include name of author, title of article, publication title, date and Web address.

Instructor: Give each student a list of 10 broad topics. Students: After doing some online research, write a one-sentence angle for a feasible story on each topic.

CHAPTER 4: ORIGINAL RESEARCH = ORIGINAL ARTICLES

In-class activities

Instructor: Ask students to go online and locate names, telephone numbers or e-mail addresses of experts on the following topics (or any topics you assign): a syndicated cartoonist who can discuss racial issues in cartoons; a middle-aged woman who has an eating disorder; an expert on DNA identification in criminal cases; an expert on autism; and a parent who has lost a child as the result of an accident caused by a drunken driver.

Instructor: On an overhead screen, review and discuss in class the electronic databases that your library offers its users. Examples: Academic Search Premier; Access World News; Biography Resource Center; Business Source Premier; Lexis Nexis: General, Business, News, Legal, People, Congressional and Environmental; Medline; CQ Researcher; CQ Weekly; and Reference USA.

Assignments

Students: Using the Internet Public Library's "Associations on the Net" directory (www.ipl.org/div/aon), find the name of a contact person for associations representing these types of groups or interests: Arab Americans, farmers, magicians, optometrists and sleep disorders. (or) Instructor: Create a separate list of topics representing students' areas of interest and ask them to find associations representing these interests.

Students: Use the Internet to find these types of primary sources: the full text of a speech, a federal court decision, a set of statistical data, recent legislation passed by Congress and an annual report. Summarize the content of each source and choose one to suggest a story idea.

CHAPTER 5: INTERVIEWS: GOAL-DRIVEN CONVERSATIONS

In-class activities

Students: Divide into teams of two. Instructor: Pass around an envelope containing the names of well-known persons currently in the news who represent a variety of fields—politics, entertainment, sports, business or religion. Each team of students should pull a name from the envelope and take 15 minutes to create a list of 10 questions that would be appropriate to ask the person during an interview. The questions should be arranged in logical order and phrased in a way to elicit thought-provoking answers.

Instructor: Display on a screen a current feature article from a Web site of a magazine or newspaper. Students: Read the article aloud and compile a list of all persons quoted in the article. Build a class discussion around these questions:

- Why did the author choose to interview each person?
- What did each interviewee contribute to the story?
- Whose "voice" was *not* heard but should have been included?
- Could any interviewee have been omitted without diminishing the value of the article?

Assignments

Students: Create a list of a dozen open-ended questions that any inter-viewer could adapt and use in almost any interview situation.

Students: Identify a person who is newsworthy because he/she is knowl-edgeable about or involved in a timely issue on campus. Interview the person and write a 500-word article that balances information about the issue with insights from the interviewee.

CHAPTER 6: FINDING THE RIGHT MARKET

In-class activities

Instructor: Create a list of lesser-known national magazines. Ask each student to choose a publication from the list, research it outside of class and prepare a brief (5- to 10-minute) "market report" to present to the class. Students: As part of your research, visit the publication's Web site, study its writer's guidelines and find its listing in one of the market guides mentioned in Chapter 6. When you deliver your market report to your classmates, emphasize the editorial formula of the magazine and evaluate the freelance opportunities.

Students: Based on each market report, brainstorm as a group and come up with two or three article ideas that might be appropriate for the publication.

Assignments

Students: Research and write a 750-word article about a trend that is evident on your campus. (Ideas: entrepreneurial students who start busi-nesses while in school; older students who return to school in hopes of making career switches; a renewed interest in foreign language among students who anticipate careers in a global economy; guys preparing for professions once dominated by women—nursing, elementary education; faculty members who practice what they teach—a government professor who is a state legislator or a drama instructor who is active on the stage.)

Students: Turn to p. 86 and reread the sidebar "How to 'Nationalize' a Story." Create a plan for turning your local trend article (above) into a story with widespread appeal that you could pitch to a national magazine. How much research would you need to do? Whom would you need to interview to broaden the scope? What magazines might be interested in your article?

CHAPTER 7: QUERY LETTERS THAT SELL

In-class activities

Students: Prepare a one-page query letter outside of class that pitches a timely article idea to a specific publication. Bring the letter to class in a form that allows everyone to view it simultaneously (either project it on a screen or distribute hard copies). The class will assume the role of the magazine's staff. After each student has presented his/her query, the magazine staff should offer feedback and render a decision: accept the proposed idea on speculation, reject it, suggest revisions to the query.

Students: Chapter 7 contains two complete query letters—one pitches a travel article about St. Petersburg, Russia, the second offers an in-depth look at coal as a source of energy. Reread the letters in class and discuss:

- How does each author convey his/her knowledge about the topic?
- How does each author convey his/her competence as a writer without sounding boastful?
- How does each author grab the editor's attention in the first paragraph?

Assignments

Students: Create a paragraph that could be used as the closing paragraph for all your query letters. In it, explain in honest but positive language your qualifications as a writer. Keep it on file for frequent use.

Students: Choose an article that you have already completed. Write a query letter that uses the first paragraph of your article as the opening paragraph of your query. Write subsequent paragraphs that summarize the story and identify your sources. Add the closing paragraph that explains your qualifications.

CHAPTER 8: HOOKS, INTROS AND LEADS

In-class activities

Instructor: Invite a guest speaker to class (preferably a feature writer or lifestyle editor from a local newspaper or magazine). Students: Conduct an in-class interview that focuses on the person's career. After the interview, divide into teams, with each team creating two possible lead paragraphs. The first lead should be a simple summary sentence; the second should be an anecdote, a scenario or an indirect quotation.

Students: Review your notes from the in-class interview and identify a strong quote that would serve as an appropriate ending for the article. With the lead and ending in place, discuss how you would organize the rest of the article.

Assignments

Instructor: Assign students to read a specific feature article in a current magazine or in the lifestyle section of a large newspaper. Students: After reading the assigned article, create at least three alternative leads. Which do you prefer?

Students: Survey the opening paragraphs of several feature articles in major magazines. Try to categorize them. Does a particular category of lead seem to dominate?

CHAPTER 9: ACTION-FILLED WRITING

In-class activities

Instructor: Give students copies of a feature story you have chosen or use one of the Pulitzer Prize-winning feature stories available at www.pulitzer.org. Students: Underline all verbs in active voice (in any tense) and circle all verbs or verb constructions in passive voice (in any tense). Discuss the passive-voice verbs and why they were probably used.

Instructor: Send students an article you have selected in a Word document and ask them to use Word's grammar and spelling check to determine its readability statistics, including: (a) average number of words per sentence; (b) average number of characters per word; and (c) percentage of sentences in passive voice. Then ask them to determine the readability statistics for one of their own stories and compare the two.

Assignments

Students: Revise the following five sentences (or others assigned by the instructor) to add action verbs and eliminate the dead constructions: "there is," "there are," "there was," "it is" and "it was."

- There were 10 women competing for the title of homecoming queen.
- There are dozens of Web sites that offer advice and tips on preparing a résumé.
- It was thrilling to watch the team win its final game.
- It will be a mistake if your cover letter and résumé are not completely truthful.
- It is important to remember that success yields to hard work.

Students: Take a notebook on a 45-minute walk around a neighborhood or campus. List the 10 most vivid impressions made on you using your senses of sight, hearing, taste and smell. Use action verbs to describe your impressions.

CHAPTER 10: THE ART OF THE ANECDOTE

In-class activities

Students: The opening anecdote in this chapter—the *Chicken Soup for the Soul* story—contains about 150 words. Edit the story to less than 100 words. Read out loud.

Instructor: Bring to class three or four published feature articles that have anecdotal leads. Read the opening paragraphs to the class and see if the students can discern the topics of the articles. Discuss whether or not the anecdotes serve as smooth and colorful introductions to the subjects that the articles examine.

Assignments

Students: Ask a friend to describe a specific moment of victory or defeat. Through follow-up questions, try to pull out as many colorful details as you can. After you have collected the information, shape it into an anecdote of three sentences. Review the material and flesh out the story to a paragraph of about 150 words. Split the anecdote in half in a way that the first half might serve as the lead of a feature article and the second half might serve as the ending of the article.

Students: Visit the Web site of the *Chicken Soup* book series (www.chickensoup.com). Follow the "Submit a Story" menu, which includes guidelines for submission. Create a possible entry that complies with the guidelines.

CHAPTER 11: IMPROVING YOUR PIZZAZZ

In-class activities

Students: Bring a selection by your favorite musical artist to class as an electronic file or downloadable attachment. Play these selections in class. Instructor: Discuss with the class how these characteristics of writing also apply to their music: (a) lead; (b) theme; (c) rhythm and pace; (d) tone; and (e) conclusion.

Instructor: Ask each student to tell a funny story based on a personal experience. After each story, discuss the main characteristic it displays: *universality, surprise, exaggeration* or *absurdity*.

Assignments

Instructor: Give students a sample of three articles chosen from magazines aimed at (a) young, (b) middle-aged and (c) senior citizens. Students: Write a summary of their style differences according to (a) viewpoint, (b) rhythm and pace, (c) tone and (d) content.

Instructor: Give students a sample of three articles chosen from magazines aimed at (a) predominantly men and (b) predominantly women. Students: Write a summary of their style differences according to (a) viewpoint, (b) rhythm and pace, (c) tone and (d) content.

CHAPTER 12: DON'T BOTCH THE BASICS

In-class activities

Instructor: Bring a newspaper article or draft of a story to class and give copies to all students. Students: Circle each correctly used comma and make an "X" by each wrongly used or unnecessary comma. Discuss wrongly used commas. For properly used commas, discuss which rules in the "Do use a comma" section of this chapter apply to each case.

Students: Bring an *AP Stylebook* to class. In groups of two or three, discuss and identify the 10 most common AP style errors that you see in the media.

Assignments

Students: Bring a first draft of your most recent story assignment to class. Working in groups of two, exchange first drafts and copy edit for grammar, punctuation and AP style errors. Discuss your mistakes with each other. Instructor: Ask students to identify the most common mistakes for class discussion.

Students: Find five punctuation or editing errors from newspapers, magazines or Web sites and copy and summarize in a written assignment. Instructor: Identify the most common mistakes and discuss in class.

CHAPTER 13: BLURBS, BRIEFS AND BRIGHTENERS

In-class activities

Students: Working in teams of two, come up with an idea for a list article appropriate for each of these audiences:

* young parents
* single female professionals
* retirees who like to travel
* college grads looking for their first job

Students: Reread the list article contained in Chapter 13 ("Seven ways to overcome 'terminal' problems"). Discuss how the author might explore the same topic (an unplanned airport layover) for a different audience. Think about what information he could retain and what information he would need to add if he were aiming the article at:

* families traveling with young children
* college students heading home for Christmas break

Assignments

Students: Pull from your files a recent article that you have written. Rewrite it, cutting its length by at least half. Working with the long version of the article, isolate an anecdote that might stand alone as a "short." Pare it down to as few words as possible without forfeiting any of its impact.

Students: Visit the library and survey several national magazines, taking note of those that publish regional editions. On a map, draw a 50-mile circle around the location of your home. Identify five points of interest within that radius. Select the one that is most appealing and write a 300-word story. Submit it to a magazine or a large-city newspaper that publishes a regional edition that includes your location.

CHAPTER 14: IN FOCUS: THE WELL-BALANCED PROFILE

In-class activities

Students: After watching the 2000 film *Almost Famous* in class, discuss the tactics that the young journalist used to produce his profile article. His first attempt was rejected by the magazine's staff. Why? What did he do wrong? What did he do right in the second version? What lessons can future writers learn from the film?

Students: Reread the question-and-answer interview with Meredith Vieira at the end of Chapter 14. If the author had not used the Q & A format, who else could she have interviewed to get another perspective on Vieira? Would you categorize the Vieira profile as a "portrait" or a "photograph?" Why? If the article ran too long for the space allotted it and the author had to delete two Q & A sequences, which ones would you recommend?

Assignments

Students: Shadow a person for a day. Meet at breakfast and follow him/her through dinner. Leave your recorder at home; take notes on your subject's quirks and habits. Pay attention to how he/she interacts with people, drives, eats, relaxes. From your notes, create a couple of anecdotes to fold into a profile article.

Students: Develop three profiles from one. First, research and write a profile article that resembles a black-and-white news photograph—an honest, accurate, "warts and all" portrayal. Second, revisit the profile, delete all negative aspects and turn it into a "portrait" article—100 percent positive. Third, take an excerpt of about 300 tightly focused words and produce a "snapshot" of the person.

CHAPTER 15: WRITING DRAMATIC STORIES

In-class activities

Instructor: Ask students to discuss some popular movies that display the common plots discussed in this chapter: (a) failure to success; (b) victim to survivor; (c) danger to safety; (d) chaos to meaning; (e) saving the world; (f) love conquers all. You may also direct them to the Web sites of some current films to look at the trailers/previews.

Students: Write a 250-word summary of a dramatic or interesting story based on your personal experience. Write with a narrative structure including the plot, resolution, time and place.

Assignments

Students: Go out and listen to a conversation or encounter between people in a public space such as a restaurant, library, store or public transportation. Record descriptions of the scene, the people and dialogue that took place, and any interesting outcome.

Students: Find one story from a newspaper, magazine or Web site that displays each of the six types of plots discussed in this chapter: (a) failure to success; (b) victim to survivor; (c) danger to safety; (d) chaos to meaning; (e) saving the world; (f) love conquers all.

CHAPTER 16: HELP! WRITING THE HOW-TO FEATURE

In-class activities

Students: Work in teams of two and compile a list of five timely how-to/ service articles that you would read if you saw them listed in a magazine's table of contents. Give each article a catchy title that would make a good cover line. Determine what kind of expert a writer would need to interview to produce each article.

Students: Choose a "crossroad" (decision point) that people in their 20s are likely to face. Come up with three how-to articles related to the crossroad.

Assignments

Students: Research and write a 750-word how-to article that offers advice that, if followed, will lead to the creation of a tangible object or an event.

Students: Research and write a 750-word how-to article that offers advice that, if followed, will result in an intangible personal change or improvement.

CHAPTER 17: CONNECTING CONTENT TO THE CALENDAR

In-class activities

Students: Brainstorm and come up with three feature article ideas with a connection to autumn. Come up with three ideas linked to May. Come up with three ideas related to Christmas. Come up with three ideas tied to the 100th anniversary of Father's Day (established in 1910).

Students: From your list of article ideas (above), choose the one you think is most marketable. What kind of research would you need to do? Whom would you need to interview? Are there any sidebar possibilities? What title would make a provocative cover line?

Assignments

Students: At the library, choose a favorite monthly magazine and review all 12 issues from one year. Jot down the calendar-related cover lines that you see.

Students: With the help of an almanac or one of the Web sites mentioned in Chapter 17, identify at least two historic events that will mark either 25- or 50-year anniversaries in the next 18 months. How might you give a current spin to the anniversary? How can you make it meaningful to today's readers?

CHAPTER 18: TRENDS, ISSUES AND CONTROVERSIES

In-class activities

Instructor: Display on a screen the Web site of a popular news site, such as msnbc.com, foxnews.com or cnn.com. Look at breaking news stories and ask students to create some feature story ideas that are related to the news, but with a potential shelf life of several months.

Students: Bring an example of a trend story to class from a magazine, newspaper or Web site. In groups of two or three, summarize your story and discuss whether you can find another story idea based on the *causes* or *consequences* of the trend.

Assignments

Students: Choose a recent trend or controversial issue and develop three angles based on the approaches discussed in this chapter: (a) central developments; (b) effects on some; and (c) reactions from others.

Students: If your library has a full-text edition of *CQ Researcher*, choose an issue discussed in a recent edition of the magazine and write a 500-word summary of key facts and viewpoints about this topic. Use this as a starting point for developing an article idea targeted at a niche magazine whose readers have specialized interests.

CHAPTER 19: WRITING TO INSPIRE AND MOTIVATE

In-class activities

Students: Reread the sample query letter on p. 252–253. Discuss how the author would need to alter it if she were proposing the article idea to an editor at a secular publication.

Students: Visit the Web site of the Amy Foundation (www.amyfound.org) and click to the page that contains the winning entries from the foundation's annual writing contest. Remembering that these cash awards go to inspirational articles published in secular newspapers and magazines, read the first-place winner. How much content would you describe as "religious?" Who might it alienate? Is it worthy of its $10,000 award? How drastically would the writer have to change the article to delete all inspirational content?

Assignments

Students: Review an article that you have written in the past and determine how—without completely rewriting the story—you could add a slightly inspirational dimension. If the article was based on interviews, what questions would you need to ask to develop a spiritual theme?

Students: Conduct a survey of the well-known news magazines (*Time, Newsweek, U.S. News & World Report*). Make a list of articles that are related to faith or religion. Are the articles promoted in cover lines? Do the writers cover religion objectively or do you detect attempts to influence readers?

CHAPTER 20: WRITING FOR PROFESSIONALS AND PRACTITIONERS

In-class activities

Students: Read a print or online issue of a B-to-B magazine. List the five most interesting articles you find and include the following information in a report: (a) title and date of magazine; (b) description of the audience; (c) name of writer and title of article; (d) a 50- to 75-word summary of each article.

Instructor: Create a list of B-to-B magazines. Ask each student to choose a publication from the list, research it outside of class and prepare a brief (5- to 10-minute) report to present in class.

Assignments

Students: Browse through the yellow pages of a telephone directory. Find five different types of businesses and call their owner or manager. Ask which B-to-B magazines they read and what types of articles they find most helpful. Instructor: Ask students to report their findings in class.

Students: Browse through the yellow pages of a telephone directory. Find five unusual businesses or occupations that might yield an interesting story. Write a one-sentence description for each story idea and locate the name of a B-to-B magazine that might consider it.

CHAPTER 21: WRITING FOR ONLINE PUBLICATIONS

In-class activities

Students: Using the search terms suggested in this chapter (writer's guidelines, submission guidelines, author guidelines, etc.) find guidelines for five Web sites that pay for freelance articles on topics you are interested in writing about.

Instructor: Display on an overhead screen a current feature article from a Web site of a magazine or newspaper. Click on each link and discuss with the class the type of information contained in each link and how it relates to the overall angle of the article.

Assignments

Students: Read an article from a print magazine or lifestyle section of a newspaper and underline key words and phrases for which a link could add additional information. Find the same article online and see how online links compare with your ideas for links.

Students: Find an article at least two pages long from a print magazine. First, highlight any content that could be extracted and used in a separate sidebar. Second, highlight material that you could summarize in a bulleted or numbered list to make it more accessible to the reader.

INDEX